A NEW FOREIGN POLICY
FOR THE UNITED STATES

HANS J. MORGENTHAU

A New Foreign Policy
for the United States

Published for the
Council on Foreign Relations
by

FREDERICK A. PRAEGER, *Publishers*
New York • Washington • London

FREDERICK A. PRAEGER, PUBLISHERS
111 Fourth Avenue, New York, N.Y. 10003, U.S.A.
5, Cromwell Place, London S.W.7, England

Published in the United States of America in 1969
by Frederick A. Praeger, Inc., Publishers

Second printing, 1969

© 1969 by Council on Foreign Relations, Inc.

Library of Congress Catalog Card Number: 68-28475

For a partial list of Council publications see pages 253–5.

Printed in the United States of America

To the memory of my Mother,
Frieda Bachmann Morgenthau
(1882–1966)

Preface

THE DEFICIENCIES of American foreign policy, epitomized by Vietnam but evident in events in many other parts of the world, result from faulty modes of thought rather than from defects of personality or errors of execution. The makers of recent American foreign policy have not always been wise, efficient, and honest, but they have always acted on basic assumptions about the world and on basic principles concerning American purposes, interests, and power. More often than not, they have taken the empirical validity of their assumptions and the philosophical and political soundness of their principles for granted, although these assumptions were frequently false and these principles dubious. Thus, they had to forgo mastery over events and reduce the conduct of foreign policy to the mechanical repetition of routines in response to unforeseen events. Sir Lewis Namier wrote:

> The effort which people put up to avoid thinking might almost enable them to think and to have some new ideas. But having ideas

produces anxiety and *malaise* and runs counter to the deepest instincts of human nature, which loves symmetry, repetition, and routine. . . . One would expect people to remember the past and to imagine the future. But in fact, when discoursing or writing about history, they imagine it in terms of their own experience, and when trying to gauge the future they cite supposed analogies from the past: till, by a double process of repetition, they imagine the past and remember the future.[1]

It is with the basic assumptions and principles of American foreign policy, rather than with specific policies, that this book is concerned. This concern is justified not only historically, in view of the shortcomings of our foreign policies, but also pragmatically, with a view toward avoiding the mistakes of the past. It is now generally admitted that our Vietnam policy has failed, but, if we were to let it go at that, we would risk applying the same faulty assumptions and principles that have brought the Vietnam disaster upon us to other situations with similarly disastrous results. Instead, we must ask what accounts for that failure and how its repetition can be avoided. These questions can be answered only through an understanding of the world as it actually is, through a return to the first principles that ought to have guided the foreign policy of the United States in the past and ought to guide it in the future. As Winston Churchill put it:

> Those who are possessed of a definite body of doctrine and of deeply rooted convictions upon it will be in a much better position to deal with the shifts and surprises of daily affairs than those who are merely taking short views, and indulging their natural impulses as they are evoked by what they read from day to day.

In short, then, this book endeavors to contribute to the development of an empirical and conceptual framework within which the foreign policy of the United States can at least attempt to control events and mold conditions in the interest of the nation and of mankind.

This book originated in a study I undertook in 1966 as Senior Research Fellow of the Council on Foreign Relations. I profited

[1] L. B. Namier, "Symmetry and Repetition," in *Conflicts: Studies in Contemporary History* (London: Macmillan & Co. Ltd., 1942), pp. 69–70.

greatly from the discussions of the study group to which I presented preliminary drafts, and I am grateful to the professional and secretarial staffs of the Council for their advice and assistance.

The American Political Science Review, Basic Books, *The Bulletin of the Atomic Scientists, Current History, Foreign Affairs, The New Republic,* and The University of Chicago Press have kindly given me permission to include revised versions of material previously published by them.

—HANS J. MORGENTHAU

November 1968

Contents

A NEW FOREIGN POLICY
FOR THE UNITED STATES

"Our business is not to speculate on what the future may bring forth, but to be certain that it will bring disaster, unless you face the facts and consent to do your duty."—DEMOSTHENES, "First Philippic," 50

1

A New Foreign Policy for the
United States: The Basic Issues

I F ONE SHOULD characterize American foreign policy in a sentence, one could say that it has lived during the last decade or so on the intellectual capital which was accumulated in the famous fifteen weeks of the spring of 1947 when the policy of containment, the Truman Doctrine, and the Marshall Plan fashioned a new American foreign policy, and that this capital has now been nearly exhausted. This exhaustion is the result of the drastic transformation of the issues which the policies of 1947 met with outstanding success. These policies have become obsolete, and the United States has been unable to devise new policies capable of dealing successfully with the issues of a different age. What is needed in 1969 is therefore a task of renovation similar to that of 1947. We must free ourselves from the burden of obsolescent policies which have become mechanical routines and embark upon a radical rethinking of the issues and of the policies adequate to them.

Five basic issues await reconsideration. We must come to terms with our allies, with the Communist world, with the uncommitted third of the world, with nuclear power, and with ourselves.

THE ATLANTIC ALLIANCE

The Atlantic Alliance was predicated upon the nuclear monopoly of the United States. Thus the origin of its crisis dates back to the fall of 1949. That is to say, the crisis of the Atlantic Alliance virtually coincides with its birth. When the Soviet Union exploded its first nuclear device in September 1949, it also undermined one of the foundation stones of the Atlantic Alliance and made it inevitable that sooner or later a new basis would have to be found for that Alliance.

When it was established, the Atlantic Alliance was for the nations of Western Europe not a matter of choice but a question of life and death. It was the political, military, and economic precondition for their survival as independent national entities. One of the preconditions was the protective umbrella which the nuclear monopoly of the United States provided for the nations of Western Europe. Thus the transformation of that monopoly into a bipolar relationship of mutual deterrence was bound to change the character of the Atlantic Alliance. In consequence of the newly acquired ability of the Soviet Union to do to the United States what the United States has been able to do to the Soviet Union since 1945—that is, to destroy it as a going concern —the Atlantic Alliance is for the European members no longer an unmixed blessing but has also become a liability. Khrushchev used to remind the nations of Western Europe from time to time of the radical change that had occurred in their relations with the United States. It is from this change that de Gaulle has tried to draw the political conclusions.

The issue de Gaulle has raised, phrased in its most elemental terms, is this: who shall die for whom under what conditions? In the pre-nuclear age, de Gaulle argues, it could be expected of a nation to support an ally at the risk of war even though its vital interests were not affected; for it risked, at worst, defeat in war with the attendant loss of territory and of a tolerable fraction of its material and human resources. What could be expected in the pre-nuclear age because it was bearable, his argument continues, can no longer be expected in the nuclear age because it is no longer bearable. A nation whose vital interests are not at stake can no longer be expected to come to the aid of an ally, if, by doing so, it risks its very existence. The reliability of alliances is thereby put into doubt. Here lies, according to de Gaulle, the crisis of the Atlantic Alliance.

De Gaulle has brought that crisis into the open through two courses of action: the development of a national nuclear capability and the pursuit of national policies regardless of the interests of France's allies. The professed aim of these courses of action has been the restoration of French independence and freedom of action on the international scene. In truth, however, de Gaulle's foreign policy is predicated upon the commitment of the American nuclear deterrent to the defense of France, a commitment to which even de Gaulle still attaches a considerable measure of credibility. The French nuclear capability serves the purpose of making that commitment operative. In other words, France enjoys its independence and freedom of action only because of the American commitment, and its nuclear capability, far from being an independent deterrent against a major nuclear power, can at best serve as a trigger to bring American nuclear power into action.

The crisis of the Atlantic Alliance will not be solved by the reiteration of slogans about "interdependence" and "partnership," for these slogans beg the question which the crisis of the Atlantic Alliance poses. Nor will it be solved by the manipulation of military technology, such as the multilateral seaborne nuclear force (MLF). Three courses of action appear to be logically possible.

It is possible to pretend that the crisis of the Atlantic Alliance really does not exist and that its appearances have been created by the contrariness of de Gaulle. This is the solution of business as usual, of the continuation of institutional arrangements and procedural routines, whose vitality has not survived the drastic change in the foundations of the Alliance referred to above. It is the course most easy to follow in the short run, and it is indeed the one we have been following since we shelved the MLF. But in the long run such inaction can only serve to strengthen the disintegrating forces, of which France has thus far been the main exponent but is not likely to remain the sole exponent for long.

It must be taken as axiomatic that the health of the Atlantic Alliance cannot be restored through attempts at preserving an unviable status quo but only through reformative action. The action will either go forward toward a much more intimate cooperation among members of the Alliance and a much closer coordination of their foreign policies, or else, as the third possibility, it will move backward to a narrower and more specific definition of the *casus foederis* than exists at present.

The present malaise within the Atlantic Alliance arises from the fact that the major allies pursue divergent policies throughout the world, and there is hardly an important issue upon which all major allies see eye to eye. It is this divergence of policies rather than the actual and threatening proliferation of nuclear weapons that has undermined the Alliance. For if there existed among the members of the Atlantic Alliance so close a community of interests that the policies of ally A would automatically be supported by ally B, and vice versa, the problem would not exist. The objectives on behalf of which A might want to threaten nuclear war would then be identical with those of B, and vice versa. In that case, the issue which de Gaulle has raised and other members of the Alliance are likely to raise in the future would no longer need to be raised because it would have lost its substance.

While from a rational point of view the alternative of congruent policies appears to be the most attractive, it is not likely to be realized in the foreseeable future. For the impetus toward supranational integration, which probably could have been transformed into fruitful political action during the first decade following the Second World War, has been replaced by a nationalism which puts in jeopardy even the existing traditional alliances. The United States can mitigate nationalistic tendencies through its own foreign policies and thereby try to mitigate these tendencies in other nations as well. Yet as long as such tendencies persist, the United States must adapt its Alliance commitments to them. We must narrow the gap between our comprehensive legal commitments and the limited sphere within which our interests and policies coincide with those of our allies. The narrowing of this gap is particularly imperative in view of actual and threatening nuclear proliferation. The opportunity nuclear proliferation provides for involving the major nuclear powers in a nuclear war against their will requires the strictest legal and political safeguards. Otherwise we shall run the risk of a catastrophe not of our making and on behalf of interests not our own.

COMMUNISM

It has become a triviality to say that Communism has lost its monolithic character and has taken on the qualities of polycentrism. It is also obvious to draw from this statement the conclusion that the transformation of Communism opens up new opportunities for the foreign policy of the United States. Yet it tells much about the power outworn ideas have over the thought and action of men that, while the truth of the two propositions is generally recognized in theory, and also in practice in our relations with Eastern Europe, in other parts of the world we continue to act as though Communism were still a monolithic force uniformly threatening the interests of the United States. Our interventions in Vietnam and the Dominican Republic are cases in point. We intervened in both countries in order to "stop Communism," taking it for granted that we knew a priori, without examining the concrete circumstances, what kind of Communist threat we were facing.

Such an attitude of instinctive opposition was indeed in order twenty or even ten years ago when any inroads Communism made anywhere were tantamount to an expansion of Soviet power hostile to the United States. This attitude has become today not only intellectually untenable but also politically useless and even counterproductive. For it is again belaboring the obvious—and that the obvious must thus be belabored indicates the defects of our foreign policy—to say that we are today in the presence of a variety of Communisms whose hostility to our interests depends upon the national interests of the individual Communist governments and parties and upon their relations to the two great Communist powers, the Soviet Union and China. The degree of their hostility on the political and military plane—in contrast to the moral and ideological one—cannot be taken for granted but must be determined in each instance through the empirical examination of the facts. Furthermore, the degree of hostility to be found in a particular case is not immutable but is susceptible to changes induced by our and other nations' policies. What is required of us, then, is a dual task: first, a subtle and admittedly risky examination of each Communist government and movement in terms of the national interests it pursues and of its relations with other Communist governments and movements, and second, the fashioning of policies which not only are appropriate to the kind of Communism encountered but also seek to minimize the negative effects that Communism might have upon the interests of the United States.

These standards must guide us in our relations not only with existing Communist governments and parties but also with revolutionary movements exposed to Communist influence. At this point the problem of our relations with Communism overlaps with that of our relations with the uncommitted third of the world. For Communism has been trying to take over the revolutionary movements and actual revolutions directed against the national and social status quo in the third world. It follows from the indiscriminate anti-Communist position we took in the aftermath of the Second World War that we must oppose these movements and revolutions because of their Communist component. Such a policy is not only unsound on theoretical grounds in that it substitutes an abstract ideological principle for the yardstick of the national interest of the United States, but it is also likely to be unsuccessful because it stands in the way of a world-wide movement supported by world-wide sympathies which cannot be suppressed by the kind of forces available and acceptable to us.

The alternatives to such a simple antirevolutionary and anti-Communist policy—either to keep one's hands off and let the revolutions take their course, or to support radical change in competition with the Communists—would be risky and could not command anything approaching unanimous support on the part of an unprepared domestic public opinion. The policy of supporting radical change, in particular, would make the highest demands on the technical skill, the moral stamina, and the political wisdom of our government. But it is the only one that promises at least a measure of success. It would also require a major modification in the conception we have developed of our role in the world and of the purposes our foreign policy is supposed to serve.

THE UNCOMMITTED NATIONS

This conception of the American role was developed in the immediate postwar period and most strikingly formulated in the Truman Doctrine of 1947, committing the United States to opposition to Communist aggression and subversion throughout the world. The unlimited global commitment was in practice narrowed down to the military containment of the Soviet Union, of which the Atlantic Alliance has been the instrument, and to the economic restoration of Western Europe through the Marshall Plan.

The tasks with which the United States is faced today in its relations with other nations are more varied and infinitely more complex than those it discharged successfully in the immediate postwar period. To the task of the military containment of the Soviet Union—which, while still fundamental to everything else, has become by virtue of its success a matter of routine to be virtually taken for granted—have been added the multifarious problems arising from our relations to Communism throughout the world and to the uncommitted nations. Yet the intellectual instruments that we have brought to bear upon these new problems are still the ones we used so sucessfully in the late 1940s: the Truman Doctrine and the Marshall Plan. In the process, the Truman Doctrine has been transformed from an ideology of military containment into a general principle of global policy, and the Marshall Plan has been transformed from a technique of economic recovery limited to Western Europe to the global principle of foreign aid. In consequence, the United States has taken upon itself global responsibilities which it cannot discharge with a chance of success and which, if it were to try to discharge them, would entail its ruin.

As I pointed out in 1951, "As a guide to political action, it [the Truman Doctrine] is the victim . . . of two congenital political weaknesses: the inability to distinguish between what is desirable and what is possible, and the inability to distinguish between what is desirable and what is essential." [1] The new globalism, which seeks to put the principle of the Truman Doctrine into practice by identifying revolution with Communism and trying to stop Communism everywhere, neglects these distinctions which are fundamental to a sound foreign policy. For while it would be desirable to contain Communism within its present limits through the efforts of the United States, it is essential that only that type of Communism hostile to the interests of the United States be so contained. Thus I have always regarded it as essential in view of the interests of the United States that the transformation of Cuba into a center of Communist subversion in the Western Hemisphere and a military and political outpost of the Soviet Union be prevented. And on the same grounds, I find the containment of Communism in Vietnam to be desirable but not essential from the point of view of the interests of the United States, especially since this Communism is likely to be an independent national Communism after the model of Yugoslavia.

This latter position is contested by some who quote General Giap, the commander of the North Vietnamese army, to the

[1] Hans J. Morgenthau, *In Defense of the National Interest* (New York: Alfred A. Knopf, 1951), p. 117.

effect that the war in Vietnam is a test case for all "wars of national liberation" and that its outcome will determine the outcome of all such wars. If this statement were correct, it would indeed follow that the containment of Communism in Vietnam is essential in view of American interests since without it Communism would triumph throughout much of the uncommitted world. However, if one subjects General Giap's statement to empirical analysis one realizes that it is devoid of merit. There is no such thing as a typical "war of national liberation" whose uniform pattern can be detected throughout the world, and which could be causally connected with all the other wars of this kind. The war in Vietnam is *sui generis,* and no comparable situation exists, or is likely to exist, anywhere else in the world. In consequence, what happens or does not happen in Vietnam can have no direct bearing upon what is going to happen elsewhere. Win or lose in Vietnam, there may still be a "war of national liberation" in, say, Indonesia or Venezuela or Greece, which may be won or lost according to what may happen in those particular countries, but certainly not according to what is going to happen in Vietnam. We are here in the presence of the kind of primitive dogmatism arguing by abstract analogy, which one thought was a peculiar weakness of the Communist mode of thought. However, this mode of thought, incapable of discriminating among divergent historic situations, is appropriate to a globalism that, as we have seen, is by its very nature averse to making such discriminating judgments.

Yet, even if one were to disregard the distinction between what is essential and what is desirable, we would still be up against the distinction between what is desirable and what is possible. We can stipulate it as desirable and we may even deem it essential in view of the interests of the United States in world peace and order that the United States should bring a modicum of order and stability to the underdeveloped nations through the instrumentality of foreign aid. Yet, after long and disappointing experiences, we must have realized by now how narrow the limits are within which we can influence the development of foreign nations. More particularly, we must have realized the extent to which the development of other nations depends upon indigenous rational and moral qualities not susceptible to deliberate foreign influence.

Similarly, if we were to stipulate the containment of all kinds of Communism as desirable or even essential, we would find that the demands such a stipulation would make upon American military power by far exceed its capabilities. We are capable of dealing simultaneously with one Vietnam and one Dominican Republic. But with how many Vietnams and Dominican Republics could we deal at the same time without straining our military resources to such a point that either we would be compelled by force of circumstances and in spite of ourselves to distinguish between what is desirable and what is essential, on the one hand, and what is possible, on the other, or else we would have to resort to nuclear war as the extreme remedy, which in its way is as lacking in discrimination as is the globalist conception of foreign policy?

In any event, such a commitment of all our military resources to the global containment of Communism would deprive our policies serving other interests of the necessary military support. Concentrating upon one aim incapable of achievement, we would incapacitate ourselves to pursue other aims in our relations with other nations. It is significant in this context that General Gallois, one of the main proponents of an independent French foreign policy, commended the U.S. interventions in Vietnam and the Dominican Republic on the ground that the commitment of large American resources to these theaters would make it possible for France to play a greater role in world affairs.

NUCLEAR POWER

Nuclear power presents itself to the United States under two different headings: the management of nuclear power and the influence of nuclear power upon the conduct of foreign and military policy.

As concerns the management of nuclear power, we must come

to terms with two interconnected problems: the abatement of the nuclear arms race and the prevention of nuclear proliferation. These issues are interconnected; for as long as the present nuclear powers continue to compete for the accumulation of nuclear weapons and delivery systems as instruments of their national policies, there appears to be no possibility to prevent other nations from following suit. Nuclear proliferation is a mere spatial expansion of the nuclear arms race. The former can be prevented only by stopping the latter.

The cessation of the nuclear arms race is required by two rational considerations. First, the unlimited accumulation of nuclear weapons, in contrast to conventional ones, is irrational, once nations have acquired the capability, as have the United States and the Soviet Union, to destroy their prospective enemies many times over even under the worst of circumstances. Second, the use of nuclear weapons as instruments of national policy, likely to call forth retaliation in kind, is irrational by virtue of their indiscriminate destructiveness. What the nuclear powers have already been doing pragmatically—that is, to refrain from the use of nuclear weapons—they ought now to do consistently and as a matter of principle: to eliminate nuclear weapons from their regular armory, so that they will not be used as instruments of national policy, and to assign to them exclusively the function of a deterrent, to be used only in suicidal desperation.

From this principle, four consequences follow for the conduct of foreign and military policy. First, since nuclear threats are inherently lacking in credibility, in so far as they are not limited to the purpose of deterrence, they ought to be eliminated from diplomatic practice. Second, for similar reasons, the use of nuclear weapons, except for deterrence, ought to be eliminated from military planning. Third, since nuclear weapons are thus irrelevant for the normal exercise of national power, foreign and military policy ought to concentrate upon the development and use of the non-nuclear instruments of national power. Fourth, among these instruments, long-range communication, delivery, and transportation systems have radically altered the importance

of the control of territory for national power. Foreign and military policy must take these changes into account.

PRIORITIES IN AMERICAN FOREIGN POLICY

Looking back on the development of American foreign policy during the last two decades, one realizes how the great innovations of 1947—containment, the Truman Doctrine, the Marshall Plan—have changed their functions under the impact of new conditions. The first postwar decade was marked by two factors: the unchallengeable supremacy of the United States, on the one hand, and the limitation of its military commitments to Europe and their hesitant extension to Asia, on the other. The second postwar decade, especially in its last years, receives its political character from the decline of the relative power of the United States, coincident with a global extension of its military commitments. The Truman Doctrine and the Marshall Plan, originally limited in their practical application to Europe, are now transformed into global commitments. These commitments have outpaced the power available to support them. It is a counsel of prudence to bring power and commitment again into harmony.

This requires, first of all, the restoration of selectivity in our commitment to national objectives in view of their essentiality and of the possibility to attain them. Second, among the objectives thus selected, a hierarchical order must be established again in view of these two standards. Both the process of selection and of hierarchical ordering require a restatement of national purposes. What is it the United States seeks to accomplish in the world, and in what order of priority? This question was answered in 1947, and the answer was translated into viable policies. The same question must be answered again in 1969.

2

The United States: Paramount or Equal?

ISOLATION AND GLOBALISM

American foreign policy has tended, in this century, to move back and forth between the extremes of an indiscriminate isolationism and an equally indiscriminate internationalism or globalism. While the two positions are obviously identified with utterly different foreign policies—indiscriminate involvement here, indiscriminate abstention there—it is important to note that they share the same assumptions about the nature of the political world and the same negative attitudes toward foreign policy correctly understood. They are equally hostile to that middle ground of subtle distinctions, complex choices, and precarious manipulations which is the proper sphere of foreign policy.

Both deny the existence of priorities in foreign policy which are derived from a hierarchy of interests and the availability of power to support them. For both extremes, it is either all or nothing, either total involvement or total abstention. Both refuse to concern themselves with the concrete issues of foreign policy on their own merits—that is, in terms of the interests involved and the power available. While isolationism stops short of these concrete issues, globalism soars beyond them. Both assume the self-sufficiency of American power to protect and promote the American national interest either in indiscriminate abstention or indiscriminate involvement. While the isolationist used to say, "We don't need to have anything to do with the world, for we can take care of our own interests on our own terms," the globalists say, "We shall take on the whole world, but only on our own terms." In short, isolationism is a kind of introverted globalism, and globalism is a kind of isolationism turned inside out. To stigmatize a position that falls short of such indiscriminate globalism as "neo-isolationism" is a polemic misuse of terms; it derives from the globalist assumption that indiscriminate involvement is, as it were, the natural stance of American policy.

Both attitudes, in different ways oblivious of political reality, substitute for the complex and discriminating mode of political thought a simple approach, which in its simplicity is commensurate with the simplicity of their picture of the political world: the moral crusade. The isolationist's moralism is naturally negative, abstentionist, and domestically oriented; it seeks to protect the virtue of the United States from contamination by the power politics of evil nations. Wilsonian globalism endeavored to bring the virtue of American democracy to the rest of the world. Contemporary globalism tries to protect the virtue of the "free world" from contamination by Communism and to create a world order in which that virtue has a chance to flourish. The anti-Communist crusade has become both the moral principle of contemporary globalism and the rationale of our world-wide foreign policy.

The anti-Communist crusade has its origins in the Truman Doctrine, formulated in President Truman's message to Congress of March 12, 1947. His message assumed that the issue between the United States and the Soviet Union, from which arose the need for aid to Greece and Turkey, must be understood not as the rivalry between two great powers but as a struggle between good and evil, democracy and totalitarianism. In its positive application this principle proclaimed the defense of free, democratic nations everywhere in the world against "direct or indirect aggression," against "subjugation by armed minorities or by outside pressure." In its negative application it postulated the containment of the Soviet Union everywhere in the world. Thus, the Truman Doctrine transformed a concrete interest of the United States in a geographically defined part of the world into a moral principle of world-wide validity, to be applied regardless of the limits of American interests and of American power.

The globalism of the Truman Doctrine was not put to the test of actual performance. Dean Acheson, President Truman's Secretary of State, in his speech before the National Press Club on January 12, 1950, trimmed the doctrine down to the size of the American national interest and of the power available to support it:

> I hear almost every day someone say that the real interest of the United States is to stop the threat of Communism. Nothing seems to me to put the cart before the horse more completely than that. . . . Communism is the most subtle instrument of Soviet foreign policy that has ever been devised, and it is really the spearhead of Russian imperialism. . . . It is an important point because people will do more damage and create more misrepresentation in the Far East by saying our interest is merely to stop the spread of Communism than any other way. Our real interest is in those people as people. It is because Communism is hostile to that interest that we want to stop it.

It was the contrast between the sweeping generalities of the Truman Doctrine and the discriminating policies actually pursued by the Truman administration that was to haunt Messrs. Truman and Acheson in the years to come. Their foreign policies, especially in Asia, were judged by the standards of the Truman Doctrine and were found wanting.

The contrast between crusading pronouncements and the actual policies pursued continued, and was even accentuated, under the stewardship of John Foster Dulles, owing, on the one hand, to his propensity for grandiose announcements and, on the other, to his innate caution and President Eisenhower's common sense. The only major practical tribute the Eisenhower administration paid to the anti-Communist crusade was alliances, such as the Baghdad Pact and SEATO, which were supposed to contain Communism in the Middle East and Asia, respectively.

Under President Kennedy, the gap between crusading pronouncements and actual policies started to narrow, because of the intellectual recognition on the part of the Kennedy administration that Communism could no longer be defined simply, as it could in 1950, as the "spearhead of Russian imperialism." Thus the crusading spirit gave way to a sober, differentiating assessment of the bearing of the newly emerged, different types of Communism on the American national interest.

THE DOCTRINE OF AMERICAN PARAMOUNTCY

Under President Johnson, pronouncements and policies were, for the first time since the great transformation of American policy in 1947, very nearly in harmony. What President Johnson only implied, the Secretaries of State and Defense clearly stated: We are fighting in Vietnam in order to stop Communism throughout the world. And the President stated with similar clarity that "we do not propose to sit here in our rocking chair with our hands folded and let the Communists set up any government in the Western Hemisphere." What in the past we had said we were doing or would do but never did, we were now in the process of putting into practice: to stop the expansion of Communism on a global scale by force of arms. We were doing this under the impact of a doctrine which asserts the temporary paramountcy of American military power. This new doctrine, underpinning the Wilsonian crusading globalism with global military power, was most cogently presented in an address to the Foreign Service Association by Professor Zbigniew Brzezinski, then a member of the Policy Planning Council of the Department of State. The doctrine, as stated by Brzezinski, opposes the common view that we have moved, since the end of the Second World War, from

American paramountcy to a bipolar and from there into a polycentric world.

> I will argue instead that in fact, if we look at the last 20 years
> there has been a shift from a period, first of all, of polycentrism in
> international affairs, to a period of bipolarity, to what is today a
> period of U.S. paramountcy. . . . The U.S. is today the only
> effective global military power in the world. Moreover . . . our way
> of life is still the most appealing way of life to most people on
> earth. Most people crave the American way of life even though
> they may reject and condemn the United States. We are the only
> power with far-flung global economic investments, economic in-
> volvement and global trade, and there is no parallel to us in the
> role our science and technology plays throughout the world! [1]

By contrast, the Soviet Union is not a global power. Khrushchev acted on the assumption that it was, but the Cuban missile
crisis proved that it was not. Brzezinski comments:

> The Soviet leaders were forced, because of the energetic response
> by the United States, to the conclusion that their apocalyptic
> power [nuclear deterrent power] was insufficient to make the So-
> viet Union a global power. Faced with a showdown, the Soviet
> Union didn't dare to respond even in an area of its regional pre-
> dominance—in Berlin. . . . It had no military capacity to fight in
> Cuba, or in Vietnam, or to protect its interests in the Congo.[2]

However, this paramountcy of American military power is not
likely to last; for the Soviet Union is in the process of becoming
a global power, too, by developing its long-range conventional
capabilities. Once that process is consummated, "great international instability" is likely. According to Brzezinski:

> This is precisely why the coming decade is a decade of opportunity
> and responsibility for the United States. This is truly the American
> decade. . . . What should be the role of the United States in this
> period? To use our power responsibly and constructively so that
> when the American paramountcy ends, the world will have been
> launched on a constructive pattern of development towards inter-
> national stability . . . The ultimate objective ought to be the shap-

1 *The Department of State Bulletin,* July 3, 1967.
2 *Ibid.*

ing of a world of cooperative communities with cooperative regional communities or cooperative communities on the basis of developmental ties as, for example, a community of the developed nations. . . . The start has already been made in Asia where, on the basis of containing Communist aggression, there are the beginnings of a community of cooperative nations which one day must include China as well. In a general way this is the task America faces in the decade of American opportunity. It may well be the last decade in which this country has such a unique opportunity to shape the future.[3]

Yet, while the doctrine postulates global stabilization as the objective of American foreign policy, it also warns us against "ideologization" and "belated anti-Communist rigidity" and enjoins us to "be very careful not to get overinvolved in conflicts with the result that we are pitched against revolutions making us appear as impediments to social change." These reservations, however, do not stand in the way of "our involvement today in the effort to create regional stability in Southeast Asia" and of our policy "of containing Communist aggression" in Asia.

This doctrine of global stabilization raises two fundamental questions for American foreign policy. How can we stabilize a world which is inherently unstable and whose stability is threatened by national and social revolutions controlled by Communism or at least having a Communist component, while at the same time eschewing anti-Communist commitments? And how can we take full advantage of our temporary paramountcy in mobile conventional forces against a primitive adversary without provoking a major hostile power into stirring up more trouble in different parts of the world than even so paramount a power as the United States can handle simultaneously, or else provoking it into trying to compensate for its inferiority in the conventional department with nuclear weapons?

Stability is obviously a neutral term. There is no more stable system of government than an autocratic or totalitarian one. Vietnam would be much more stable than it is today, in consequence of our intervention on behalf of stability, if the Communists were to govern all of it. Obviously we are not called upon to establish and support any kind of stability throughout the world, but only a stability that favors our interests. If it were otherwise, we could afford to sit back and allow an unstable world to find its own stability, Communist or otherwise. What we are against is not instability per se, but an instability of which Communism, and, through it, the Soviet Union, China, and Cuba might take advantage. Thus the doctrine of stabilization reveals itself as an ideology of the status quo, opposed to social and national revolutions because of their Communist auspices or components. As Alexander I and Metternich invoked Christianity against the liberal revolutions, so the new doctrine invokes the abstraction of stability against contemporary revolutionary change. By doing this, the doctrine evades the real issue facing American foreign policy. That issue is not how to preserve stability in the face of revolution, but how to create stability out of revolution.

Furthermore, the new doctrine dangerously misjudges the nature of American military power and overestimates its effectiveness. It does so in two different respects. First, the mobile conventional power of the United States is no doubt superior to that of the Soviet Union, but it is not likely to remain so for long; for the Soviet Union has made a concerted effort to increase the mobility of its conventional forces, especially in the air and on the sea. However, even this temporarily superior conventional power has by no means proven effective in support of American policies. It has not proven so in Vietnam where an enormous superiority in conventional weapons, which in the air and on the sea amounts to a virtual monopoly, has produced nothing better than a stalemate. It has not proven effective even with regard to Cuba. As concerns the Middle East, it is the Soviet Union, not the United States, that has brought its mobile conventional capabilities to bear upon the distribution of military power.

The explanation for this failure is threefold. First, the conventional military power of the United States is quantitatively limited, while the opportunities for revolutionary upheavals are numerous. This quantitative disproportion paralyzes the United States, fully committed in Vietnam, in other parts of the world.

Second, it is precisely the enormous qualitative superiority in the variety and sophistication of modern weapons that renders American conventional military power ineffective against primitive enemies. This qualitative disproportion paralyzes our military and political judgment and makes us compensate for the frustration of our military efforts with ever-renewed quantitative increases in our efforts, thereby increasing the disproportion and frustration.

Finally and most important—and here is the second fundamental military misjudgment of the new doctrine—it is an illusion, born of nationalistic blindness, to attribute the restraints and failures of the Soviet Union to its inferiority in mobile conventional power and our daring and successes to our superiority in this department. The Soviet Union has conventional superiority with regard to Berlin, and the United States has conventional superiority with regard to Cuba and Vietnam. The Soviet Union has made no use of that superiority with regard to Berlin for the same reason we have made less than full use of ours with regard to Cuba and Vietnam: because both superpowers are afraid of the escalation of conventional war into a nuclear one. The new doctrine completely misses this point. It assumes that "apocalyptic power [i.e., nuclear power] is not effectively usable power unless you allow yourself to be terrified by it. And it does not seem likely that the Americans will become terrified by it." In other words, the doctrine assumes that it is possible to proceed with the use of conventional military power as though nuclear power did not exist because it is not "usable." However, it does not follow that because nuclear power has not been used by the United States and the Soviet Union against each other and because such use would be utterly irrational, it could never be so used in the future. Both superpowers proceed on the assumption that under certain extreme conditions nuclear weapons might be used. This is the only assumption that can make plausible the development of defenses against nuclear attack.

One such set of extreme conditions can arise from the firm commitment of one superpower to a particular course of action pursued with conventional weapons and opposed with equal firmness by the other superpower with similar weapons. The superpower that is unable to emerge victorious from this conventional confrontation and sees no chance for a compromise between the status quo and revolution must choose between retreat and resort to nuclear weapons. While it is not a foregone conclusion that it will choose the latter alternative, it is also not a foregone conclusion that it will choose the former. The decision will depend upon the importance, real or imagined, of the stakes; the character and wisdom of the rulers; and, more particularly, their ability to resist the illusion that it is possible to wage a successful or even a tolerable nuclear war.

The two superpowers have thus far been able to avoid the confrontation allowing for only these two alternatives. They have done so because they are indeed "terrified" by each other's nuclear power. But if the United States were to follow the advice of the new doctrine and cease being so "terrified," one of the major impediments to nuclear war would indeed have been removed. The probability of such an "apocalyptic" dénouement would become particularly acute during that period of "great international instability" which the new doctrine foresees when "the American decade" has come to an end. For then, to believe the new doctrine, the United States will confront the Soviet Union throughout the world on equal terms in so far as mobile conventional capabilities are concerned. From that confrontation there would then result a number of stalemated contests, irresolvable with conventional means. The two superpowers would then have to come to terms with the two alternatives of retreat or nuclear war. Both superpowers, for different reasons, would have an incentive to push matters to the rim of that abyss: the United States because of the false assurance that nuclear power is not "usable," and the Soviet Union because, as we shall see, the weakness of its government's legitimacy makes it more dependent upon success than are other governments more firmly grounded.

The Anti-Communist Crusade

The new doctrine, by postulating the paramountcy of American military power on behalf of prerevolutionary stability and at the risk of nuclear war, raises by implication three fundamental issues with which the foreign policy of the United States must come to terms: First, what is the purpose of foreign policy when it must deal not, or not only, with a hostile power, but with a hostile political movement transcending national boundaries? Second, what is the bearing of the world Communist movement upon the national interests of the United States? Third, how can the United States deal with the revolutions that might be taken over by Communism?

These questions, more vexing than those with which foreign policy must ordinarily come to terms, are typical for a revolutionary age. Twice before in modern history, such questions had to be answered. They first arose during the last decade of the eighteenth century in England on the occasion of the expansionist policies of revolutionary France. Three great political minds —Edmund Burke, Charles James Fox, and William Pitt—debated how to deal with the expansionism of a great power which was also the fountainhead of a universal political religion. Fox held that England was not at all threatened by France or, for that matter, by the principles of the French Revolution, which were a mere domestic concern of France, and that therefore England had no reason to be at war with France. Burke, on the other hand, looked at the issue as

> . . . the cause of humanity itself. . . . It is not the cause of nation as against nation; but, as you will observe, the cause of mankind against those who have projected the subversion of that order of things, under which our part of the world has so long flourished. . . . If I conceive rightly of the spirit of the present combination, it is not at war with France, but with Jacobinism. . . . We are at war with a *principle,* and with an example, of which there is no shutting out by fortresses or excluding by territorial limits. No lines of demarcation can bound the Jacobin empire. It must be extirpated in the place of its origin, or it will not be confined to that place.[4]

[4] *Correspondence of the Right Honourable Edmund Burke,* edited by Charles William, Earl Fitzwilliam, and Sir Richard Bourke (London: Francis and John Rivington, 1844), IV, 138–41. Reprinted in *Principles and Problems of International Politics,* edited by Hans J. Morgenthau and Kenneth W. Thompson (New York: Alfred A. Knopf, 1950), p. 333.

It was for Pitt, the Prime Minister, to apply the standard of the national interest:

> The honorable gentleman defies me to state, in one sentence, what is the object of the war. In one word, I tell him that it is security—security against a danger, the greatest that ever threatened the world—security against a danger which never existed in any past period of society. . . . We saw that it was to be resisted no less by arms abroad, than by precaution at home; that we were to look for protection no less to the courage of our forces than to the wisdom of our councils; no less to military effort than to legislative enactment.[5]

The other issue arose after the Napoleonic Wars, when the absolute monarchies of Europe were threatened, on the one hand, by liberal revolutions and, on the other, by the imperial ambitions of Russia claiming to fight liberalism anywhere in the name of the Christian principles of government. Faced with this dual danger, Lord Castlereagh, the British Foreign Secretary, opposed the expansion of Russia and refused to oppose or support liberal revolutions per se. He said to the Russian ambassador in 1820:

> It is proposed now to overcome the *revolution;* but so long as this revolution does not appear in more distinct shape, so long as this general principle is only translated into events like those of Spain, Naples and Portugal—which, strictly speaking, are only reforms, or at the most domestic upsets, and do not attack materially any other State—England is not ready to combat it.[6]

At the same time he wrote to his brother:

> It is not possible for the British Government to take the field in fruitlessly denouncing by a sweeping joint declaration the revolutionary dangers of the present day, to the existence of which they are, nevertheless, sufficiently alive. Nor can they venture to embody themselves *en corps* with the nonrepresentative Governments in what would seem to constitute a scheme of systematic interfer-

[5] *The Parliamentary History of England, from the Earliest Period to the Year 1803* (London: T. C. Hansard, 1819), XXXIV, 1442–45. Reprinted in Morgenthau and Thompson, *op. cit.,* p. 349.

[6] C. K. Webster, *The Foreign Policy of Castlereagh, 1815–1822* (London: G. Bell & Sons, 1925), pp. 282–84. Reprinted in Morgenthau and Thompson, *op. cit.,* p. 353.

ence in the internal affairs of other States; besides, they do not regard mere declarations as of any real or solid value independent of some practical measures actually resolved upon; and what that measure is which can be generally and universally adopted against bad principles overturning feeble and ill-administered governments, they have never yet been able to divine.[7]

Castlereagh's foreign policy was so unpopular that he was driven to suicide; in the streets of London, the people celebrated the news of his death. While Castlereagh did not enjoy what we now call "consensus," he enjoys the historic reputation of a very great and successful statesman. The Austrian Chancellor Metternich, on the other hand, a champion of the status quo against liberalism, saw his political world disappear in the revolutions of 1848.

A foreign policy that takes for its standard the active hostility to a world-wide political movement, such as Jacobinism, liberalism, or Communism, confuses the sphere of philosophic or moral judgment with the realm of political action, and for this reason it is bound to fail. For there are narrow limits, defined by the interests at stake and the power available, within which a foreign policy has a chance to succeed, and a foreign policy that would oppose Communist revolution and subversion throughout the world oversteps those limits. It does so in three different respects.

First, as pointed out before, the conventional resources of even the most powerful nation are limited. Second, the task such a foreign policy sets itself is unending. You suppress Communism in South Vietnam, and it raises its head, say, in Thailand; you suppress it in the Dominican Republic, and it raises its head, say, in Colombia. The successful suppression of revolution in one spot does not discourage revolution elsewhere, provided the objective conditions are favorable. The conjunction between an objective revolutionary situation in large parts of the world and a world-wide political ideology and organization committed to exploit it makes piecemeal attacks upon individual, acute trouble spots a hopeless undertaking.

Third, the attack upon a particular revolution as part of a

7 *Ibid.*

world-wide, antirevolutionary campaign is bound to have world-wide repercussions. Local successes against a particular revolution may have to be paid for by loss of support elsewhere and even by the strengthening of revolutionary forces throughout the world.

The only standard by which a sound foreign policy must be informed is not moral and philosophic opposition to Communism as such, but the bearing a particular Communism in a particular country has upon the interests of the United States. That standard was easily applied in 1950 when Communism anywhere in the world could be considered a mere extension of Soviet power and be opposed as such. The task is infinitely more difficult today when Soviet control of the world Communist movement has been successfully challenged by the competition of China and the reassertion of their particular national interests by Communist governments and parties throughout the world. Yet, while the task is very complex, it can be left undone only at the risk of an exhausting and ultimately fruitless crusade which, by dint of its lack of discrimination, is likely to be counterproductive as well; for it tends to restore the very unity of the Communist camp that it is in our interest to prevent.

A sound anti-Communist policy would ask itself at every turn what the relations of this particular Communist government or movement are likely to be with the Soviet Union and China, and how those relations are likely to be influenced by our choice of policy. It would choose a different approach to Cuba from that taken to North Vietnam, for Cuba is a military and political outpost of the Soviet Union in the Western Hemisphere that pursues revolutionary foreign policies at odds with those of the Soviet Union, while North Vietnam maintains an uneasy balance in its dependence upon the Soviet Union and China and would prefer not to be subservient to either. Such a policy no doubt entails considerable risks, for the analysis may be mistaken or the policy may fail through miscalculation. Furthermore, and most important, such a policy is faced with a real dilemma. That dilemma is presented by the prospect of the rise of revolutionary movements in Asia, Africa, and Latin America, most, if not all, of which are likely to have a Communist component. In other words, any of these revolutionary movements risks being taken over by Communism.

In the face of this risk, we think we can choose between two different courses of action. On the one hand, we can oppose all revolutionary movements around the world. But in consequence of such opposition and in spite of our reformist intentions, we shall then transform ourselves into the antirevolutionary power per se, after the model of Metternich's Austria of 150 years ago, and we will find ourselves defending a status quo that we know to be unjust and in the long run indefensible. For we know, of course, that the rational choice open to us is not between the status quo and revolution, but between non-Communist and different types of Communist revolutions. But it is our fear of Communism that forces us into an antirevolutionary stance.

On the other hand, if we refrain from intervening against those revolutionary movements, we risk their being taken over by the Communist component. It would then be left to our skill in political manipulation to prevent a Communist take-over from coming about, or if it should come about, to prevent such a Communist revolution from becoming subservient to the Soviet Union or China. The United States would then have to compete with the Soviet Union and China in the sponsorship of revolutions, taking the risk that not all those revolutions would remain under American sponsorship.

In comparison with the moral, political, and technical demands such a policy would make, the alternative, the anti-Communist crusade, is simplicity itself. The domestic "consensus" supports it, and it makes only minimum demands on moral discrimination, intellectual subtlety, and political skill. Its implementation is in essence a problem of military logistics: how to get the requisite number of armed men quickly to the theater of revolution. That task is easy, and we have shown ourselves adept at it. Yet the achievement of that task does not solve the problem of revolution. It smothers, as it were, the fire of revolution under a military blanket; but it does not extinguish it. And when that fire breaks out again with increased fury, the assumptions of our policy have left us with no remedy but the commitment of more and more armed men to try to smother it again.

This policy is bound to be ineffective in the long run against the local revolution to which it is applied. It is also ineffective in its own terms of the anti-Communist crusade. For the very logic that makes us appear as the antirevolutionary power surrenders to Communism the sponsorship of revolution everywhere. Thus the anti-Communist crusade achieves what it seeks to prevent: the exploitation of the revolutions of the age by the Soviet Union and China.

Finally, our reliance upon a simple anti-Communist stance and its corollary, military intervention, is bound to corrupt our judgment about the nature and the limits of our power. We flatter ourselves to defend right against wrong, to discharge the self-imposed duty to establish a new order throughout the world, and to do so effectively within the limits of military logistics. Thus we may well come to think that all the problems of the political world will yield to moral conviction and military efficiency, and that whatever we want to do we shall be able to do because we possess those two assets in abundance. Edmund Burke warned his countrymen in 1793 under similar conditions:

> Among precautions against ambition, it may not be amiss to take one precaution against our *own*. I must fairly say, I dread our *own* power and our *own* ambitions; I dread our being too much dreaded. . . . We may say that we shall not abuse this astonishing and hitherto unheard-of power. But every other nation will think we shall abuse it. It is impossible but that, sooner or later, this state of things must produce a combination against us which may end in our ruin.[8]

Pitt and Castlereagh heeded that warning. Our future and the future of the world will depend on our heeding it as well.

[8] H. Edmund Burke, "Remarks on the Policy of the Allies with Respect to France." *Works*, Vol. IV (Boston: Little, Brown, 1899), p. 457.

3

The Foreign Policy of Communism

WHEN IN 1947 the United States reluctantly concluded that its involvement with a hostile world had become permanent, it had to face up to two challenges: the expansionism of the Soviet Union and the spread of Communism. Each of these challenges would have been sufficient to tax the ingenuity and adaptability of a traditionally uncommitted, if not isolationist, nation which suddenly and to its surprise had to shoulder the responsibilities of the most powerful nation on earth. What has made the conduct of American foreign policy particularly baffling ever since has been the coincidence of hostile great-power aspirations with the promotion of Communist world revolution. The Soviet Union and China are great powers pursuing their national interests, but they are also competitive claimants for the leadership of the world Communist movement.

In view of this dualism of the foreign policies of the two great Communist powers, the soundness of American foreign policy is predicated upon the correct assessment of the kind of challenge the United States faces in each concrete instance. What is it we are facing in Vietnam? Is it Russian or Chinese imperialism, or is it Soviet or Chinese Communism? Is it a combination of two or more of these elements, or is it none of these? If we give the wrong answers to questions such as these, our foreign policy is bound to be intellectually unsound and can be successful only by accident.

The distinction between the great-power and Communist character of Soviet and Chinese foreign policies overlaps, but is not identical, with the distinction between the monolithic and polycentric character of the world Communist movement. Logically, it is possible to distinguish between a monolithic and polycentric great-power policy, as well as between a monolithic and polycentric Communist policy. And what is logically possible is empirically observable. Poland, for instance, pursues a European policy that derives from its distinct national interests, yet that policy is monolithically subordinated to that of the Soviet Union because of the identity of national interests and the distribution of power between the two countries. Romania, on the other hand, pursues a national foreign policy that is polycentrically distinct from that of the Soviet Union by dint of the distinctiveness of the national interests involved. China pursues, at least outside Asia, a Communist foreign policy that is polycentrically distinct from that of the Soviet Union. Albania pursues a Communist foreign policy that is monolithically a replica of that of China.

The diversity of the types of interaction between Communism and national interest is matched, if not surpassed, by the complexity of the functional relations existing between the two factors. We have tended to neglect both this diversity and the complexity and to base our foreign policies upon a simplistic interpretation of the foreign policy of Communist nations. Such an interpretation is congenial to a nation that has been accustomed, and until two decades ago could afford, to conceive of the political world in the stark and simple contrasts between good and evil, law-abiding and aggressor nations. Thus we have tended to go from one extreme to another.

During the first decade following the Second World War, we

perceived the Communist world as a monolith dominated by a Soviet Union bent upon world revolution. Now we look at it as a conglomeration of nation-states each pursuing its separate national interests. Thus Dean Rusk could say in 1951:

> We do not recognize the authorities in Peiping for what they pretend to be. The Peiping regime may be a colonial Russian government—a slavic Manchukuo on a larger scale. It is not the Government of China. It does not pass the first test. It is not Chinese! [1]

On the other hand, Professor Brzezinski could say in 1967: "Communism, the principal, and until recently most militant, revolutionary ideology of our day is dead. Communism is dead as an ideology in the sense that it is no longer capable of mobilizing unified global support." [2] However, the Communist world was never as Communist-oriented and monolithic as Dean Rusk thought it was, nor is it now as devoid of Communist aspirations and as polycentric as Professor Brzezinski appears to think it is.

COMMUNIST PHILOSOPHY AND POLITICAL POWER

The Charismatic Legitimacy of Communism

In order to understand the subtle and intricate relations that exist between the philosophy of Communism and the foreign policy of Communist nations, taking the Soviet government as the prime example, it is necessary to understand the functions Communist philosophy performs for the exercise of political power at home and abroad.

All civilized political regimes must justify themselves in philosophic and moral terms in order to be able to govern at all; no such government can govern for any length of time by brute force alone. A political order must rest on one of three foundations of legitimacy: traditional—here the government rules in the name of a "natural order"; constitutional—here the government rules by virtue of a set of pre-established rational rules of

[1] *Vital Speeches* XVII, No. 17 (June 15, 1951), 515.
[2] *The Department of State Bulletin,* July 3, 1967.

conduct; charismatic—here the government rules because of a special endowment of wisdom, virtue, and power. The Soviet government belongs to the last category. Paradoxically enough, its charismatic character is a function of the scientific pretense of Marxist-Leninist philosophy.

Marxism-Leninism conceives of itself not as just another political philosophy, superior to the others but not essentially different from them. Quite to the contrary, it claims to be the only science of society worthy of the name, the repository of all the truth there is to be had about man and society. In other words, it lays claims to a monopoly of truth and, through it, to a monopoly of virtue. The claim of the government to govern derives from the monopolistic access to that truth.

The truth of Marxism-Leninism must be made relevant to the concrete issues of the day; it must be interpreted, developed, and applied. This is the task of the government. Certain individuals, such as Lenin, Stalin, and Khrushchev, or certain elitist collectives, such as the Politburo, the Central Committee, or the party as a whole, are supposed to stand in a special relationship to that truth. Endowed with extraordinary qualities of mind and character, they are the authentic guardians, interpreters, and augmenters of the Marxist-Leninist truth. They have the same monopolistic access to that truth as priests have to the truth of revealed religion. Hence their infallibility in thought and action, hence their right to govern and the citizen's duty to obey.

From this relationship between the philosophy of Marxism-Leninism and the legitimacy of government, two interrelated consequences follow: the inevitability of the "cult of personality" and the successful exercise of power as the ultimate test of the legitimacy of government.

The "cult of personality"—that is, the singling out of individual leaders as the incarnation of Communist truth and virtue—is on the face of it incompatible with the basic Marxist conception of the proletariat as the "chosen" class which will bring salvation to mankind by putting into practice that truth, impersonal and objective, by dint of its scientific nature. The very polemic use of the term in the post-Stalinist era expresses that incompatibility by trying to make it appear as though the Stalinist "cult of personality" was a mere deviation from Marxist-Leninist orthodoxy. However, Marx had already emphasized the importance of an elite, from which bourgeois elements were not excluded, for making the amorphous mass of the proletariat conscious of itself as a class and of its historic mission. For Lenin, the tightly organized elite of revolutionary cadres became the mainstay of Bolshevist revolution and government, and Trotsky went one step further by stressing the crucial importance of the revolutionary leader. The very importance that in a positive or negative sense the Communist tradition attributes to such personalities as Marx, Engels, Liebknecht, Bernstein, Kautsky, Lenin, Trotsky, Stalin, Tito, Khrushchev, and Mao Tse-tung militates against the pretended anonymity of Communist science and the deviationist quality of the "cult of personality."

The inevitability of the "cult of personality" or of the "exorcism of personality" as its negation results from the claim to infallibility of the political leader and the gap that of necessity exists between the truths of Communism and the requisite political action. Communism tells us that the capitalistic system will be overthrown by the proletarian revolution, once it has exhausted its inherent potentialities and has therefore become ripe for revolution. This is a truth all Communists can accept. That truth gives us the abstract criteria by which the necessity of revolution must be judged, but it tells us nothing about whether this particular capitalistic system has actually reached the state of decomposition, making the proletarian revolution inevitable. This issue must be decided not by logical deduction from abstract propositions, but by practical political judgment assessing the concrete circumstances of the case.

Yet Marxism-Leninism, pretending to a monopolistic possession of all the truth about man and society, must also pretend that the answer to that question is not extraneous to itself but is of necessity in the possession of the faithful. The truth is revealed once and for all in the writings of Marx and Lenin; it only needs to be applied to concrete cases. That is the task of the elect few who, because of charismatic endowment, speak to the issues of the

day in the voices of Marx and Lenin. Hence, they have a right to bask in the reflected glory of the founders, to share in that "cult."

The truth of Marxism-Leninism is, then, not really scientific; for it is not in the nature of tentative propositions to be tested against reality and discarded if they do not meet that empirical test. Rather, it is composed of dogmatic assertions that have passed the empirical test once and for all and, hence, must be applied to reality without any further examinations as to their correctness. Marxism-Leninism is actually a dogma, a body of pseudo-theological propositions which, in accord with the secular and scientist spirit of the times, demands acceptance in the name of science.

Since there can be only one truth, the one propounded by the official interpreters of Marxism-Leninism, dissent from the official truth is bound to be illegitimate. Since the truth has already been revealed, there can be no room in the marketplace for the dissenter to compete with the official view in the discovery of the truth. The dissenter is an outcast by definition. He is not to be argued with on rational grounds or overruled because he is pragmatically mistaken. He is to be denounced as a saboteur and traitor and ostracized as a "deviationist." Thus, as the monopolistic pretense of Marxism-Leninism is of necessity tantamount to a pseudo-theological dogmatism in theory, so this dogmatism calls forth in practice the monolithic structure of Communist society. Here, however, we must make a sharp distinction between non-Communist and Communist societies. In the former, Marxism-Leninism is monolithic in pretense only, but sectarian—i.e., pluralistic—in fact; whereas in the latter it is monolithic both in pretense and in fact. The difference results from the availability of political power to enforce the monolithic character of Communist society in one case and the absence of such political power in the other.

The history of Marxism-Leninism has from the very beginning been the story of interminable pseudo-theological controversies and squabbles about the true meaning of the doctrine. Custodians of the doctrinal truth, from Marx to Mao, have argued not so much in terms of what is feasible and therefore ought to be done in view of concrete political circumstances, but of what is required by the truth of Communism, correctly interpreted. Where no political power has been available to enforce a particular view of the truth—that is, in non-Communist societies—unresolved conflicting claims to the monopolistic possession of the truth have called into being fanatical sects ostracizing each other. Social Democrats and independent Socialists, Socialists and Communists, Mensheviks and Bolsheviks, Stalinists and Trotskyites, Khrushchevites and Maoists, each laying claim to the monopolistic possession of the truth, have fought each other, sometimes literally, to the death. Faced with the beginnings of this sectarianism, intellectually sterile and politically ineffectual, Marx was moved to write to his son-in-law, Paul Lafargue: *"Moi, je ne suis pas Marxiste."*

Where political power is available to establish and maintain the monolithic character of Communist society by enforcing conformity with the official version of the truth, basic disagreements over policy lead on the individual level to the political purge and criminal punishment and, if they are widespread, to a crisis of the regime itself. In so far as the truth of Marxism-Leninism, as officially interpreted, is not accepted by virtue of its rational persuasiveness, political power forces its acceptance.

The periodic purge is the instrument through which the truth of Marxism-Leninism is reaffirmed and, if need be, restored and the governing elite's monopolistic possession of that truth is reasserted. However, it bespeaks the pervasive force this pretense to the monopolistic possession of the truth once had, that the doomed dissenters of the Stalinist period testifying in court did not challenge that pretense but affirmed it by "confessing" their sins against it. In other words, the dissenters did not dissent from the basic assumptions of Marxism-Leninism but remained within their framework. They dissented from the interpretation which the powers-that-be had given to one or the other of the tenets of Marxism-Leninism, and that interpretation was accepted as true by all concerned since its claim to truth was supported by a monopoly of political power. Here we are in the presence of the distinctive nature of the Communist charisma.

The Peculiar Nature of the Communist Charisma

What sets a Communist government apart from other types of government and exerts a subtle influence upon its policies, domestic and foreign, is the peculiar character of the charisma by which it rules. All types of government contain a charismatic element; for they all require an implicit belief in the superior endowment of the rulers with wisdom, virtue, and power. Thus the legitimization of government by tradition, as is the case in monarchical and aristocratic forms of government, assumes that there is something hallowed about tradition itself, bestowing those superior qualities on those who rule by virtue of it. Similarly, a type of government such as democracy, which derives its legitimacy from the rational constitutional processes by which the rulers are chosen and govern, assumes that the will of the majority is endowed with those superior qualities: *vox populi, vox Dei.*

What distinguishes the charismatic type of legitimacy from the others is the primary and determining character of the charisma. The charismatic element supports traditional and constitutional legitimacy, but it is not essential to it; tradition and law, as fountainheads of order in their own right, are capable of supporting a regime even when the charismatic element is weakened or has disappeared altogether. Conversely, tradition and law perform a similar supporting function in the charismatic type of legitimacy. Napoleon derived the legitimacy of his rule from the charismatic qualities of his person, proven in action and visible to the people; each victory confirmed the people's belief in his charismatic right to rule. But Napoleon tried to underpin the charismatic legitimacy of his rule by connecting it with both the tradition of monarchy and the rational order of legal codes and administrative organization. His rule could not survive the destruction of his charisma through defeat in war, while ironically the tradition he had revived and the legal and administrative system he had established became the primary basis of the legitimacy of his successors.

The Napoleonic type of charismatic leader depends for the legitimacy of his rule upon continuing success. For it is in success, especially against seemingly insuperable odds, that his charisma reveals itself. In consequence, the legitimacy of his rule and, more likely than not, his rule itself cannot survive persistent failure. This was as true of Hitler and Mussolini as it was of Napoleon. In this respect the modern charismatic leader differs sharply from the premodern one, whose charisma was typically established by a religious sanction. The legitimacy of the rule of a Pope, his election by his fellow cardinals as an expression of the divine will, survives failure in this world since his charisma does not depend upon success; the same was true of the Emperor of the Holy Roman Empire, chosen by the Electors and anointed by the Pope. Premodern charismatic legitimacy enjoys a degree of stability which is lacking in modern charismatic leadership. The former derives from an objective order, as does traditional and legal legitimacy; none of them depends exclusively, except under particularly primitive conditions, upon the personal achievement of a leader. On the other hand, Hitler's suicide and Mussolini's aimless flight into death were consistent with the nature of their rule. There was nothing for them to claim once they had failed, while a premodern charismatic leader or a traditional or constitutional ruler can go into exile and claim his throne or maintain his constitutional right to govern by invoking the objective order from which his legitimacy derives.

Communist legitimacy occupies an intermediate position between these two types. It derives from an objective order, the truth of Marxism-Leninism. But that truth, unlike the truth of revealed religion, is not to be taken on faith alone, by virtue of having been revealed. It pretends to be "scientific" truth and hence must submit to the test of experience. The Christian can wait without a time limit for the Second Coming, for it has been divinely revealed that Christ will come again. His faith will survive delay as long as he believes in the revelation itself. The Communist cannot indefinitely maintain his faith in the "withering away of the state" and the coming of the classless society or in the triumph of Communism throughout the world; for these prophecies are subject to historical verification, not at the end of time but, if not here and now, certainly tomorrow or the day after.

Thus Marxism-Leninism contains within itself the seeds of its own destruction; it becomes the victim of the self-same dialectic from which it deduced the inevitable doom of all historical phenomena. For the very scientific pretense of Marxism-Leninism makes the confrontation of the pseudoscientific dogma with empirical reality inevitable. Sophisticated arguments may stave off the confrontation for the time being, but "the science of society," in contrast to an otherworldly religion, cannot evade the empirical "moment of truth" forever.

The prophecies of Marxism-Leninism are indeed vague and contingent enough to stretch the time span within which their fulfillment can be expected. The successful Communist leaders have been able to protect their charisma by reformulating and reinterpreting the tenets of Marxism-Leninism and, more particularly, by explaining delays in the fulfillment of the Marxist-Leninist prophecies in terms of Marxism-Leninism itself. This has been the technique that Marxist-Leninists have consistently used in order to reconcile the integrity of the dogma with the deficiencies of actual performance.

The issue arose at the very beginning of the Bolshevist regime, and the pattern for its solution was set then. The Bolshevist leaders were faced with the task of making peace with Germany, and they had decided that if they could not obtain satisfactory conditions they would simply wait for the proletarian revolution to break out in Germany, which would bring the war to an end. However, the German soldiers gave no sign of making common cause with the Russian Bolshevists against their masters. The great majority of the Bolshevist leaders, faithful to the doctrine, were in favor of rejecting the German terms and waiting for the inevitable German revolution to occur. Yet, realizing that the Soviet Union needed peace, revolution or no revolution, Lenin in January 1918 made an emendation to the doctrine.

The state of affairs with the socialist revolution in Russia must form the basis of any definition of the international task of our Soviet power. The international situation in the fourth year of the war is such that the probable moment of the outbreak of revolution and of the overthrow of any one of the European imperialist governments (including the German Government) is completely incalculable. There is no doubt that the socialist revolution in Europe is bound to happen and will happen. All our hopes of the *final* victory of socialism are founded on this conviction and on this scientific prediction. Our propaganda activity in general and the organization of fraternization in particular must be strengthened and developed. But it would be a mistake to build the tactics of the socialist government on attempts to determine whether the European, and in particular the German, socialist revolution will happen in the next half year (or in some such short time) or will not happen.[3]

Similarly, Stalin could reassure the comrades who at the Eighteenth Party Congress in 1939 had raised the question why, after the destruction of the class enemies within the Soviet Union, the state was not withering away, as Marx, Engels, and Lenin had said it would, by asserting that Marx and Lenin did not foresee everything and that while the state was no longer needed for domestic purposes it was still essential in order to defend the "Fatherland of Socialism" against capitalistic encirclement. Or the delay in the world-wide triumph of Communism can be explained either by the revisionism of the Soviet leaders or the adventurism of the Maoists. And the diversity of polycentric Communisms, apparently challenging the monopolistic pretense of the fountainhead of Marxist-Leninist truth, can be justified in terms of "several roads to Communism," the monopolistic pretense being maintained for the end result in which the different roads inevitably will converge.

But there are obvious limits to such postponements. Sooner or later, a science of society claiming a monopoly of the truth must either make good on its claim or lose its credibility. Thus the

[3] Quoted in E. H. Carr, *The Bolshevik Revolution 1913–1923*, III (New York: Macmillan, 1953), 34.

charisma of Communism not only contains an objective element by virtue of being grounded in the science of Marxism-Leninism; but, by virtue of being so grounded, it also contains a subjective element in that it depends upon the success of those who act in its name. The charisma of a Stalin or a Khrushchev is not as exposed to the corroding influence of failure as is that of a Hitler or Mussolini, but it is not as immune from it as is the charisma of a traditional monarch or of a constitutional democracy.

The peculiar character of the Communist charisma, its relative stability because of its derivation from dogma and its relative instability because of its dependence upon political success, also accounts for the peculiarities of the succession to supreme power in Communist states. In contrast to the radical disruption of legitimacy in the case of the Napoleonic or Fascist charismatic leader, Communism has been able to maintain the continuity of its legitimacy and its institutions. That continuity corresponds to the objectivity of the dogma from which legitimacy derives and in whose name the institutions operate.

Succession has two facets: the removal of the incumbent and the choice of a successor. As concerns the former, the issue has thus far arisen in the Soviet Union only with regard to Khrushchev since Lenin and Stalin died in office. The decision to remove Khrushchev was rendered by the Central Committee in accordance with pre-established constitutional processes and was obviously the result of pragmatic considerations. Khrushchev had failed in stabilizing the European empire of the Soviet Union by challenging the Western powers in Berlin. He had failed to restore the monopoly of the Soviet Union as the fountainhead of Marxism-Leninism by coming to terms with China. His long-range strategic success in Cuba was overshadowed by the spectacular character of his tactical defeat. His agricultural policies were an unmitigated failure. And perhaps most important, by his denunciation of Stalin, he put into question, as we shall see, the legitimacy of the Soviet regime itself.

On the other hand, in contrast to the modern types of traditional and constitutional legitimacy, the determination of the person of the successor is inevitably the result of a naked struggle for power and even survival. While the decisions were rendered through the institutional instrumentality of majority votes of the highest organs of the Communist Party, the substantive issue was actually decided through the distribution of military and para-military power. In this respect, Communist succession resembles a type of monarchical succession which is strong in tradition but weak in constitutional rationality, as was the case in England in the fourteenth and fifteenth centuries. Monarchical legitimacy derived from tradition remains here intact; but the designation of the person to succeed to the throne hallowed by tradition depends upon who can kill whom or at least who can defeat whom in battle. Similarly, Stalin and Khrushchev rose to, and maintained themselves in, supreme power either through a series of outright assassinations, as in the case of Trotsky, or of assassi-nations, legally disguised as executions, as in the case of the purges of the 1930s and of Beria. That the struggle for succession did not degenerate into a civil war and was at worst in the nature of a *coup d'état* resulted from the extreme inequality in the distribution of military power among the contenders. The armed forces at the disposal of Beria as Minister of Internal Affairs were no match for the regular armed forces at the disposal of the majority of the Central Committee. Khrushchev owed his success in the struggles for supreme power—both in the original assumption of it and in subsequent challenges to it—to his con-trol of the armed forces. This is true not only in general with regard to the control of effective power within the state, which in the last analysis is military, but also as concerns his technical ability to bring his supporters in military transports to Moscow for a decisive vote of the Central Committee.

The Three Crises of Marxism-Leninism

The effectiveness of the Communist charisma is dependent upon the success of the policies undertaken in its name. This is true of modern charismatic leadership in general, as it is, broadly speak-ing, of any modern type of government. As Max Weber put it, without limiting his observation to the premodern era: if the charismatic leader "is for long unsuccessful, above all if his leadership fails to benefit his followers, it is likely that his charismatic authority will disappear." [4] It is to this risk that the Communist charisma is exposed with particular force; for, as we have seen, its claim to scientific infallibility invites continuous testing against actual experience. Communism has failed that test in three areas vital to its legitimacy. Major prophecies of Marxism-Leninism have been denied by historic experience. The validity of the Communist charisma itself has been authoritatively denied from within the Soviet Union. The claim of Marxism-Leninism to completeness, if not infallibility, as a guide to political action has been denied by the development of a plurality of Communisms, independent from, if not hostile to, the monopolistic claims of the Soviet guardians of the doctrine.

Historic Disavowal. The first denial Marxism-Leninism suffered at the hands of history occurred in 1914 at the outbreak of the First World War. It had been one of the basic assumptions of Marxism-Leninism, both in theory and in practice, that the solidarity of the international proletariat was stronger than the loyalty of individual proletarians and proletarian parties to their respective nations and governments. Thus before 1914 all European socialist parties as a matter of principle voted against military appropriations for their respective governments. The proletarian masses were expected to follow this example of their elected representatives and refuse to fight against their proletarian comrades on the other side of the frontier if their respective governments should declare war against each other. Rather, they would jointly rise against these governments; thus war would issue in revolution. Yet in August 1914 the proletarians of the world did not unite, but started to kill each other on behalf of their respective nations and governments.

The second denial was suffered by Marxism-Leninism at the end and in the aftermath of the First World War. According to

[4] Max Weber, *The Theory of Social and Economic Organization*, Translated by A. M. Henderson and Talcott Parsons (New York: Oxford University Press, 1947), p. 360.

the strict principles of the doctrine, the October Revolution of 1917 should not have occurred in Russia, a backward country which was still half feudalistic and whose early capitalist system, far from mature, had not yet produced a large industrial proletariat. When it occurred, the doctrine had to conceive it not as an isolated event but as the initial stage of world revolution. World revolution was required not only by the doctrine, but also by the security of the Soviet Union, surrounded as it was by hostile capitalistic powers. Yet Communist revolution failed everywhere, and the Soviet Union survived within "capitalistic encirclement."

Marxist-Leninist prophecies were denied a third time when decaying capitalistic systems took refuge in Fascism. Inflation, the Crash of 1929, and mass unemployment proletarianized the middle classes and drove the proletariat to despair. Out of this endemic economic crisis appeared to evolve the classic Marxist-Leninist juxtaposition between a small group of desperate monopoly capitalists and their mercenaries, on the one hand, and the proletarianized masses, on the other. According to Marxist-Leninist principles, the consciousness of the proletarianized middle classes should have reflected their economic position: they should have become Marxists. Yet something very un-Marxist happened: revolting against their proletarianization, they became Fascists. Their consciousness did not follow their material conditions but revolted against them. When this happened, in contrast to what ought to have happened according to the doctrine, Fascism was welcomed with a measure of "scientific" approval as a historic necessity: the last stage of capitalism, preparatory to, and inevitably followed by, the Communist revolution. Finally, the Ribbentrop-Molotov pact of 1939, amounting to an implicit alliance between Nazi Germany and the Soviet Union, bestowed upon the "Fascist beasts" a respectability and upon their rule an assumption of permanence, both utterly at odds with what Communists had been taught to believe.

The import of these successive blows that the Marxist-Leninist prophecies received from history could be temporarily concealed by the spectacular increase in political and military power with which the Soviet Union emerged from the Second World War. That power, revealed not only in military victory but also in the Communization of the nations of Eastern Europe, appeared to provide empirical proof both for the national achievements of the Soviet Union and for the superiority of Marxism-Leninism as a philosophy and system of government. However, with a dialectic "ruse of the idea" that Hegel would have enjoyed, this very triumph revealed Communisms's inner weakness and ushered in its destruction as a monolithic system of philosophy and government.

The beginning of the end of Communism as a unified system dates from Stalin's expulsion of Yugoslavia from the Communist camp in 1948. Tito's establishment of an autonomous "national Communism" not only as a doctrine but, more important, as a going concern confronted Stalin with a crucial dilemma. On the one hand, he could not recognize the legitimacy of such an autonomous Communism, independent of the Soviet Union in source, doctrine, and operation, without putting into question the legitimacy of his own rule. Thus Stalin had to expel Tito as a heretic. But on the other hand, Stalin had to demonstrate in actual performance his monopolistic possession of the truth of Marxism-Leninism and the invalidity of the Titoist counter-claims; for the very existence of a dissident Communist regime was a denial of his monopolistic pretense. He tried to destroy the Titoist regime and failed. Thereby he showed that, as the monopoly of Communist truth in the hands of the Soviet government is a function of the unchallengeable power of the rulers, so the monolithic domination of world Communism by the Soviet Union is a function of Soviet power. The validity of the Marxist-Leninist truth, as interpreted by the Soviet government, is coterminous with the reach of Soviet power; that truth conquered Eastern Europe on the bayonets of the Red Army, not by dint of its own inner persuasiveness. However, Tito owes his power not to the Red Army but to indigenous sources of military and political strength. Thus he could successfully maintain his own brand of Communism in spite of Soviet opposition. Stalin had to assert his monopolistic claim through the instrument of Soviet power and, by failing, showed the limits of that power.

This failure was embarrassing to the monopolistic claims of the Soviet Union, but it was not necessarily dangerous to the legitimacy of the Soviet regime as long as it was limited to one particular country, such as Yugoslavia, whose foreign policies, at the very least, were not spectacularly different from those of the Soviet Union. However, that legitimacy suffered grievous and irreparable damage when Khrushchev denounced Stalin at the Twentieth Party Congress in 1956. That attack is the decisive turning point in the history of Soviet legitimacy.

Stalin's Repudiation. Stalin was blessed with a dual charisma: one institutional, the other personal. As Lenin's successor to supreme power, he was the authoritative guardian, interpreter, and augmenter of the Marxist-Leninist heritage. And, by virtue of his unique personal qualities, he was worshipped as the greatest statesman, the greatest strategist, the greatest economist, the greatest linguist, the greatest genius of mankind, the incomparable teacher of progressive humanity. This giant of a man, almost the equal of Marx and Lenin, in Khrushchev's polemic words, "a superman possessing supernatural characteristics akin to those of a god," [5] was denounced by his successor as a bloodstained tyrant, the despoiler of the principles of Marxism-Leninism. Khrushchev thus performed three interconnected destructive deeds. By destroying the myth of Stalin's greatness in Marxist-Leninist terms, he cast doubt upon the legitimacy of any ruler or regime governing in the name of Marxism-Leninism. And in doing this, he impaired the monolithic character of Soviet rule with the Soviet Union and destroyed it abroad.

If a blood-stained tyrant could rule supreme for twenty years in the name of Marxist-Leninist legitimacy, how trustworthy was the test by which the successors of Marx and Lenin were chosen? That question was bound to be raised with regard not only to Stalin, but to any Communist regime tracing its legitimacy to

---

[5] Quoted in Bertram D. Wolfe, *Khrushchev and Stalin's Ghost* (New York: Frederick A. Praeger, 1957), p. 98.

Marxism-Leninism. And when Khrushchev raised it with regard to Stalin, he made sure that it would also be raised with regard to himself. It was raised in 1957 by a majority of the Presidium of the Central Committee, although Khrushchev managed through the plenum of the Central Committee to give a successful answer. He was less lucky in October of 1964. The question, however, is bound to be raised again with regard to his successor and his successor's successor, and the answer is likely to depend less and less upon conformity with the teachings of Marx and Lenin and more and more upon the pragmatic test of success and of the sheer ability to hold on to power.

It is admittedly hazardous, in view of the at best fragmentary nature of hard evidence, to speculate on the meaning of the "cultural revolution" in China. However, it is possible to see a similarity between Khrushchev's attack upon Stalin and Mao's attack upon the bureaucracy. Both tried to restore the original charisma of Marxism-Leninism by eliminating what they regarded as a corrupting deviation. For Khrushchev, that deviation was the tyrannical rule of one man, for Mao, the pragmatism of the many. In both instances, the attack upon the despoilers of the charisma could not help but impair the charisma itself. In the case of China in particular, indecisive factionalism, calling forth anarchy in theory and practice, must cast doubt upon all claims to legitimacy in Marxist-Leninist terms.

Khrushchev's attack upon Communist legitimacy from within could not fail to be more damaging than were the denials Marxism-Leninism suffered from historic experience. The doctrine could be defended at least with a certain measure of plausibility against the denial one or another of its tenets had suffered from historic experience. Thus Lenin could defend the integrity of the doctrine during the First World War by branding the leaders of the European proletariat fighting on behalf of their respective nations as "social-patriotic" traitors. He could explain the isolated character of the Bolshevist Revolution as a kind of temporary interlude due to the remaining strength of reactionary forces throughout the world and of a treasonous proletarian leadership. It was then left to Stalin to extend that interlude *ad infinitum* by proclaiming "socialism in one country." The shock to the Communist faith that the staying power of Fascism and, more particularly, the pact with Nazi Germany constituted was mitigated and in good measure obliterated by the transformation of the Second World War in June 1941 from an imperialistic struggle into the "Great Patriotic War."

In contrast, Khrushchev's attack upon Stalin went to the very heart of Communist legitimacy. By destroying Stalin's reputation, it impaired his own ability and that of his successors to govern in the name of Marxism-Leninism. The supporters of Khrushchev and the defenders of Stalin found themselves in the same leaking boat: They could not help but cast doubt upon the validity of a doctrine and the legitimacy of a political system that brought such leaders to the fore. And the doctrine had no plausible argument with which to dispel that doubt.

That doubt, on the part both of the governors and of the governed, is the source of what is called the internal "liberalization" of the Soviet regime. It is the peculiar nature of charismatic legitimacy, as pointed out before, that it is particularly vulnerable to failure. As it is a "gift from heaven," so it must at the very least guard against the exposure of being of this world. Once it is so exposed, it is emptied of its substance. The governors may continue to govern in its name, and the subjects may still pay obeisance to it. But both the rulers and the ruled have lost faith in the wisdom, the virtue, and the unchallengeable power of the government, which faith is the vital force of any legitimacy. They go through the motions of mouthing worn tenets and observing empty rituals, which at best serve the purpose of providing justifications and rationalizations for the actions of the government. However, this is not what now makes those actions acceptable to the governed. That acceptance now rests effectively only upon the power of the government to enforce its will and upon the benefits the governed receive from them.

This is indeed the essence of the "liberalization" of the Soviet regime. The Soviet government can no longer impose its will with the same totalitarian ruthlessness that was characteristic of Lenin and Stalin's rule. It has lost that ability not because it no longer has the physical power to impose its will upon a recalcitrant citizenry, but because it no longer firmly believes in the charismatic source of its own legitimacy. It can no longer maintain the monolithic character of Soviet society because it is no longer monolithic itself. It no longer purges and kills dissenters, not because it lacks the power, but because it lacks the moral conviction of its own legitimacy to overcome the new moral conviction of the dissenters in its midst. Instead of purging them, it must accommodate the dissenters. Thus Khrushchev's exposure of monolithic Stalinism has inevitably issued in a pragmatic pluralism within the Soviet government characterized by the competition among individuals and groups, all equal in legitimacy, for the determination of Soviet policies within a common Marxist-Leninist framework.

A government thus beset by doubt about its own legitimacy must govern a citizenry similarly doubtful. The pluralism from which its action springs is reflected in the nature of the action itself; typically, it will be lacking in that singleminded and ruthless decisiveness, which reflects unquestioning faith in the wisdom, virtue, and power of the actor. And it encounters among the citizens the same pluralism it had to cope with in its own midst. While the difficulties in coping with the former pluralism are in good measure hidden behind the veil of official secrecy and will be revealed only, if at all, when the controversy has faded into history, the dilemma the Soviet government faces in coming to terms with the latter is a matter of public record. On the one hand, the Soviet government is morally incapable of suppressing dissent after the fashion of Lenin and Stalin, and, on the other, it must continue to exert a considerable measure of monolithic control in order to maintain its monopoly of political power. It cannot afford morally to suppress dissent altogether, nor can it afford politically to allow dissent free reign. Thus it vacillates between the reassertion of monolithic control and "liberalization," i.e., granting a measure of freedom to express dissent. This dilemma is a function of the divorce of political power from the legitimacy that gave it birth. The monopoly of political power in the hands of the Soviet government is the political expression of the monopolistic pretense of Marxism-Leninism. The monopoly of political power has survived the monopolistic pretense. It is power denuded of legitimacy. As such, it is uncertain of itself, indecisive in application, and of dubious durability.

By denying explicitly the legitimacy of Stalin's rule, Khrushchev had implicitly put into question the legitimacy of Soviet rule. That question was from then on to be raised explicitly not only within the Soviet Union but throughout the Communist world. The negative answer given to it within the Soviet Union resulted in the "liberalization" of the Soviet regime. The same negative answer given abroad transformed polycentrism from the isolated Yugoslav instance into a universal phenomenon.

Polycentrism. Yugoslavia was the first and isolated example of polycentric Communism—that is, a Communism whose character and policies are determined not by the power or example of the Soviet Union but by the peculiar national qualities and needs of the country concerned. What characterizes this type of Communism is its national orientation and its consequent independence from the Soviet Union as well as from all other extraneous Communist models. This orientation may call forth institutions and policies similar or dissimilar to those of the Soviet Union, as the case may be. What is important is that this relationship, positive or negative, is not inherent but coincidental in a particular national Communism. Soviet Communism is essentially irrelevant to national Communism. Its monopolistic claims are rejected in so far as this particular nation is concerned; but, as a matter of principle, they are left intact with regard to all other nations.

Thus polycentrism is in the nature of a defection from the universal church, but it is not an outright attack upon the claim to universality itself. It is only by implication that universality is impaired in the very existence of the defector. The impairment becomes explicit when defection is transformed from an isolated instance, an exception to the monolithic rule, into a universal phenomenon.

That development started dramatically in the fall of 1956 with the revolts in Poland and Hungary, both of which reasserted the independence of Communist nations against the monolithic control of the Soviet Union. Both challenged the power of the Soviet state within its established and recognized sphere of influence. The Polish challenge was limited as to both means and ends. Poland, tied by its security interests to the Soviet Union, only sought to regain a measure of domestic autonomy and used political and military pressure, controlled by the government, to that end. Thus the Soviet Union could afford to retreat halfway since it did not have to meet a total challenge to its hegemony. This was indeed what the Soviet Union had to face in the Hungarian revolution; for here a popular revolt brought a government to power that opted out of the Soviet orbit altogether, and Soviet power had to be restored by means of a suppression commensurate with the challenge.

The Hungarian revolution proved that a Communist state was willing to challenge the power of the Soviet Union and all it stands for by way of monopolistic pretenses, and that the Soviet Union, with power and determination, was able to destroy the challenge. The latter hardly needed to be proven, but the demonstration of the former has indeed been of far-reaching historic importance. For the Hungarian revolution, in spite and in a profound sense perhaps because of its defeat, ushered in the era of polycentric Communism as a world-wide phenomenon. What many Communists throughout the world had felt, thought, and said in private, the Hungarians had made manifest: The monopolistic claims of Soviet Communism are dubious, and that they had to be supported by tanks and legalized murder only served to strengthen the doubts about their intrinsic validity. A charismatic legitimacy whose monopolistic claim to scientific rationality needs fire and sword to be persuasive cannot but appear as a contradiction in terms.

Once Poland and Hungary had set the example, it remained for others to seek less provocative ways of following suit. This is the road Romania has most consistently and openly taken—and the road Czechoslovakia has tried to take. Other Communist governments and parties throughout the world have done the same, though, except for China and Cuba, less consistently and openly. The cumulative effects of this multitude of polycentric deviations and defections have been qualitatively different from the isolated defection of Yugoslavia. For the assertion of national interests and independent judgments by scores of Communist governments and parties, none challenging the monopolistic claim of the Soviet Union explicitly, amounts to a collective denial of that claim. It also amounts to a collective assertion of the limits of Soviet power.

That denial and assertion were for all practical purposes formalized in the repeated refusal of a number of Communist governments and parties to consent to a World Communist Congress at which the Soviet Union would obtain confirmation for its monopolistic possession of Communist truth against China's contrary claims. Opposition to the convocation of that Congress serving this purpose is tantamount to a refusal to recognize the validity of the Soviet claim. That the number of opponents is sufficiently large and influential to have delayed and thus far prevented the convocation of such a Congress as originally intended indicates the decline of the legitimacy and of the power of the Soviet regime in the eyes of the Communist world.

The Chinese position is different from the genuine polycentric one in that it not only disregards the Soviet version of Communism as irrelevant for itself, but that it replaces it with one whose universal relevance it proclaims. In other words, China challenges explicitly the monopolistic pretense of the Soviet Union and opposes it with a monopolistic pretense of its own. Three factors enabled it to take that position.

First, like Yugoslavia, China received Communism not on the bayonets of the Red Army but through victory in a civil war that owed little to the doctrinal and material support of the Soviet Union. Quite to the contrary, by relying upon the peasants rather than the industrial proletariat, Mao deviated radically from the teachings of Marxism-Leninism and disregarded the advice he received from the Soviet Union as well. Thus the Chinese Communists never recognized in practice Moscow's monopoly of the truth of Marxism-Leninism, and in consequence Stalin had good reason for declaring that the Chinese Communists were not Marxist-Leninists at all.

Secondly, while all the other Communist governments and parties are to a greater or lesser extent dependent upon the political, military, and economic support of the Soviet Union, China possesses indigenous national resources commensurate with its objectives at home and abroad. Striving to become a power of the first rank, it welcomed Soviet assistance, especially in the nuclear field. But when the Soviet Union in the late 1950s confronted it with a choice between renunciation of this national objective and permanent subordination, on the one hand, and the independent pursuit of that objective, on the other, China could afford to choose the latter alternative.

Finally, after Khrushchev had put into question the legitimacy of Moscow's monopolistic successorship to the mantle of Marx and Lenin by denigrating Stalin, Mao became by force of circumstance the natural pretender to that mantle. For he alone among the major Communist leaders was untainted by association with either Stalin's or Khrushchev's rule. Furthermore, and most important, his interpretation of Marxism-Leninism had succeeded in practice under conditions seemingly similar to those prevailing elsewhere in Asia, Africa, and Latin America.

By exposing Stalin as an impostor, Khrushchev had attacked the charismatic legitimacy of Soviet rule itself; that attack was rendered plausible by the consequent disintegration of monolithic Soviet rule in the form of "liberalization" at home and polycentrism abroad. Mao identified himself with, and accentuated, the negative results of Khrushchev's argument, in so far as the monopolistic pretense of the Soviet Union was concerned. But he turned it against Khrushchev by exposing him as the impostor and reasserting the legitimacy of Stalin's rule. Khrushchev, not Stalin, was accused of having deviated from the teachings of Marxism-Leninism, and Mao remained the sole legitimate successor to Lenin and Stalin, the defender of the true faith, the beneficiary and guardian of the Marxist-Leninist charisma.

In consequence of this competition for the monopolistic possession of the truth of Marxism-Leninism, the same fanatical sectarianism which we found to have split the Marxist parties everywhere before 1917 and after that in non-Communist states now divides Communist states as well. The same epithets, such as "revisionists," "adventurists," "social reactionaries," "traitors," which formerly only Communist factions hurled against one another, or Communist governments used against foreign Communist factions, now are used by Communist governments against each other to discredit their respective philosophies and policies.

The rivalry between two great Communist nations, each claiming a monopoly of Communist truth, resembles the rivalry among Communist factions in that there is no way of objectively testing the validity of these claims except by success—that is, power. Here, however, the similarity ends. The relative power of factions can be tested by a variety of social contrivances, such as intraparty or parliamentary elections, competition for membership, exclusions and fusions, ostracism and assassination. On the other hand, states may compete for influence and power throughout the world. Any success a state will have anywhere in the world will be interpreted as empirical proof of the validity of its monopolistic claim, and vice versa. Yet such competition is bound to be inconclusive. For as long as a state exists, pretending to be in the monopolistic possession of Communist truth, it puts into question, by its very existence, the validity of the counterclaims on the part of another Communist state. They cannot both be valid, and there is no way of proving empirically, short of a decisive war, which is. Yet, while both claims cannot be valid, they can both be spurious. And that is exactly the conclusion a drawn-out, inconclusive conflict must suggest.

Here we are in the presence of still another significant distinction between other-worldly religions and a secular religion, such as Communism, that claims to be *the* science of society. Rival claims of religious dogmas concern the correct interpretation of the divine will, especially as regards the sure road to salvation. They are in the nature of things not susceptible to empirical tests, short of the primitive one of ordeals and the working of miracles, and hence, can go on forever without impairment of their plausibility. The plausibility of a political doctrine, claiming to provide a blueprint for successful political action, cannot survive consistent failure. It cannot avoid being weakened by the consistent inconclusiveness of empirical tests. Thus the inconclusiveness of the doctrinal rivalry between the Soviet Union and China is bound to have a debilitating effect upon the plausibility of either claim.

Between the genuine polycentrism of which Yugoslavia, Czechoslovakia, and Romania are the prototypes, and the rival monopolistic claims of China, the Communism of Cuba occupies an intermediate position. It is genuinely polycentric in that it aims to reflect the interests, and meet the opportunities, of individual nations. But it conceives of these interests and opportunities not as peculiar to a particular individual nation but as being typical of a number of nations similarly situated, of which Cuba is the prototype. Cuba's polycentrism, then, possesses a distinct expansionist quality; for Cuba offers itself as a model and as a fountainhead of truth and support rivaling the Soviet Union and China—not, it is true, to the whole Communist world, but to all those Communist movements which might profit from the Cuban example and support. Consequently, the impairment of the universalistic claims of the Soviet Union and China is here quantitatively greater than that caused by the polycentrism of a number of individual nations, such as Yugoslavia, Czechoslovakia, or Romania. For it is not one particular nation that puts its national interests above the Soviet or Chinese claims; but a potentially indefinite number of nations, having certain characteristics in common, imitate Cuba in choosing a road to Communism different from that of the Soviet Union and China.

This indefinite quantity of potential polycentric defections is bound to have a negative qualitative impact upon the monopolistic claims of the Soviet Union and China. For the quantitative limitation of the validity of these monopolistic claims, if it becomes large enough, deprives them of all substantive significance. It exposes the monopolistic claims as empty pretense and reduces them in practice to just another polycentric version of Communist dogma. The Communist world, which is supposed to be one world, formed by the one truth of Marxism-Leninism, then is transformed into a pluralistic universe in which at best different polycentric Communisms live peacefully side by side or at worst struggle for predominance with each other. In any event, regardless of whether there will be rivalry for "spheres of influence" or peaceful coexistence among several polycentric Communists, such pluralism would empty the monopolistic claims of all substance.

THE FOREIGN POLICIES OF COMMUNISM

Thus the Communist world appears to have reverted to the traditional pluralistic pattern in which individual nations cooperate or compete with each other for the protection and promotion of their respective interests. This is the accepted meaning of polycentrism. The observation is correct as far as it goes. But it does not go far enough; for it does not take into account the fact that this polycentric world is composed of nations whose Communist character qualifies the polycentric orientation of their foreign policies. Because this polycentric world is also a Communist world, the foreign policies of its members cannot be explained by exclusive reference to their traditional national interests. Communism has introduced three new dimensions into traditional foreign policy: it has provided new instruments with which to support traditional interests; it has created new interests; and it has changed the style of foreign policy.

Stalin: Communism as an Instrument of Russian Power

The transformation of the tenets of Communism into instruments for Russia's traditional foreign policy was the great innovative contribution Stalin made to the foreign policy of the Soviet Union. The nature of this contribution has been widely misunderstood. The Western world has looked upon Stalin as an orthodox Bolshevik, the fanatical proponent of a "rigid theology," [6] bent upon spreading the Communist gospel indiscriminately and by hook or crook to the four corners of the earth. Those who hold this view judge Stalin as though he were Trot-

[6] The words are those of Arthur Schlesinger, Jr., who, in *The New York Review of Books* VII, No. 6 (October 20, 1966), 37, reaffirmed the popular assessment of Stalin as a fanatical promoter of Communism for its own sake.

sky: They confuse Stalin's means, which, among others, indeed comprise the classic Communist methods, ruthlessly applied, with his ends, which were in the tradition of Czarist expansionism rather than of the Marxist-Leninist promotion of world revolution as an end in itself. In truth, as concerns its relations to Marxism-Leninism, Stalin's foreign policy is distinct from Lenin's and Trotsky's, on the one hand, and from that of Khrushchev and his successors, on the other.

Lenin saw in Russian Bolshevism the doctrinal and political fountainhead of the Communist world revolution and in the success of that revolution the precondition for the survival of the Bolshevist regime in Russia. Russian Bolshevism was the "base" of world revolution; that was its historic function and justification in Marxist terms, as world revolution was Russian Bolshevism's inevitable sequel and the guarantee of its success. On this doctrinal foundation, as developed in Lenin's *Left-wing Communism: An Infantile Disorder,* the Soviet Union stood in its earliest years as a guide and instigator of violent revolution throughout the world. Trotsky gave an extreme characterization to this first phase of Bolshevist foreign policy when he declared on his appointment as People's Commissar for Foreign Affairs: "I will issue a few revolutionary proclamations to the people of the world and shut up shop." [7]

However, in contrast to Marx and the other Marxists, Lenin used Marxism not as a blueprint to be superimposed intact upon a recalcitrant reality but as an instrument for the acquisition of power. He reversed the priority between Marxism and power, traditional with the Marxists. One could say that he loved Marx, but he loved power more; he was a practitioner of power before he was an interpreter of Marx. Thus he decided what needed to be done for the sake of power, and then he used his version of Marx to justify what he was doing. One only has to read Lenin's polemics against Kautsky in order to realize how completely Marxism has here changed its traditional function. We are no longer in the presence of a doctrinaire disputation in search of the Marxist truth for its own sake. Rather, we are witnessing a

[7] Quoted in Carr, *op. cit.,* p. 16.

phase in the conquest of power undertaken by a man who uses the doctrine with passionate fury as a hammer with which to obliterate views that, if accepted, might bar him from that conquest. What Lenin perfected for the domestic politics of the Soviet Union—the transformation of *the* science of society into an instrument for the acquisition of power—Stalin achieved for the foreign policies of the Soviet Union.

Both the consolidation of the Bolshevist regime within Russia and the collapse of the attempts at world revolution gave birth to Stalin's policy of "socialism in one country." Stalin's foreign policy in its first phase, lasting until victory in the Second World War, served the purpose of protecting the Soviet experiment from hostile outside intervention. During that period, Soviet foreign policy was haunted by the nightmare of a united front of the capitalistic powers seeking the destruction of the Soviet Union. The means Stalin employed to that end—clandestine military cooperation with Germany, temporary support of the League of Nations, the 1935 alliance with France, the implicit 1939 alliance with Germany—were in the classic tradition of power diplomacy. What was new was the additional power the Soviet Union could draw from its monolithic control of Communist parties throughout the world. The promotion of popular fronts and the Soviet intervention in the Spanish Civil War were the main manifestations of this new opportunity for the expansion of Soviet power.

How effective this use of world Communism for the purposes of the Russian state has been is strikingly revealed in the testimony of British and Canadian members of the Gouzenko spy ring before the Royal Commission investigating the case.[8] When asked why they had betrayed their own countries to the Soviet Union, almost all the members replied that they had done it for the sake of humanity, that concern for humanity supersedes loyalty to any individual nation, and that the interests of humanity and those of the Soviet Union are identical. Communist internationalism and Russian nationalism are here brought into

8 *Royal Commission To Investigate Disclosures of Secret and Confidential Information to Unauthorized Persons,* (Ottawa: HMSO, 1946).

harmony. The Soviet Union appears endowed with a monopoly of truth and virtue, which sets it apart from, and above, all other nations. It may be pointed out in passing that here the Soviet Union is assigned the same privileged position among the nations that the proletariat occupies in Marxist philosophy among the classes.

From 1943 onward, with Soviet victory over Germany assured, the main purpose of Soviet foreign policy changed from security to territorial expansion. Stalin sought to expand Soviet control primarily into territories adjacent to Russia, the traditional objectives of Russian expansionism. The conquest of Eastern Europe and of part of the Balkans, the pressure on Turkey for control of the Dardanelles and its northern provinces, the attempts to gain footholds on the eastern shore of the Mediterranean and in northern Iran and to draw all of Germany into the Russian orbit, the recovery of the Russian interests in China—all these moves follow the lines of expansion traced by the Czars. The limits of Stalin's territorial ambition were the traditional limits of Russian expansionism. The former even fell short of the latter when political and military considerations appeared to make that retraction advisable. Thus Stalin honored the agreement with Great Britain of 1944, dividing the Balkans into spheres of influence, recognized explicitly on the occasion of the Greek civil war that Greece was in the British sphere, and he lived up to that recognition in the policies he pursued. As Stalin put it to Eden during the Second World War: "The trouble with Hitler is that he doesn't know where to stop. I know where to stop."

These traditional purposes of Stalin's foreign policy, as well as their misunderstanding by the West, are clearly and dramatically revealed in the confrontation at Yalta between Stalin and Roosevelt. From that confrontation Stalin emerged as the power politician who, unencumbered by considerations of ideological advantage, sought to restore and expand Russia's traditional sphere of influence, while Roosevelt defended an abstract philosophic principle, incapable of realization under the circumstances. Poland, said Stalin, is "a question . . . of life and death for the

Soviet State." [9] Roosevelt's philosophy was most strikingly expressed in his report on the Yalta Conference to Congress on March 1, 1945:

> The Crimean Conference . . . spells the end of the system of unilateral action and exclusive alliances and spheres of influence and balances of power and all the other expedients which have been tried for centuries—and have failed.
>
> We propose to substitute for all these a universal organization which all peace-loving nations will finally have a chance to join.[10]

Yet it was through this "system of unilateral action . . . and all the other expedients" of traditional power politics that Stalin intended to secure Russia's predominance in Eastern Europe.

The incompatibility of these two conceptions of the postwar world came to a head in the controversy over the kind of governments to be established in the nations of Eastern Europe. Stalin insisted that these governments be "friendly." Roosevelt and Churchill conceded that they should be "friendly" to the Soviet Union, but they insisted that they should also be "democratic." Stalin clearly saw the inner contradiction of that position. "A freely elected government in any of these countries," he said, "would be anti-Soviet, and that we cannot allow." [11] Stalin could not help but interpret the Western position as implacable hostility to Russian interests, while the West saw in the ruthless transformation of the nations of Eastern Europe into Russian satellites empirical proof for the unlimited ambitions of Soviet Communism.

This misunderstanding resulted from the combination of two factors: the actual Communization of Eastern Europe and the attempted Communization of much of the rest of Europe, and the use of Communist parties throughout the world on behalf of Soviet policies justified by Soviet spokesmen in terms of Marxism-

[9] Quoted in James F. Byrnes, *Speaking Frankly* (New York: Harper & Brothers, 1947), p. 32.

[10] *Nothing To Fear: The Selected Addresses of Franklin Delano Roosevelt 1932–1945*, edited by Ben Zevin (Cambridge, Mass.: Houghton Mifflin, 1946), p. 453.

[11] Quoted in Philip E. Mosely, *The Kremlin in World Politics* (New York: Vintage Books, 1960), p. 214.

Leninism. Thus, by taking the Soviet government at its Marxist-Leninist word, one could not fail to conclude that Stalin was on his way to achieving what Lenin and Trotsky had been attempting in vain: to make the Marxist-Leninist prophecy of the Communization of the world come true. Haunted by the spectre of Communism, Western opinion found it hard to appreciate the extent to which Stalin used Communist governments and parties as instruments for the ends of Russian power. He needed governments in Eastern Europe "friendly" to the Soviet Union. He did not care about the ideological character of these governments and parties as long as they were "friendly." Thus he tried to install aristocratic German generals in Germany and to come to terms with the Romanian monarchy and a freely elected Hungarian government, and failed. On the other hand, he established a stable *modus vivendi* with a non-Communist government in Finland. Yet he realized that, save for that exception, the only people in Eastern Europe who were willing to serve the interests of the Soviet Union were Communists. In private conversations, he heaped scorn upon the fools and knaves who allowed themselves to be used by him, but he used them because there was nobody else to use. And he was as hostile to Communist nationalists as he was to non-Communist ones. He purged the Communists of Eastern Europe who refused to do his bidding, and for the same reason was at best indifferent to Chinese Communism, exorcised and tried to bring down the Communist government of Yugoslavia, and opposed the projected federation of Communist Balkan states. For him, then, Communist orthodoxy was a means to an end, and the end was the power of the Russian state traditionally defined.

It is perhaps only in retrospect—by searching for the meaning of Stalin's policies in his private statements and kept commitments rather than in his public pronouncements, by comparing what Stalin did with what he could have done but did not do, and finally by comparing Stalin's policies with those of his predecessors and successors—that one can assess correctly the nature of Stalin's foreign policy. And it is only in retrospect that one can savor the irony of the pope of Marxism-Leninism manipulating the tenets of the doctrine with cynical pragmatism on behalf of the national interests of Russia, while his Western opponents, more serious about the doctrine than he, sought the meaning of his deeds in the tenets of the doctrine.

Khrushchev: Communism as Ends and Means of Soviet Foreign Policy

It was a similar penchant for taking the words for the deeds, or at least those words which sound pleasant to the ear, that was responsible for the misunderstanding of Khrushchev's foreign policies. It is generally held that the foreign policies of Khrushchev were less "aggressive"—that is, less expansionist—than Stalin's, and hence less dangerous to the interests of the West. This view derived primarily from two terms Khrushchev introduced into the vocabulary of foreign policy: "relaxation of tensions" and "peaceful" or "competitive coexistence." Yet these propositions do not seek a peaceful state of affairs as an end in itself; rather they aim at a concrete political result, made attractive by the pacific terms in which it is presented. Thus, when Khrushchev spoke of relaxation of tension, he wanted the West to stop challenging the European territorial status quo of 1945. In order to force the West to do this, he himself challenged the status quo of West Berlin twice at the risk of war. On the other hand, in order to maintain the status quo of the Soviet empire, he went to war with Hungary with methods as ruthless as any Stalin had ever used.

When Khrushchev spoke of "peaceful" or "competitive coexistence," he expressed his resolution to avoid a direct confrontation between the United States and the Soviet Union in Europe and to try to settle the issues outstanding between the two superpowers in favor of the Soviet Union through competition for the allegiance of the uncommitted third of the world. He tried to minimize the risk of nuclear war during the last years of his premiership by bypassing Europe, where the vital interests of the two superpowers were directly at stake in the form of a military confrontation. Instead, he undertook to channel the conflict with the United States into directions that would lead the Soviet

Union to victory either through the piecemeal erosion of the American positions or the filling of political and military vacuums.

Those who rely for the analysis of Soviet foreign policy upon verbal propositions alone and who take comfort from those mentioned must come to terms with another set of such propositions which give a concrete political meaning to terms such as "relaxation of tension" and "peaceful" or "competitive coexistence." It was Khrushchev, not Stalin, who expressed the conviction that he would witness in his lifetime the world-wide triumph of Communism and looked forward to the day when "we will bury you." It was Khrushchev, not Stalin, who proclaimed Soviet support for "wars of national liberation." We are here in the presence of a mode of thought typical of the Soviet version of Marxism-Leninism when the Soviet Union must face a political situation to which the tenets of Marxism-Leninism do not apply. While the integrity of the prophecy is maintained, its fulfillment is relegated to a more or less distant future. Thus Khrushchev professed again, in accord with his predecessors, the faith of orthodox Marxism-Leninism in the ultimate transformation of the world in the Communist image. Yet, while Stalin had relegated the fulfillment of that prophecy to an indefinite future, at the very least not visibly connected with action taken here and now, Khrushchev drastically shortened the span between prophecy and consummation, and, in contrast to Stalin and in accord with Lenin and Trotsky, he set to work to make that prophecy come true.

The debt that Khrushchev's foreign policy owes to Marxism-Leninism is both greater and more complex than Stalin's. Stalin discovered the uses of Marxism-Leninism as a tool to enlarge Russia's power and to weaken its enemies; it was for him not a guide for action by virtue of its inherent truth. Khrushchev is the restorer of Marxism-Leninism as to its ends and the innovator as concerns the means to achieve those ends. There is not only a quantitative but also a qualitative contrast between Stalin's expansion of Soviet power into territories adjacent to Russia, ruthless in the choice of means but limited by Russian tradition in the choice of objectives, and Khrushchev's political, military, and economic support for Egypt, Syria, Cuba, Guinea, Mali, Somalia, and Tanzania. These objectives owe nothing to the traditional interests of Russia; they are manifestations of the world-wide aspirations of Marxism-Leninism.

Khrushchev's pursuit of the unlimited aspirations of Marxism-Leninism was subject to two limiting factors: the protection and promotion of Russia's traditional interests in Europe and Asia and the avoidance of a direct military confrontation with the United States. It was these limitations which exposed Khrushchev to the Chinese reproach of "revisionism." Khrushchev tried to stabilize the European territorial status quo, proclaimed as provisional by the West (particularly by West Germany) by raising the issue of West Berlin. And following in Stalin's footsteps, he envisaged in private conversations the inevitability of an Eastern orientation of all of Germany, directed against the West. He preferred a break with China and the consequent split in the world Communist movement to Soviet cooperation in making China a great power, potentially superior to the Soviet Union. His support of "wars of national liberation" stopped short of a direct military confrontation with the United States. Thus he was willing to accept a tactical defeat over Cuba, more spectacular than the strategic victory he had won.

However, the original contribution of Khrushchev lies in the sphere of the means he chose to support his ends. Both Lenin and Stalin had to rely in the main upon foreign Communist parties to achieve those of their respective goals which were not susceptible to immediate military pressure. Aside from military pressure, their methods were limited to manipulation, subversion, and revolution. Khrushchev had at his disposal a new weapon: the economic and technological achievements of the Soviet Union and the prestige resulting therefrom. Thus his methods ran the whole gamut from military intervention and threats to diplomatic pressure, foreign aid and trade, support of subversion, and the propagandistic exploitation of the new technological prestige of the Soviet Union. Most important, Khrushchev was the first leader of Communism who could point to the actual achievements of the Soviet Union as empirical proof of the truth of Marxism-Leninism. The Communist prophets from Marx to Stalin had to argue philosophically for the foreordained triumph of Communism, the Communist salvation of mankind that would inevitably occur, in however distant a future. Khrushchev could point to what was occurring in the Soviet Union as a token of the correctness of that prophecy. Thus he argued from actual and contemporary experience rather than from the sacred texts. That shift in the nature of the argument gave a new lease on life to the charisma of Marxism-Leninism, enfeebled as it was by the blows it had received from history and the exposure of Stalin's rule. From the actual achievements of the Soviet Union, Khrushchev gained the confidence, on the one hand, to challenge the foremost capitalist nation at its own game of technology and production and, on the other, to offer Communism to the other nations, especially the backward ones, as a universal principle of social organization, a model to emulate.

For Khrushchev, then, Marxism-Leninism was the embodiment of unquestioned truth, as Marxism had been for Lenin. Yet, while Lenin tried to force a resistant reality into the Marxist mold, Khrushchev thought he witnessed an existing reality that received its meaning from Marxism-Leninism and in turn bestowed plausibility upon it. Sputnik owed nothing to the teachings of Marx and Lenin, yet the Communist claim to the monopolistic possession of the truth drew sustenance from this technological success. While Lenin had worked in vain for the fulfillment of the Marxist prophecies, Khrushchev only needed to make the technological success of the Soviet Union intelligible as the partial fulfillment of these prophecies. Marx had tried to understand the world in order to change it; Lenin tried to practice what Marx had preached; and Khrushchev tried to make the changes accomplished in the name of Marxism-Leninism into a model of universal application.

The Burden of a Moribund Charisma

Khrushchev's prophecies did not fare any better at the hands of history than those of Marx. His personal charisma, like that of the doctrine, was at the mercy of short-term success, and his failures in foreign policy were as spectacular as his claims and objectives. Unlike Stalin, he did not know when to stop, or he learned it only toward the end of his career, in 1962, when he had to beat a humiliating tactical retreat. It fell to his successors to draw the practical lessons from his failures. They have continued Khrushchev's policies of "relaxation of tensions" and "peaceful" or "competitive coexistence." But they have done so with two significant and interconnected shifts of emphasis. Following Stalin's example, they have tried to restore the interests of the Russian state as the rationale of Soviet foreign policy, and erecting the lesson Khrushchev had learned in 1962 into a general principle of Russian statecraft, they have made the avoidance of a direct military confrontation with the United States the overriding concern of Soviet foreign policy.

The new orientation of Soviet foreign policy toward the Russian national interest has come to the fore in its contrast with, and opposition to, the policies pursued by China outside Asia and by Cuba in Latin America. Their policies seek national or regional revolution as an intermediate step toward world revolution in the classic Marxist-Leninist sense, and they try to instigate and support revolution with the classic methods of Communist manipulation and subversion. There is no connection whatsoever between these policies and the traditional national interests of the nations pursuing them. These policies are the outgrowth of Marxism-Leninism in its pure form.

On the other hand, where the Soviet Union has been faced with a choice between support for a revolutionary Communist movement and the pursuit of its national interests, it has with ever more blatant consistency chosen the latter, despite the destructive effects such a policy might have for the chances of Communist revolution. Thus the Soviet Union has supported the Egyptian government, which has outlawed the Communist Party and put its leaders in jail. It has tried to enter into large-scale trade relations with Latin American governments at the risk of strengthening the forces of the status quo against incipient revolutionary movements. At the very least, it does not oppose, if it does not actually support, those Latin American Communist parties which have washed their hands of the revolutionary guerrillas whom Cuba supports. While China has sought to prevent a peaceful settlement of the "war of national liberation" in Vietnam, the Soviet Union has indicated a desire for such a settlement, if it has not actually tried to bring it about. It is again ironic that "the Fatherland of Socialism" has unobstrusively and effectively expanded its political and military influence in the eastern Mediterranean, the Middle East, South Asia, the Indian Ocean, and its commercial influence throughout the world [12] in

12 See, for instance, "The Russians Capitalize on the Suez Closure," *The Financial Times,* February 14, 1968:

> As far as the U.S.S.R. is concerned, however, there is also quite a lot of commercial advantage to gain from a continuation of the Suez obstacle. The huge land mass of the Soviet Union lies across "straightline" routes from Western Europe to most of Asia, and the Russians are now beginning to exploit this fact.
> Already they have developed two alternative water routes of their own to the East—the waterway system linking the Baltic Sea with the Caspian, and the Northern Sea Route from Europe through the Arctic Ocean to the Pacific. Distances by these routes are shorter than via Suez (unlike the corresponding Cape journeys) and in the event of a long closure could well capture some of the traffic permanently.
> Iran's use of the Baltic-Caspian waterway has reached an advanced stage already. This route, passing from Leningrad through various lakes, rivers, and canals and thence down the Volga into the Caspian, is cutting 2,700 miles off the Suez route between Germany and Iran. Cargo times have fallen from 50 to 25 days.
> Iran sent 400,000 tons of transit goods across the Soviet Union in 1966, mainly along this route. This was a big increase on the 1965 figure and 1967 is likely to show another large increase. Transport costs are claimed to be lower than via Suez. . . . Russia announced last spring that she would also be opening her previously tightly guarded Arctic shipping lane across the top of Siberia to foreign ships. Last August the Soviet cargo boat *Novovoronezh* docked in Yokohama with 2,000 tons of merchandise from Hamburg after making what was heralded as the inaugural run on a new international sea route from Europe to Japan through these icy but strategic waters in only 28 days. . . . Japanese boats, already frequent callers at Soviet ports in eastern Siberia, should especially benefit from the route's opening to foreign ships. Yokohoma is about 12,500 miles from London by way of Suez; via the Northern Sea Route the distance is cut to about 8,500 miles. . . . These new developments [new

the best tradition of great power politics, while the foremost capitalistic nation has been hypnotized by the Communist aspect of the Vietnam war to such an extent as to be oblivious to this expansion of Soviet power.

This policy of promoting and supporting "wars of national liberation" and Communist revolutions (at best, very selectively), and of actually trying to prevent or abate many of them, results primarily from a pragmatic approach to foreign policy that is indifferent to the ends and means of Marxism-Leninism. But it also owes something to the overriding concern of Soviet foreign policy: the avoidance of situations that might lead to a direct military confrontation between the United States and the Soviet Union in the form of nuclear war. At the height of his power, Khrushchev could present his opponents with ultimatums and threaten them with atomic destruction. Although he was cautious enough to refrain from following up his threatening words with corresponding actions, one could not be absolutely sure that he would. Since his downfall, ultimatums and nuclear threats have disappeared from the vocabulary of the Soviet government, and now when the interests of the Soviet Union and the United States clash, as they did in the Middle East in the spring of 1967, both superpowers assure each other of their peaceful intentions. While Cuba would like to involve the United States in a number of simultaneous Vietnams—an involvement that would be likely to overtax America's conventional resources and thereby confront the United States with a choice between retreat and nuclear war—the Soviet Union, by the same token, has sought to end or at least limit the war in Vietnam.

On the face of it, then, the foreign policy of the Soviet Union appears to have come full circle. Communism was the end and revolution the means of Lenin's foreign policy. Stalin used Communism as a tool to serve the interests of the Russian state.

---

land and air connections across the Soviet Union] all go to indicate the U.S.S.R.'s key geographical position as the great land bridge between East and West, Soviet cities like Novosibirsk, Khabarovsk and Tashkent could well become as familiar to the international jet set as Beirut, Teheran or Delhi in the near future.

Khrushchev used the power of the Russian state to further the interests of Communism. And now both ends and means of Soviet foreign policy appear to be determined by the interests and power of the Russian state. This analysis is correct as far as it goes, but it leaves one last question unanswered: How do Khrushchev's successors define the interests of the Russian state?

In order to answer this question, we must return to the point from which we started and remind ourselves of the nature of the legitimacy from which the Soviet government derives its authority. The Soviet government still governs in the name of Marxism-Leninism. It is clear that the Marxist-Leninist pretense to the monopolistic possession of scientific truth has not survived the blows the doctrine received from historic experience, from Khrushchev, and from dissident Communists. The science of society, which in its monopolistic pretense has always been nothing more than a dogma, has lost its intellectual persuasiveness for all concerned. It has been reduced to a ritual, mechanically invoked for ideological and polemic purposes. And it is so invoked by leaders who do not even pretend, as their predecessors did, to anything approaching a personal charisma.

Still, this ruin of a once imposing edifice is all the legitimacy the Soviet government has got and can afford to have. The Soviet regime is not old enough to invoke the pre-Bolshevist tradition of Russia, even though Stalin, not without reason, tried to connect his rule with that of the great Czars, being indeed himself in the tradition of both Ivan the Terrible and Peter the Great. Nor is the Soviet regime old enough to invoke a Bolshevist tradition, leaving aside the difficulty of fashioning a tradition spanning half a century of which three decades are identified with the deviant Stalin and one with the fumbling Khrushchev. The Soviet regime cannot invoke constitutional rationality without risking the loss of its monopoly of power. Thus it has nothing left to clothe its power with but the threadbare charismatic vestments of Marxism-Leninism. From the weakness of this legitimacy, two consequences follow for Soviet foreign policy, one concerning its substance, the other its style.

Soviet foreign policy pursues two disparate kinds of objectives:

those dictated by the traditional interests of Russia, such as friendly governments in Eastern Europe, a neutral or friendly Germany, access to the Mediterranean, the security of the Asian frontiers; and those provided by Communism, such as Vietnam, Cuba, Somalia. One is reminded of the distinction Talleyrand made in 1808 in a conversation with Alexander I: "The Rhine, the Alps, and the Pyrenees are the conquests of France; the rest, of the Emperor; they mean nothing to France." Yet it was the Emperor who governed France, superimposing his interests upon those of France, as Communists govern the Soviet Union, adding Communist interests to those of Russia.

The Soviet Union cannot afford to shed the claim, however implausible it has become on empirical grounds, that it is not just a nation among others but the model of a nation built upon the principles of Marxism-Leninism. It cannot shed that claim without destroying the moral foundation of legitimacy, upon which its government rests. Yet, as we have seen, neither can the Soviet government effectively govern by invoking that claim. Thus, both at home and abroad, it must strike an uneasy and unstable balance between the demands of the claim and the requirements of pragmatic policies. At home, it endeavors to give a limited measure of satisfaction to popular aspirations to free-dom and prosperity within the unchanged framework of mono-lithic rule, at the risk of either losing its monopoly of power or having to revert to its Stalinist misuse.

A similar dilemma faces the Soviet Union in its relations with other Communist governments, especially those of Eastern Eu-rope. That dilemma appears in two different configurations. First, the Soviet Union has a traditional national interest in seeing the nations of Eastern Europe governed by friendly gov-ernments, which can only be Communist governments. The uni-versal trend toward polycentric pluralism compels the Soviet Union to allow these governments considerable leeway in their domestic and foreign policies, provided they remain Communist (i.e., friendly). Yet the Soviet Union, by having to reconcile itself to a measure of liberalization in its relations with these govern-ments, runs the risk of either losing control altogether or having to restore it with the methods Khrushchev used in Hungary in 1956. This is the dilemma the Soviet Union faced in 1968 in Czechoslovakia.

Second, while the Soviet Union can no longer prove the claim to uniqueness in Marxist-Leninist terms in relation to other Communist governments and movements, it can still try to prove it—and this is its sole opportunity—in competition with the foremost capitalist nation, the United States. However, these policies may be irrelevant or even detrimental to the traditional national interests of Russia. The Soviet government must then try to strike a balance between two distinct if not contradictory claims, the Communist commitment and the Russian national interest. The Soviet support of Cuba and North Vietnam are cases in point.

The support of Cuba to the estimated tune of a million dollars a day presents a dual paradox. It is not compensated for by any tangible advantage in terms of the Russian national interest and only by the intangible one of honoring Khrushchev's commitment to the support of a Communist government. Furthermore, this support strengthens, and perhaps keeps in power, a competitive Communist regime whose policies in favor of violent revolution are diametrically opposed to those of the Soviet Union.

Similarly, the fate of Vietnam, North and South, has no bearing upon the traditional national interests of Russia. But it bears acutely upon the interests of the Soviet Union as the "Fatherland of Socialism." The Soviet Union cannot afford to sit idly by while the United States destroys the Communist regime of North Vietnam, or to concede to China a monopoly of support; for doing so would jeopardize its claims to legitimacy abroad and at home. However, while the Soviet Union cannot afford to disengage itself from these conflicts, it cannot afford to acerbate them either, because it must avoid a direct military confrontation with the United States. While, on the one hand, it fulfills its Communist commitments, it must, on the other, exert a restraining influence upon the "fraternal Socialist governments." Thus it has tried—so far unsuccessfully—to persuade Castro to give up his support for violent revolution in Latin America and has impressed upon the North Vietnamese government the need for a negotiated settlement.

Here the Soviet Union faces a dilemma which it has in common with the other great nuclear power. Both support their national interests with the threat or the use of force. But neither of them can afford to resort to nuclear force, and since 1962 they have foregone even the threat to use it. Their ability to achieve their ends, then, depends upon the use of conventional force. Consequently, they must forego success and be willing to accept failure or stalemate if the relentless pursuit of their advantage would conjure up the possibility that the losing side might want to redress its fortunes by resort to nuclear arms. In other words, the side that has the advantage must avoid confronting the other side with a choice between ignominious retreat and resort to nuclear arms. Such a policy requires restraint in the use of the conventional instruments, diplomatic and military. It must allow both sides avenues of retreat while saving face. The settlement of the Cuban crisis of 1962 is a classic example of this technique.

Such a policy is difficult for any nation to pursue; for it requires a new mode of thinking which accepts compromise as a substitute for victory and thereby exposes itself to the reproach of weakness. Such a policy is particularly difficult for the Soviet Union to pursue; for, as we have seen, the legitimacy of the Soviet regime is in a peculiar sense predicated upon its success at home and abroad. The charisma of Marxism-Leninism having been drained of its substance, the legitimacy of the Soviet government is predicated at the very least upon the appearance of success. The Soviet government cannot afford the risk of consistent failures without risking its downfall and endangering the regime itself. This being so, it is tempted, if not compelled, sooner or later to compensate for failures with a spectacular success even at risks which the rational calculation of the distribution of interests and power might find prohibitive.

The very feebleness of Soviet legitimacy makes for its vulnerability to failure. A regime secure in its legitimacy is not only able to absorb failures but may even emerge strengthened from them; the personal charisma of de Gaulle was confirmed by his ability to liquidate the Algerian war. But for the Soviet government, which has nothing left to go on except success, every failure puts a question mark behind its claim to legitimacy. It must demonstrate, even at considerable risks, its ability to govern successfully in order to be able to govern at all.

THE MEANING OF CZECHOSLOVAKIA

When the military forces of the Soviet Union and of four other members of the Warsaw Pact occupied Czechoslovakia, in August 1968, the weakness of the Soviet Union as the fountainhead of international Communism and both its weakness and strength as the predominant military power in Eastern Europe were clearly revealed. All Communist governments of Eastern Europe are in a dual sense beholden to the Soviet Union. There would be no Communist governments anywhere in Eastern Europe if the Soviet Union had not established them in the immediate aftermath of the Second World War and sustained them military, economically, and politically ever since. Secondly, whatever legitimacy these governments possess is derived from that of the Soviet government. These governments govern in the name of the same philosophic and political principles which are most eminently represented by the Soviet Union.

Czechoslovakia defaulted this dual indebtedness to the Soviet Union in 1968 by attempting to liberalize its domestic regime to a degree unprecedented in the Communist world. That liberalization, had it been consummated, could have brought into being a pluralistic society, challenging the Communist monopoly of political power. That challenge would have been tantamount to a challenge to the political, economic, and military orientation of Czechoslovakia toward the Soviet Union. Thus Czechoslovakia might have been able to do through a gradual process of domestic liberalization what Hungary did for a fleeting moment in 1956 through a single revolutionary act: to drop out of the Soviet orbit. The Soviet Union intervened in Hungary in 1956 in order to undo that act, and it intervened in Czechoslovakia in 1968 in order to forestall it.

The Soviet Union felt itself threatened in both instances as the "Fatherland of Socialism"—that is, as the fountainhead of Communist wisdom and virtue, and as the paramount power of its empire. However, it felt itself more acutely threatened by the possibility of the Czechoslovak defection than by the actuality of the Hungarian one. The reason lies in the nature of the Czechoslovak reforms as well as in the geographic position of Czechoslovakia. Hungary's was a single act of defiance, hardly to be duplicated elsewhere. The Czechoslovak reforms conjured up the specter of slow erosion which, given the weakness of Communist legitimacy everywhere, could spread throughout the Communist world, destroying the monopoly of political power of the Soviet Communist Party itself. Furthermore, while Hungary is isolated from the West, except for a common border with Austria, Czechoslovakia has a long border with Austria and Germany, East and West. Here is indeed the nub of the matter as seen by the Soviet Union.

Once polycentrism gained sway in Eastern Europe and the nationalism of the Communist nations of Eastern Europe reasserted itself, the Soviet Union could maintain its ascendancy in the region only by one of two devices: the convergence of the national interests of these nations with its own, or the imposition of its will upon recalcitrant nations by military force. This convergence has existed in the relations of the Soviet Union with some of the nations of Eastern Europe, but by no means with all of them.

Poland, almost extinguished by the German *Drang nach Osten*, seeks the protection of the Soviet Union. East Germany, an artificial creation serving the Kremlin's interests, depends for its very life on Soviet support. The need of the other East European nations for Russian assistance, however, is not so clear-cut. They have a freedom of maneuver that is foreclosed to Poland and East Germany. And therein lies the threat to the security of the Soviet Union.

It is an existential fact, which has determined the fate of the nations of Eastern Europe for centuries, that none of them can stand on its own feet but must lean on one or the other of its powerful neighbors. One of these neighbors is Russia; the other, Germany. In the measure that a nation such as Czechoslovakia moves away from the Soviet Union, therefore, it must move closer to Germany. To paraphrase Stalin's statement quoted above, this the Soviet Union cannot allow.

For it is another existential fact, which has dominated the fate of Europe, East and West, that Germany—by virtue of its geographic position, size and quality of population, political organization, and industrial potential—is the most powerful nation on the Continent. This is true even of truncated West Germany today. Consequently, Germany exerts a natural attraction upon its weaker neighbors, especially those to the east. While the attraction has been powerfully counteracted by the terror the Nazi armies spread throughout the region, it testifies to its force that it is making itself felt again.

This attraction terrifies the Soviet Union. There is, of course, no doubt that much of the verbal attacks the Soviet Union has launched against West Germany is propaganda and therefore is not to be taken seriously. But underneath the verbal excess there is a genuine fear nourished by both the history of a century and the experiences of World War II. Germany provides, by dint of its very existence, the natural alternative to the Russian orientation of the nations of Eastern Europe. The Soviet Union regards this alternative as a threat to its security and the stability of Europe. It is resolved to oppose even the beginnings of the realization of this alternative by all means, fair or foul. Thus the "Joint Letter from Leaders of Parties and Governments of Socialist Countries to the Central Committee of the Communist Party of Czechoslovakia" (July 16, 1968) declared: "We shall never agree to have imperialism, using ways peaceful and nonpeaceful, making a gap from the inside or from the outside in the Socialist system and changing in imperialism's favor the correlation of forces in Europe." And the White Book published by the Soviet government on September 22, 1968, stated that rather than "open to imperialism its favorite road to the East . . . thereby imperiling the achievements of world Socialism and of the gains of the Second World War," the Socialist countries would "erect an impassable barrier to a new *'Drang nach Osten'* . . . again showing the world that no one can change the postwar borders."

If this interpretation of the Soviet move in Czechoslovakia is correct, then that move constitutes not so much an affirmation of Communism as a denial of some of its basic tenets. It demonstrates, first of all, that Communist governments after the Soviet model are not expressions of the popular will but creatures of an elite monopolizing political power. Secondly, it demonstrates that the Soviet Union is not the "Fatherland of Socialism" tied to other Communist governments and movements by a natural harmony of interests, but that it has been trying to impose its will upon these movements and governments in order to be able to use them for the purposes of the Russian state.

These two revelations are bound to have far-reaching consequences. They discredit once more the Marxist-Leninist philosophy, and to the extent that they do, they weaken the political movements and governments whose legitimacy derives from that philosophy. This is especially true of the government of the Soviet Union both at home and abroad.

The "secularization" of the Soviet state has taken another big step forward. The Soviet Union now stands revealed as just one state among others, compelled to pursue its aims with a particular ruthlessness, since its claim to the spontaneous support of all Socialist peoples has proven to be false. The Soviet rulers, unable to rely upon that support and faced with the hostility of peoples thirsting for freedom, have no recourse other than brute force to keep themselves in power.

But power thus maintained is bound to be precarious. A ruling group armed with the modern technologies of communication, transportation, and warfare can keep itself in power against a rebellious population only if the spirit of freedom does not affect the ruling group itself. It is upon this proviso, aside from the success of its policies to which we have referred before, that the future of Communist government depends.

4

The United States and the Developing World

America as Model for the World

The postulate of self-restraint in the use of American power runs counter to innate tendencies of the American character, on the one hand, and to opportunities for successful intervention which the developing world appears to offer to American good intentions and power, on the other. From the very beginning of American history, an organic relationship has existed between the character of American society and its relations with other nations. It was as an example for other nations to emulate that America offered itself to the world. The very creation of the United States was regarded both by the founders and by foreign observers as an experiment which had a meaning not only for that country but for all the world. America, wrote Thomas Paine, "made a stand not for herself only, but for the world, and looked beyond the advantages which herself could receive. Even the Hessian, though hired to fight against her, may live to bless his defeat; and England, condemning the viciousness of its government, rejoice in its miscarriage." [1] "A just and solid republican government maintained here," Thomas Jefferson wrote to John Dickinson on March 6, 1801, "will be a standing monument and example for the aim and imitation of the people of other countries; and I join with you in the hope and belief that they will see from our example that a free government is of all others the most energetic, and that the inquiry which has been excited among the mass of mankind by our revolution and its consequences will ameliorate the condition of man over a great portion of the globe." [2] And in the words of Lincoln: "The Declaration of Independence . . . [gave] liberty, not alone to the people of this country, but hope to the world for all future time. It was that which gave promise that in due time the weights should be lifted from the shoulders of all men." [3] Responding to these American expectations, the French statesman Turgot wrote to Dr. Price on March 22, 1778, as follows:

> All right-thinking men must pray that this people may arrive at all the prosperity of which they are capable. They are the hope of the human race. They should be the model. They must prove to the world, as a fact, that men can be both free and peaceful and can dispense with the trammels of all sorts which tyrants and charlatans of every costume have presumed to impose under the pretext of public safety. They must give the example of political liberty, of religious liberty, of commercial and industrial liberty. The asylum which America affords to the oppressed of all nations will console the world. The facility of profiting by it, in making escape from the consequences of bad governments, will compel the European powers to be just, and to see things as they are. The rest of the

[1] Thomas Paine, *The Rights of Man* (New York: E. P. Dutton, 1951), p. 151.

[2] *The Writings of Thomas Jefferson*, edited by A. Lipscomb (Washington, D.C.: Thomas Jefferson Memorial Association, 1905), X, 217.

[3] Speech in Philadelphia, February 22, 1861, in *The Collected Works of Abraham Lincoln*, edited by Roy P. Basler, (New Brunswick, N.J.: Rutgers University Press, 1959), IV, 240.

world will, by degrees, have its eyes opened to the dispersion of the illusions amidst which politicians have been cradled. But, for that end, America herself must guarantee that she will never become (as so many of your ministerial writers have preached) an image of our Europe, a mass of divided powers disputing about territories or the profits of commerce, and continually cementing the slavery of peoples by their own blood.[4]

This conception of America as a model to be emulated by other nations did not at first affect the foreign policy of the United States. It only imposed upon America the obligation to arrange its domestic affairs in such a way as to serve as an example for mankind. At the turn of the century, in consequence of the territorial acquisitions following the Spanish-American War, an activist conception of America's mission in the world was added to this passive one.

America as Missionary for the World

The promise of universal happiness, implicit in the American experiment, obviously did not mean that all men could achieve it by simple imitation, but it did mean that no group of men was a priori excluded from achieving it and that, as a matter of principle, given favorable circumstances, all men could achieve it. Such circumstances were of two kinds: the objective conditions of existence—that is, empty spaces and natural wealth such as had favored the Americans—and the ability of a people ingenious and partial to innovation to make use of these objective conditions.

From this conception of the American experiment's relation to the world at large it was only a step to the acceptance, on the part of America, of the positive obligation to assist less favored peoples, subject to American influence, to achieve the happiness enjoyed by Americans. Thus the territorial expansion of America, hesitating and embarrassed, beyond the boundaries of the continent at the turn of the century goes hand in hand with the

[4] *The Life and Writings of Turgot*, edited by W. Walker Stephens (London and New York: Longmans, Green, 1895), p. 303.

self-confident and vigorous expansion of the American principles and practices of government. In that fashion territorial expansion could be justified as serving the American mission, and so too could the liquidation of empire after the mission seemed to have been achieved. It then appeared that America had not just stumbled upon the Philippines, Cuba, and Puerto Rico without knowing what it was doing, but that these historic accidents became, if they were not from the beginning, instruments through which America used its power for the benefit of other peoples. The hyperbolic moralisms with which American expansion has been traditionally justified, then, contain elements not only of subjective sincerity but also of objective truth. The idea of the American mission to the less fortunate peoples of the world is certainly a political ideology, a rationalization and justification of policies that were undertaken for other and primarily selfish reasons. But that idea expresses also a serious commitment to a mission that is merely the American mission projected beyond the territorial limits of America and circumscribed only by the reach of American influence.

Senator Albert J. Beveridge of Indiana summarized this missionary philosophy when he said in the Senate on January 9, 1900:

> Self-government and internal development of other lands will be the dominant notes of our second century. And administration is as high and holy a function as self-government, just as the care of a trust estate is as sacred an obligation as the management of our own concerns. Cain was the first to violate the divine law of human society which makes of us our brother's keeper. . . .
>
> The Declaration of Independence does not forbid us to do our part in the regeneration of the world. If it did, the Declaration would be wrong. . . .
>
> He [God] has given us the spirit of progress to overwhelm the forces of reaction throughout the earth. He has made us adept in government that we may administer government among savage and senile peoples. Were it not for such a force as this the world would relapse into barbarism and night. And of all our race He has marked the American people as His chosen nation to finally lead in the regeneration of the world. This is the divine mission of

America, and it holds for us all the profit, all the glory, all the happiness possible to man. We are trustees of the world's progress, guardians of its righteous peace.[5]

America as Crusader

The missionary conception of the relationship between our domestic situation and our foreign policy here blends into the third, the crusading one. As missionaries of the American experiment, we would offer our assistance to others, who were free to accept or reject it. As crusaders, we would impose it on the rest of the world, with fire and sword if necessary. The actual limits of such a crusade would be the limits of American power, its potential limits would be the limits of the globe. The American example is transformed into a formula of universal salvation by which right-thinking nations would voluntarily abide and to which the others must be compelled to submit. The classic example of this new relationship between America's domestic purpose and its foreign policy was Woodrow Wilson's crusade for universal democracy.[6]

Had Wilson's United States conceived of itself as just a power among others, it would, like other powers, have looked to its own

[5] Quoted in Ruhl J. Bartlett, *The Record of American Diplomacy* (New York: Alfred A. Knopf, 1947), pp. 386 ff.

[6] Before the conflict among them came to a head in this century, Calhoun saw clearly the dynamic relationship that exists between these three conceptions of America's role in the world, on the one hand, and the American experiment at home, on the other:

> It has been lately urged in a very respectable quarter that it is the mission of this country to spread civil and religious liberty over all the globe, and especially over this continent—even by force, if necessary. It is a sad delusion. . . . To preserve it [liberty], it is indispensable to adopt a course of moderation and justice toward all other countries; to avoid war whenever it can be avoided; to let those great causes which are now at work, and which by the mere operation of time, will raise our country to an elevation and influence which no country has ever heretofore attained, continue to work. By pursuing such a course, we may succeed in combining greatness and liberty . . . and do more to extend liberty by our example over this continent and the world generally, than would be done by a thousand victories. (*The Works of John C. Calhoun*, edited by Richard K. Cralle [New York: Appleton, 1854], IV, 416, 420.)

advantage and competed with its allies for the spoils of victory. For Wilson, the First World War was the instrument through which America would achieve the purpose for which it was created: to bring the blessings of its own political system to all the world. America would free all the world, as it had freed itself, from the scourge of authoritarian government, power politics, the balance of power, armaments races, alliances, spheres of influence, and the rest. The purpose of the war was not only to end war, but to end power politics as well.

Thus American participation in the First World War revealed itself as the very consummation of the American experiment. America would remain faithful to its purpose in a negative way by not seeking any advantage, territorial or otherwise, for itself; and it would remain faithful to its purpose in a positive way by not only offering its own equality in freedom as a model to be emulated, but also spilling its blood and spending its treasure to make the world safe for democracy—that is, to enable the world to emulate America. In Wilson's thought and action the democratic crusade was thus a logical extension of the American experiment, adapted to the circumstances of the twentieth century.

Toward the close of the Second World War and in its immediate aftermath, the United States took upon itself the task of the reconstruction of the world by reviving the Wilsonian conception. Emerging from the war as the most powerful nation on earth, without whose global involvement the political world could not be reconstructed or its national interests safeguarded, the United States now faced the Wilsonian problem without the benefit of the isolationist escape. With only two power centers left in the world, the second one being the Soviet Union, the choice of 1920 was no longer open to the United States; that choice would now have meant anarchy in Europe and Asia to be followed by the establishment of order under the auspices of Communism.

If the United States could no longer isolate itself from a world infected with what it chose to call power politics, it had to decontaminate the world from that infection so that it might be safe for the United States to become permanently involved with it.

Our leaders therefore anticipated and prepared for a postwar world where, in the words of Secretary of State Cordell Hull, "there will no longer be need for spheres of influence, for alliances, for balance of power, or any other of the special arrangements through which, in the unhappy past, the nations strove to safeguard their security or promote their interests." [7] These expectations, voiced in 1943 after Great Britain, the Soviet Union, and the United States had agreed upon the establishment of the United Nations, moved President Roosevelt to declare on March 1, 1945, in his report to Congress on the Yalta Conference:

> The Crimean Conference . . . spells the end of the system of unilateral action and exclusive alliances and spheres of influence and balances of power and all the other expedients which have been tried for centuries—and have failed.
>
> We propose to substitute for all these a universal organization in which all peace-loving nations will finally have a chance to join in.[8]

When Wilson prepared for the postwar world with similar expectations, his contemporaries could still try to restore the traditional hemispheric limitations of the American purpose by returning to isolationism. They simply disavowed him by turning their backs on America's involvement in the affairs of the world. No such disavowal of Roosevelt's and Hull's expectations was necessary, and no such return to isolationism was possible at the end of the Second World War. The Soviet Union's interpretation of the Yalta agreements in terms of the expansion of Russian power and not of international cooperation revealed the utopian character of Roosevelt's and Hull's expectations and threatened the European balance of power and, through it, the vital interests of the United States. Thus it was obvious that for the United States the fruit of victory was to be neither a minimal normalcy without power politics nor the safety of hemispheric isolation. The expansion of Russian power, threatening the security of the

[7] Report to Congress on Moscow Conference, *The New York Times*, November 19, 1943, p. 4.

[8] *Nothing To Fear: The Selected Addresses of Franklin Delano Roosevelt 1932–1945*, edited by Ben Zevin (Cambridge, Mass.: Houghton Mifflin, 1946), p. 453.

United States, ushered in a new and formidable crisis of the American purpose abroad.

The crisis proceeded in three distinct stages. The first was a period of adaptation, of restoration, of creation, culminating in the "fifteen weeks" of the spring of 1947 during which a whole new system of American foreign policy was devised from a radically new conception of the American purpose abroad. The first stage came to an end with the conclusion of the armistice in the Korean War in 1953. The second stage differed sharply from the first one. Rather than being a crisis of restoration and of achievement, as in the first stage, it was a crisis of perplexity, of seeming inability to continue the process of adaptation, restoration, and creation, so auspiciously begun. The novel problems of the immediate postwar world were at first successfully met in one great creative effort, and now the nation settled down to meeting the novel problems of the 1950s with the remedies of yesterday, many of which had outlived their usefulness, and transformed yesterday's creative effort into today's routines.

This period seemed to come to an end in 1961 when the Kennedy Administration embarked upon an intellectual effort at laying the groundwork for a new foreign policy appropriate to new political conditions. But while these efforts were translated into eloquent political rhetoric, they hardly influenced the actual conduct of American foreign policy. After this brief and inconsequential interlude, the routines of the 1950s were continued with renewed vigor. They were now put at the service of a revived globalistic conception of America's role in the world: to bring the blessings of the Great Society to the developing third of the world. The conception is Wilsonian in content, but it is underpinned by a new conception of American power. It is this marriage between Wilsonian globalism and the belief in the paramountcy of American power that characterizes the third postwar period of American foreign policy. While that marriage was consummated under the Johnson Administration, the psychological longings and political forces that gave it life continue to exert a powerful influence upon America's conception of its relations to the developing world.

The Great Society and the American Mission Abroad

The projection of the Great Society onto the international scene is clearly in line of succession to Wilson's and Roosevelt's conception of America's mission abroad. It is missionary in theory and crusading in practice. The theory was formulated in general terms in Ambassador Arthur Goldberg's speech to the U.N. General Assembly on September 23, 1965:

> In my own country we are embarked under the leadership of President Lyndon B. Johnson in a search for a "Great Society."
>
> This vision of a just democratic order is based on consent of the governed and due process of law, on individual dignity, on economic diversity and on the just satisfaction of political, economic and social aspirations.
>
> We in the United States reject reactionary philosophies of all extremes. We seek to build instead on what we regard the most enlightened and progressive philosophy in human history, that the aim of government is the maximum self-fulfillment of its citizens and that the good life should be within the reach of all, rather than a monopoly of the few. Both domestically and in international affairs there can be no island of poverty in seas of affluence.
>
> We espouse equality not only as a principle. We seek equal opportunity for all as an accomplished reality. And we are resolved to enrich the life of our society by developing human, as well as natural, resources. And we are determined not merely to increase material production but to assure such equality to guarantee genuine social and economic justice, to eliminate poverty and also to realize qualitative improvements in the life of our citizens —in more attractive and functional cities, in a more beautiful countryside and through learning and the arts.
>
> And this is not the program of any one group or one class or one political party in our country. Nor is the vision it proclaims exclusively American. It is a vision common to all mankind. It fell to my lot for twenty-five years to represent the great labor movement of our country. And one of the great labor leaders with whom I was long associated, Philip Murray, when I asked, what was the aim of the labor movement, to which he dedicated his life, paused and thought and said the aim of the labor movement is a society in which each man shall have a rug on the floor, a picture on the wall, and music in the home. And I think that is a good goal for all of mankind.

So what we seek for our own people in a Great Society at home, we seek for all mankind.

This statement of principles was elaborated in President Johnson's speech of September 16, 1965, at the Smithsonian Institution: "We mean to show that this nation's dream of a Great Society does not stop at the water's edge. It is not just an American dream. All are welcome to share in it. All are invited to contribute to it." Johnson committed the United States to "a broad and long-range plan of world-wide educational endeavor" and announced the appointment of a task force for that purpose, headed by the Secretary of State and with the Secretary of Health, Education, and Welfare as a member. The President enumerated the five components of this plan: assistance to developing countries in their educational efforts; help to American schools and universities to "increase their knowledge of the world and the people who inhabit it"; international exchange of students and teachers; increase of "the free flow of books and ideas and art, works of science and imagination"; the organization of "meetings of men and women from every discipline and every culture to ponder the common problems of mankind."

In his State of the Union message of January 12, 1966, President Johnson expanded his program for the global Great Society:

This year I propose major new directions in our program of foreign assistance to help those countries who will help themselves.

We will conduct a worldwide attack on the problems of hunger and disease and ignorance.

We will place the matchless skill and the resources of our own great America, in farming and in fertilizers, at the service of those countries committed to develop a modern agriculture.

We will aid those who educate the young in other lands, and we will give children in other continents the same head start that we are trying to give to our own children. To advance these ends I will propose the International Education Act of 1966.

I will also propose the International Health Act of 1966 to strike at disease by a new effort to bring modern skills and knowledge to the uncared-for, those suffering in the world, and by trying to wipe out smallpox and malaria and control yellow fever over most of the world during this next decade; to help countries trying to control population growth, by increasing our research—and we will earmark funds to help their efforts.

In the next year, from our foreign aid sources, we propose to dedicate one billion dollars to these efforts, and we call on all who have the means to join us in this work in the world.

The philosophic roots of this program for the global Great Society were discussed in a report by *Time* magazine of September 3, 1965, concerning the influence of Barbara Ward's *The Rich Nations and the Poor Nations* [9] upon the President's thinking. *Time* referred to this book as "the LBJ selection of the century" and "Baedecker to the great Global Society." It quoted the President as having said: "I read it like I do the Bible," and that the book "excites and inspires me." Miss Ward was quoted as returning the compliment by saying: "His profound and compassionate understanding of the roots of poverty gives a unique dimension to the leadership he offers the world." *Time* characterized the book as "messianic materialism" and found its influence in the President's speeches.

Reading Miss Ward's book with one's expectations thus aroused, one is bound to be disappointed. None of the great moral and intellectual issues, to which the relations between the rich and poor nations give rise, is explicitly posed and validly discussed. The moral and intellectual foundation of the book's thesis—that the rich nations must help the poor nations to overcome their poverty—is taken for granted. Thus the very conception of the relations between rich and poor nations as being nothing more than a quantitative extension of the relations between rich and poor individuals within the same society is posited as self-evident. So is the moral conclusion that the rich nations are obligated to help the poor nations. So is the practical expectation that the quantitative extension of foreign aid is actually capable of eliminating poverty on a world scale. There is no awareness of the cultural conditions from which stems the persistent poverty of many new nations, nor is there any awareness of the political issues to be settled before foreign aid can become effective in countries whose governments have a political

[9] New York: W. W. Norton, 1962.

stake in the status quo of poverty and backwardness. Yet the capacity of foreign aid to bring the Great Society to all mankind depends upon the examination of these assumptions and the elucidation of these conditions and issues.

FOREIGN AID

Six Types of Foreign Aid

The first prerequisite for the development of a viable philosophy of foreign aid is the recognition of the diversity of policies that go by that name. Six such policies can be distinguished which have only one thing in common: the transfer of money and economic services from one nation to another. They are humanitarian foreign aid, subsistence foreign aid, military foreign aid, bribery, prestige foreign aid, and foreign aid for economic development.

Of these different types of foreign aid, only humanitarian foreign aid is per se nonpolitical. The aid that governments have traditionally extended to each other in case of natural disasters, such as floods, famines, and epidemics, falls in that category. So do the services, especially in the fields of education, medicine, and agriculture, which private organizations, such as churches and foundations, have traditionally provided in Asia, Africa, and Latin America. And so do the activities of the Peace Corps, which provides humanitarian foreign aid on an institutionalized basis under government auspices.

While humanitarian aid is defined as nonpolitical, it can indeed perform a political function when it operates within a political context. The foreign aid that private organizations provide will be attributed, for better or for worse, to their respective governments insofar as humanitarian aid emanating from abroad is recognized by the recipient country to perform a political function. Thus the agricultural aid that the Rockefeller Foundation has provided for many years to certain Latin American countries is likely to take on under contemporary conditions a political function it did not perform previously. The same has been true, from the beginning, of the work the Ford Foundation has been doing in India. By the same token, humanitarian aid extended by a government may have political effects.

Subsistence foreign aid is extended to governments that do not command the resources to maintain minimal public services. The donor nation makes up the deficit in the budget of the recipient nation. Subsistence foreign aid seeks to prevent the breakdown of order and the disintegration of organized society itself. It performs the political function of maintaining the status quo. It maintains it without, as a rule, increasing its viability. Where there is a political alternative to an unviable regime, subsistence foreign aid diminishes its chances of materializing.

Bribes proffered by one government to another for political advantage were, until the beginning of the nineteenth century, an integral part of the armory of diplomacy. Statesmen did not hesitate to acknowledge the giving and accepting of bribes. It was proper and common for a government to pay the foreign minister or ambassador of another country a pension. Lord Robert Cecil, the Minister of Elizabeth I, received one from Spain. Sir Henry Wotton, British Ambassador to Venice in the seventeenth century, accepted one from Savoy while applying for one from Spain. The documents that the French revolutionary government published in 1793 show that France subsidized Austrian statesmen between 1757 and 1769 to the tune of 82,652,479 livres; the Austrian Chancellor Kaunitz received 100,000.

Nor was it regarded less proper or less usual for a government to compensate foreign statesmen for their cooperation in the conclusion of treaties. In 1716, the French Cardinal Dubois offered the British Minister Stanhope 600,000 livres for an alliance with France. He reported that Stanhope, while not accepting the proposition at that time, "listened graciously without being displeased." After the conclusion of the Treaty of Basel of 1795, by virtue of which Prussia withdrew from the war against France, the Prussian Minister Hardenberg received from the French government valuables worth 30,000 francs and complained of the insignificance of the gift. In 1801, the Margrave of Baden spent 500,000 francs in the form of "diplomatic presents," of which French Foreign Minister Talleyrand received 150,000. It was originally intended to give him only 100,000, but the amount was increased after it had become known that he had received from Prussia a snuffbox worth 66,000 francs as well as 100,000 francs in cash. The Prussian Ambassador in Paris summed up well the main rule of this game when he reported to his government in 1802: "Experience has taught everybody who is here on diplomatic business that one ought never to give anything before the deal is definitely closed, but it has only proved that the allurement of gain will often work wonders."

Much of what goes by the name of foreign aid today is in the nature of bribes. The transfer of money and services from one government to another performs here the function of a price paid for political services rendered or to be rendered by the recipient. These bribes differ from the traditional examples given above in two respects: They are justified primarily in terms of foreign aid for economic development, and money and services are transferred through elaborate machinery fashioned for genuine economic aid. In consequence, these bribes are a less effective means for the purpose of purchasing political favors than were the traditional ones.

The compulsion to substitute for the traditional business-like transmission of bribes the pretense and elaborate machinery of foreign aid for economic development results from a climate of opinion which accepts as universally valid the proposition that the highly developed industrial nations have an obligation to transfer money and services to underdeveloped nations to foster economic development. Thus, aside from humanitarian and military foreign aid, the only kind of transfer of money and services that seems to be legitimate is the one made for the purpose of economic development. Economic development has become an ideology by which the transfer of money and services from one government to another is rationalized and justified.

However, the present climate of opinion assumes not only that affluent industrial nations have an obligation to extend foreign aid for economic development to nations of the third world. It also assumes as a universally valid proposition that economic development can actually be promoted through such transfer of money and services. Thus economic development as an ideology requires machinery that makes plausible the assumption of the efficacy of the transfer of money and services for the purpose of economic growth. In contrast to most political ideologies, which operate only on the verbal level and whose effects remain within the realm of ideas, this ideology, in order to be plausible, requires an elaborate apparatus serving as an instrument for a policy of make-believe. The government of nation *A,* trying to buy political advantage from the government of Nation *B* for, say, the price of $20 million, not only must pretend, but also must act out in elaborate fashion the pretense, that what it is actually doing is giving aid for economic development to the government of nation *B.*

The practice of giving bribes as though they were contributions to economic development necessarily creates expectations, in the donor and the recipient, which are bound to be disappointed. Old-fashioned bribery is a straightforward transaction: Services are to be rendered at a price, and both sides know what to expect. Bribery disguised as foreign aid for economic development makes of donor and recipient actors in a play which in the end they can no longer distinguish from reality. In consequence, both expect results in economic development which, in the nature of things, could not have been forthcoming. Thus both are bound to be disappointed, the donor blaming the recipient for his inefficiency and the recipient accusing the donor of stinginess. The ideology, taken for reality, gets in the way of the original purpose of the transaction, and neither side believes that it has received what it is entitled to.

Foreign aid for military purposes is a traditional means for nations to buttress their alliances. Rome used to receive tribute from its allies for the military protection it provided. The seventeenth and eighteenth centuries were the classic period of military subsidies, by which especially Great Britain endeavored to increase the military strength of her continental allies. Glancing through the treaties of alliance of that period, one is struck by the meticulous precision with which obligations to furnish troops, equipment, logistic support, food, money, and the like were defined. This traditional military aid can be understood as a division of labor between two allies who pool their resources, one supplying money, material, and training, the other providing primarily manpower.

In contrast to traditional practice, military aid is today extended not only to allies but also to certain uncommitted nations. The purpose here is not so much military as political, for political advantage is sought in exchange for military aid. This kind of aid obligates the recipient to the donor. The latter expects the former to abstain from a political course that might put in jeopardy the continuation of military aid, which is thus really in the nature of a bribe.

What appears as military aid may also be actually in the nature of prestige aid, to be discussed below. The provision of jet fighters and other modern weapons for certain underdeveloped nations can obviously perform no genuine military function. It increases the prestige of the recipient nation both at home and abroad. Being in the possession of some of the more spectacular instruments of modern warfare, a nation can at least enjoy the illusion that it has become a modern military power.

As bribery appears today in the guise of aid for economic development, so does aid for economic development appear in the guise of military assistance. In the session of 1967, Congress, for instance, appropriated $600 million for economic aid to strategic areas, and it is likely that in the total appropriations for military aid in excess of $1 billion other items of economic aid were hidden. This mode of operation results from the reluctance of Congress to vote large amounts for economic aid in contrast to its readiness to vote virtually any amount requested for military purposes. Yet the purposes of aid for economic development are likely to suffer when they are disguised as military assistance, as we saw the purposes of bribery suffer when disguised as aid for economic development. The military context within which such aid is bound to operate, even though its direct administration may be in the hands of the civilian authorities, is likely to deflect such aid from its genuine purposes. More particularly, it

strengthens the ever-present tendency to subordinate the requirements of aid for economic development to military considerations.

Prestige aid has in common with modern bribes that its true
purpose, too, is concealed by the ostensible purpose of economic
development. The unprofitable or idle steel mill, the highway
without traffic and leading nowhere, the airline operating with
foreign personnel and at a loss but under the flag of the recipient
country—they ostensibly serve the purposes of economic development and under different circumstances could do so. Actually,
however, they perform no positive economic function. They owe
their existence to the penchant, prevalent in many underdeveloped nations, for what might be called "conspicuous industrialization," an industrialization that produces symbols of, and monuments to, industrial advancement rather than satisfying the objective economic needs of the country. This tendency sheds an
illuminating light upon the nature of what is generally referred
to as the "revolution of rising expectations."

We are inclined to assume that the "revolution of rising expectations"—that is, a people's urgent desire to improve their lot by
means of modern technology and industry—is a well-nigh universal trend in Asia, Africa, and Latin America. Actually, however, it is universal only in the sense that virtually all underdeveloped nations want the appearance of having achieved industrialization, while only a fraction of the population, and frequently only small elite groups within it, in fact seek the social
and economic benefits of industrialization and are willing to take
the measures necessary to achieve them. For many of the underdeveloped nations the steel mill, the highway, the airline, the
modern weapons perform a function that is not primarily economic or military but psychological and political. They are
sought as symbols and monuments of modernity and power.
They perform a function similar to that which the cathedral
performed for the medieval city and the feudal castle or the
monarch's palace for the absolute state. Nehru is reported to
have said, when he showed Chou En-lai a new dam: "It is in
these temples that I worship." And the more underdeveloped

and less viable a nation is, the greater will generally be its urge to prove to itself and to the world through the results of prestige aid that it, too, has arrived.

The advantage for the donor of prestige aid is threefold. He may receive specific political advantages in return for the provision of aid, very much after the model of the advantage received in return for a bribe. The spectacular character of prestige aid establishes a patent relationship between the generosity of the giver and the increased prestige of the recipient; the donor's prestige is enhanced, as it were, by the increase of the recipient's prestige. Finally, prestige aid comes relatively cheap. A limited commitment of resources in the form of a spectacular but economically useless symbol of, or monument to, modernity may bring disproportionate political dividends.

The donor of foreign aid must perform the task of distinguishing between prestige aid and aid for economic development. It is in the nature of prestige aid that it is justified by the prospective recipient in terms of genuine economic development. The prospective donor, unaware of the distinction, is likely to fall into one of two errors. By mistaking prestige aid for aid for economic development, he will either waste human and material resources in support of the latter, while the purpose of prestige aid could have been achieved much more simply and cheaply. Or else he will reject out of hand a request for prestige aid because it cannot be justified in terms of economic development, and may thereby forego political advantages he could have gained from the provision of the aid requested. The classic example of this error is the American rejection of the Afghan request for the paving of the streets of Kabul as economically unsound. It may be noted in passing that the Soviet Union, pursuing a politically oriented policy of foreign aid, paved the streets of Kabul, even though that measure had no bearing upon the economic development of Afghanistan.

Foreign Aid for Economic Development in Particular

None of the types of foreign aid discussed thus far poses theoretical questions of the first magnitude; rather they raise issues for practical manipulation which can be successfully met by common sense tested by experience. Foreign aid for economic development has been the primary area for theoretical analysis and speculation, primarily of an economic nature. Economic thought, true to its prevailing academic tradition, tends to look at foreign aid as though it were a self-sufficient technical enterprise to be achieved with the instruments, and judged by the standards, of pure economics. And since Western economic development, from the first Industrial Revolution onward, has been the result of the formation of capital and the accumulation of technical knowledge, we have tended to assume that these two factors would by themselves provide the impetus for the economic development of the underdeveloped nations of Asia, Africa, and Latin America. This tendency has been powerfully supported by the spectacular success of the Marshall Plan, conceived and executed as a strictly economic measure for the provision of capital and technological know-how. Yet it is not always recognized that this success was made possible only by the fact that, in contrast to the underdeveloped nations of Asia, Africa, and Latin America, the recipients of Marshall aid were among the leading industrial nations of the world, whose economic systems were only temporarily in disarray.

The popular mind, on the other hand, and, through it, much of the practice of foreign aid have proceeded from certain unexamined assumptions, no less dubious for being deeply embedded in the American folklore of politics. Thus correlations have been established between the infusion of capital and technological know-how into a primitive society and economic development, between economic development and social stability, between social stability and democratic institutions, between democratic institutions and a peaceful foreign policy. However attractive and reassuring these correlations may sound to American ears, they are borne out neither by the experience we have had with our policies of foreign aid nor by general historic experience.

The first of these assumptions implies that underdevelopment is at least primarily the result of lack of capital and technological know-how. Underdevelopment is regarded as a kind of accident or at worst as a kind of deficiency disease, which can be taken care of through the infusion of capital and technological know-how. Yet a nation may suffer from deficiencies, some natural and insuperable, others social and remediable, which no amount of capital and technological know-how supplied from the outside can cure. The poverty of natural resources may be such as to make economic development impossible. Many of the nations that are the permanent recipients of subsistence aid are likely to fall in that category.

A nation may also suffer from human deficiencies which preclude economic development. As there are individuals whose qualities of character and level of intelligence make it impossible for them to take advantage of economic opportunities, so are there nations similarly handicapped. To put it bluntly: As there are bums and beggars, so are there bum and beggar nations. They may be the recipients of charity, but short of a miraculous transformation of their collective intelligence and character, what they receive from the outside is not likely to be used for economic development.

Some nations are deficient in the specific kind of character and intelligence that go into the making of a modern economic system, but their general qualities of character and level of intelligence qualify them for the necessary transformation. They are, to use a rough analogy, in a medieval stage of cultural development, still awaiting the equivalent of the moral and intellectual revolutions which in the sixteenth and seventeenth centuries created the cultural preconditions for the economic development of the West. Yet we tend to take the existence of these preconditions for granted, forgetting that without the secularization and rationalization of Western thought and society the industrialization of the West would not have been possible.

A civilization, for instance, which deprecates success in this world because it stands in the way of success in the other world, puts a cultural obstacle in the path of industrial development which foreign aid by itself cannot overcome. Saving—that is, the preservation of capital or goods for future use—has become so integral a part of our economic thought and action that it is hard for us to realize that there are hundreds of millions of people in the underdeveloped areas of the world who are oblivious to this mode of operation, indispensable to economic development. We have come to consider the productive enterprise as a continuum in which the individual owner or manager has a personal stake. Yet in many underdeveloped areas the productive enterprise is regarded primarily as an object for financial exploitation, to be discarded when it has performed its function of bringing the temporary owner a large financial return in the shortest possible time. Foreign aid poured into such a precapitalistic and even prerational mold is not likely to transform the mold, but rather it will be forced by it into channels serving the interests of a precapitalistic or prerational society.

The economic interests that stand in the way of foreign aid being used for economic development are typically tied in with the distribution of political power in underdeveloped societies. The ruling groups in these societies derive their political power in good measure from the economic status quo. The ownership and control of arable land, in particular, is in many of the underdeveloped societies the foundation of political power. Land reform and industrialization are therefore an attack upon the political status quo. In the measure that they are successful, they are bound to affect drastically the distribution of economic and political power. Yet the beneficiaries of both the economic and political status quo are the typical recipients of foreign aid given for the purpose of changing the status quo! Their use of foreign aid for this purpose requires a readiness for self-sacrifice and a sense of social responsibility that few ruling groups have shown throughout history. Foreign aid proffered under such circumstances is likely to fail in its purpose of economic development and, as a bribe to the ruling group, rather will strengthen the economic and political status quo. It is likely to accentuate unsolved social and political problems rather than bring them closer to solution. A team of efficiency experts and public accountants might well have improved the operations of the Al

Capone gang; yet, by doing so, it would have aggravated the social and political evils that the operations of that gang brought forth.

Given this likely resistance of the ruling group to economic development, foreign aid requires drastic political change as a precondition for its success. Foreign aid must go hand in hand with political change, either voluntarily induced from within or brought about through pressure from without. The latter alternative faces the donor nation with a dual dilemma. On the one hand, to give foreign aid for economic development without stipulating conditions that maximize the chances for success maximizes the chances for failure. On the other hand, to give aid "with strings" arouses xenophobic suspicions and nationalistic resentments, to be exploited both by the defenders of the status quo and by the promoters of Communist revolution.

Furthermore, once it has been decided to bring about political change in opposition to the ruling group, the alternative group must be identified as the instrument of this change. Sometimes, it may be a choice among different alternative groups that are equally unattractive. Sometimes, and not infrequently, the absence of any alternative group leaves no choice.

Finally, the promotion of drastic social change on the part of the donor nation creates the precondition for economic development, but it also conjures up the specter of uncontrollable revolution. In many of the underdeveloped nations, peace and order are maintained only through the ruthless use of the monopoly of violence by the ruling group. Determined and skillful foreign intervention may not find it hard to weaken the power of the ruling group or to remove it from power altogether. While it may be able to control events up to this point—that is, to instigate drastic reform and revolution—it may well be unable to control the course of the revolution itself. More particularly, a democratic nation such as the United States is greatly handicapped in competing with Communists in the control of the revolution. The revolution may start, as did the Cuban, under the democratic auspices of the unorganized masses dedicated to social reform and supported by the United States, and may in the course of its development be taken over by the highly organized and disciplined Communist minority, the only organized and disciplined revolutionary group available.

Successful foreign aid for economic development may have similarly unsettling political results. Economic development, especially by way of industrialization, is likely to disrupt the social fabric of the underdeveloped nation. By creating an urban industrial proletariat, it loosens and destroys the social nexus of family, village, and tribe, in which the individual had found himself secure. And it will not be able, at least not right away, to provide a substitute for this lost social world. The vacuum thus created will be filled by social unrest and political agitation. Furthermore, it is not the downtrodden masses living in a static world of unrelieved misery who are the likely protagonists of revolution, but rather those groups that have begun to rise in the social and economic scale but not enough to satisfy their aroused expectations. Thus, economic development is bound to disturb not only the economic status quo but, through it, the political status quo as well. If the change is drastic enough, the social and political effects of economic development may well amount to a prerevolutionary or revolutionary situation. And while the United States may have started the revolutionary process, it will again be uncertain under whose auspices it will be ended.

The United States faces a number of formidable handicaps in the task of controlling social and political change in the underdeveloped nations either as a prerequisite for, or a result of, foreign aid for economic development. First of all, the United States is a Western capitalistic nation. It appears to the underdeveloped nations as a conservative power both domestically and internationally. In both its civilization and its social and economic structure, it belongs to that complex of nations which until recently were able to hold Africa, Latin America, and most of Asia in a condition of colonial or semicolonial dependency. It is tied by military alliances to some of these nations, and while it has generally shunned and even opposed outright colonial policies, it has actively and successfully participated in the semicolonial exploitation of backward nations. Thus the resentment against the former colonial powers attaches also to the United States, and its policies of foreign aid are frequently suspected of serving in disguise the traditional ends of colonialism.

Furthermore, the United States, by dint of its pluralistic political philosophy and social system, cannot bring to the backward nations of the world a simple message of salvation, supported first by dedicated and disciplined revolutionary minorities and then by totalitarian control. In the nature of things the advantage lies here with the Communist powers. They are, as it were, specialists in exploiting a revolutionary situation, which is bound to cause us embarrassment. For while the Communists are able to direct a revolution into the desired channels through their use of a disciplined minority, we, even if we are convinced that revolution is inevitable and therefore do not oppose it, tend to look with misgivings upon it since we cannot control the direction it will take.

The Communist powers have still another advantage over the United States in that their problems and achievements are more meaningful, at least on the surface, to the underdeveloped nations than are ours. The Soviet Union has achieved, and Communist China attempts to achieve, what the more enlightened underdeveloped nations seek: a drastic increase in the standard of living through rapid industrialization. The Communist powers use totalitarian control as their instrument and Communist doctrine as rationalization and justification. Seeking the same results, the underdeveloped nations are understandably attracted by the methods that achieved these results elsewhere. In contrast, the slow process of industrialization, stretching over centuries, through which the nations of the West achieved a high standard of living must appeal much less to them. That appeal is lessened even more by the economic processes of the free market and the political processes of liberal democracy through which, in large measure, Western industrialization was achieved. For these processes require a degree of moral restraint and economic and political sophistication that is largely absent in the underdeveloped nations. The simple and crude methods of totalitarianism must appear much more congenial to them.

Thus we arrive at the disconcerting conclusion that successful foreign aid for economic development can be counterproductive if the donor nation's goal is the recipient's social and political stability. In some cases at least, the failure of American aid for economic development may have been a blessing in disguise in that it did not disturb a status quo whose continuing stability was our main interest. Such aid, intended for economic development, actually performs the function either of a bribe or of prestige aid. Here again, however, these functions are likely to be impaired by disappointed expectations of economic development of the donor and the recipient nations.

It is equally a moot question whether or not successful foreign aid for economic development is conducive to the development of democratic institutions and practices. This is obviously not the place to raise *ex professo* the issue of the relationship between democracy and economic development; but that no necessary relationship exists between the two, recent history has made clear. The most impressive example is the Soviet Union. Its rapid economic development has gone hand in hand with totalitarian government, and a case could well be made for the proposition that the former would have been impossible without the latter. It is more likely than not that where the intellectual and moral preconditions for economic development are lacking in the population at large and are present only in a small elite, as is the case in many of the underdeveloped nations, the imposition of the will of that small minority upon the majority of the population is a precondition not only for the start of economic development but also for sustained economic growth.

As concerns the promotion of a peaceful foreign policy, economic development is likely to be counterproductive, provided a political incentive for a belligerent foreign policy is present. The contrary conclusion derives from the popular, yet totally unfounded assumption that "poor" nations make war on "rich" nations for economic advantage and that "rich" nations are by definition peaceful because they have what they want. In truth, of course, most wars have been fought not for economic but political advantage, and, particularly under modern technological conditions, only economically advanced nations are capable of waging modern war. We did not consider the Soviet Union a military threat as long as it was economically underdeveloped; it became such a threat at the very moment its economic development had transformed it into a modern industrial power. Similarly, Communist China today is only a potential military threat by virtue of its economic potential, both waiting to be activated by economic development.

Foreign aid for economic development, then, has a very much smaller range of potentially successful operation than is generally believed, and its success depends in good measure not so much upon its soundness in strictly economic terms as upon intellectual, moral, and political preconditions, which are not susceptible to economic manipulation, if they are susceptible to manipulation from the outside at all. Furthermore, the political results of successful foreign aid for economic development may be either unpredictable or counterproductive in terms of the goals of the donor nation. In any event, they are in large measure uncontrollable. Foreign aid proffered and accepted for purposes of economic development may turn out to be something different from what it was intended to be, if it is not oriented toward the political conditions within which it must operate. Most likely, it will turn out to be a bribe or prestige aid, or else a total waste. To do too much may here be as great a risk as to do little, and "masterly inactivity" may sometimes be the better part of wisdom.

Conclusions for Policy

The major conclusions for policy to be drawn from this analysis are three: the requirement of identifying each concrete situation in the light of the six different types of foreign aid and of choosing the quantity and quality of foreign aid appropriate to the situation; the requirement of attuning, within the same situation, different types of foreign aid to each other in view of the over-all goals of foreign policy; and the requirement of dealing with foreign aid as an integral part of political policy.

The task of identifying specific situations in terms of the appropriate foreign aid requires concrete answers to specific questions. Can a prospective recipient country not survive without foreign aid? Is its government likely to exchange political advantages for economic favors? Would our military interests be served by strengthening this nation's military forces? Does this country provide the noneconomic preconditions for economic development to be supported by foreign aid? Are our political interests likely to be served by giving this nation foreign aid for purposes of prestige? Can a case be made for foreign aid in order to alleviate human suffering? What kind and quantity of foreign aid is necessary and sufficient to achieve the desired result?

To answer these questions correctly demands first of all a thorough and intimate knowledge and understanding of the total situation in a particular country. But it also requires political and economic judgment of a very high order, and in two different areas. On the one hand, it is necessary to anticipate the susceptibility of the country to different kinds of foreign aid and their effects upon the country. On the other hand, when this task has been performed, it is then necessary to select from a great number of possible measures of foreign aid those most appropriate to the situation and hence most likely to succeed.

In most situations, however, the task is not that simple. Typically, an underdeveloped country will present a number of situations calling for different types of foreign aid to be given simultaneously. One type of foreign aid given without regard for the effects it may have upon another type risks getting in the way of the latter. One of the most conspicuous weaknesses of our past foreign-aid policies has been the disregard of the effect different types of foreign aid have upon each other. Bribes given to the ruling group, for instance, are bound to strengthen the political and economic status quo. Military aid is bound to have an impact upon the distribution of political power within the receiving country; it can also have a deleterious effect upon the economic system, for instance, by increasing inflationary pressures. Similarly, subsistence foreign aid is bound to strengthen the status quo in all its aspects. In so far as the donor nation desires the foregoing effects or can afford to be indifferent to them, they obviously do not matter in terms of its over-all objectives. But in so far as it has embarked upon a policy of foreign aid for economic development that requires changes in the political and economic status quo, the other foreign-aid policies can be counterproductive in terms of economic development; for they can strengthen the very factors that stand in its way.

This problem is particularly acute in the relations between prestige aid and aid for economic development. The donor nation may seek quick political results and use prestige aid for that purpose; yet it may also have an interest in the economic development of the recipient country, the benefits of which are likely to appear only in the distant future. At best, prestige aid is relevant to economic development only by accident; it may be irrelevant to it, or it may actually impede it. What kind of foreign aid is the donor to choose? If it chooses a combination of both, it must take care to choose an innocuous kind of prestige aid and to promote economic development, the benefits of which are not too long in coming. Afghanistan was the classic example of this dilemma. The Soviet Union, by paving the streets of Kabul, chose a kind of prestige aid that was irrelevant to economic development. The United States, by building a hydroelectric dam in a remote part of the country, chose economic development, the very existence of which is unknown to most Afghans and the benefits of which are slow in coming.

It follows, then, from the very political orientation of foreign aid, that its effect upon the prestige of the donor nation must always be in the minds of the formulators and executors of foreign-aid policies. Foreign aid for economic development, in particular, whose benefits to the recipient country are immediate and patent, is a more potent political weapon than aid whose benefits are obscure and lie far in the future. Furthermore, the political effects of foreign aid are lost if its foreign source is not obvious to the recipients. For it is not aid as such or its beneficial results that create political loyalties on the part of the recipient, but the positive relationship that the mind of the recipient establishes between the aid and its beneficial results, on the one hand, and the political philosophy, the political system, and the political objectives of the donor, on the other. That is to say, if the recipient continues to disapprove of the political philosophy, system, and objectives of the donor, despite the aid he has received, the political effects of the aid are lost. The same is true if he remains unconvinced that the aid received is a natural, if not inevitable manifestation of the political philosophy, system, and objectives of the donor. Foreign aid remains politically ineffectual as long as the recipient says either, "Aid is good, but the politics of the donor are bad," or "Aid is good, but the politics of the donor—good, bad, or indifferent—have nothing to do with it." If a positive psychological relationship between donor and recipient is to be established, the procedures through which aid is given, and the subject matter to which it is applied, must lend themselves to the creation of a connection between aid and the politics of the giver which reflects credit upon the latter.

The problem of foreign aid is insoluble if it is considered as a self-sufficient technical enterprise of a primarily economic nature. It is soluble only if it is considered an integral part of the political policies of the donor country, which must be devised in terms of the political conditions, and for its effects upon the political situation, in the receiving country. In this respect, a policy of foreign aid is no different from diplomatic or military policy or propaganda. They are all weapons in the political armory of the nation.

As military policy is too important a matter to be left to the generals, so foreign aid is too important a matter to be left to the economists. The expertise of the economist is needed to analyze certain facts, devise certain means, and perform certain functions of manipulation for foreign aid. But the formulation and overall execution of foreign-aid policy is a political function that must be performed by the political expert.

It follows from the political nature of foreign aid that it is not a science but an art. What that art requires by way of mental predisposition is political sensitivity to the interrelationship among the facts, present and future, and between ends and means. The requirements by way of mental activity are twofold. The first requirement is a discriminatory judgment of facts, ends, and means and their effects upon each other. However, an analysis of the situation in the recipient country and, more particularly, its projection into the future and the conclusions from the analysis in terms of policy can be arrived at only in part through rational deduction from ascertainable facts. When all the facts have been ascertained, duly analyzed, and conclusions drawn from them, the final judgments and decisions can be derived only from subtle and sophisticated hunches. The best the formulator and executor of a policy of foreign aid can do is to maximize the chances that his hunches turn out to be right. Here as elsewhere in the formulation and conduct of foreign policy, the intuition of the statesman rather than the knowledge of the expert will carry the day.

The Global Great Society and Its Enemies

Yet, even if the foreign-aid policies of the United States are able to maximize their chances for success, what are the chances that the vision of a global Great Society can be achieved in practice? Four factors stand in the way of its achievement. Each one of them would suffice to make the achievement unlikely, and the four combined make it well-nigh impossible.

We have tried to show elsewhere that the Great Society cannot be realized without serious political conflicts and that the refusal to recognize the inevitability of political conflict will doom the Great Society. Yet what is true for the United States is true in particular for those nations to which the global Great Society addresses itself primarily—that is, the developing ones. Their poverty and general backwardness are in good measure not the result of injustices imposed from without or deficiencies of the natural environment, but are to a great extent caused by factors impervious to foreign aid. On the one hand, they result from, if not ethnic, at least cultural deficiencies which can be overcome, if at all, only through slow transformation from within. On the other hand, they result from the fact that the ruling groups have a vital stake in the continuation of backwardness, for their political power is a function of the poverty and illiteracy of the majority of the people. The attempt to remedy these deficiencies from the outside is tantamount to an attack upon the political status quo, to be resisted by the powers-that-be. The frustrations of the Alliance for Progress and of much of foreign aid in general can be traced to this political factor. The cultural and political receptivity of the nation being aided sets a limit to the American mission.

Secondly, the achievements of America as an example to the world were rendered possible by a natural environment—a politically empty, rich and fertile continent isolated from the centers of international strife—singularly conducive to the development of an open society, horizontally and vertically mobile. Furthermore, these gifts of nature required a people endowed with the moral and rational qualities to take advantage of them. Few nations throughout history have been so favored by nature, and few nations have been morally and rationally equipped for the task nature presented to them. It has been the besetting weakness of America's conception of its global mission from Wilson to Johnson that it has endeavored to separate the American achievements from its uniquely American roots and to erect it into a principle of universal applicability. Wilson and his epigones lifted the American purpose up to the skies, divorced from the concrete conditions of American existence. Yet, while they could divorce the American experiment from the American experience, they could not divorce it from the experience of the world. From the former they took it, to the latter they sought to apply it. And in this Wilson failed, as his successors are bound to fail.

Thirdly, the very universalization of the Great Society impairs its plausibility as an example to the world. The plausibility of the American experiment and the possibility of its achievement were from the beginning dependent upon the objective conditions of American existence which drew out certain qualities of the people and rewarded them with success. This unique concatenation of objective and subjective conditions, bringing forth unique results, could plausibly be held up as a model for others to emulate only if conditions elsewhere were not totally different from those prevailing in the United States. Even in conditions not completely dissimilar American principles could apply only as ideal guideposts, not as blueprints to be imitated to the letter. The failure of the attempt to demonstrate in action that what had proved possible in America was possible elsewhere, given good will and material resources, cast doubt upon the suitability of the American experiment to serve as a model under any conditions.

This impairment of the plausibility of the American experiment through its universalization is aggravated when the experiment itself lacks intrinsic plausibility. This is indeed the case of the Great Society. Its qualitative substance remains undefined and its realization is dubious even within the American context. How can so vague and uncertain an experiment serve as a model for other nations to emulate, let alone as a vehicle for a universal mission?

Finally, the plausibility of the Great Society for other nations is altogether destroyed by its involvement in wars on the soil of developing nations. The conception of a national experiment as a model for the world to emulate has the tendency to transform itself into a missionary endeavor to persuade and help other nations to emulate the example, and such a missionary enterprise tends to transform itself into a crusade that will force laggard and benighted nations for their own good to emulate the example. Thus the New Freedom issued in the Fourteen Points, giving meaning to the First World War; the New Deal, in the Four Freedoms and the United Nations, giving purpose to the Second World War. Thus the Great Society issues in the anti-Communist crusade seeking to preserve the freedom of nations, threatened by Communism, to choose the Great Society if they so wish, thereby giving meaning to the intervention in the Dominican Republic and the war in Vietnam.

However, the contemporary crusade differs significantly from those that preceded it. The latter were carried forward by a victorious army, whose victory seemed to provide empirical proof for the validity of the crusading principles in whose name it was fought. The former must compete, and fight against, a rival conception of the Great Society, more relevant to the experiences and needs of many developing nations than ours. For the anti-Commumnist crusade on behalf of the Great Society, war is not the ultimate manifestation of its victory or of the validity of its principles. Rather, it is the instrument with which the Great Society tries to defend its global scope against the onslaught and subversion of its rival.

The very need of a political philosophy claiming universal applicability to defend itself against a rival by force of arms leaves at the least the validity of that claim in abeyance. Furthermore, the peoples to be preserved for the global Great Society are likely to be more impressed with the potency of American arms than with the promises of the Great Society. The voice of the arms is clear and its power is not open to doubt, while the message of the Great Society is faint and inarticulate. What is true of the nations immediately concerned is likely to be true also of the world at large: The clatter of arms drowns out the message of the Great Society.

The connection between the Great Society and war is also bound to have a deleterious effect upon the Great Society at home. No nation, however rich and powerful, can simultaneously create the Great Society at home, spread it abroad, and wage war in order to defend the Great Society's opportunity to spread. Governments must distinguish between goals that are desirable and those that are necessary, and they must give priority to the latter. Of necessity, the successful waging of war takes precedence over the achievement of the Great Society at home and abroad. Thus, in the end, war fought to make the world safe for the Great Society makes the achievement of the Great Society impossible.

What the crusade for a world-wide Great Society has achieved is, then, quite different from what was intended. Aside from the issue of war waged on behalf of the Great Society, foreign aid has become in good measure a world-wide philanthropic undertaking engaged in competitively by the developed nations and even by some developing ones, such as India. The economic exploitation of their colonies by the metropolitan powers is here replaced by the attempt at the economic exploitation of the developed nations by the former colonies. The philosophy of the world-wide Great Society discussed above is in essence the ideological justification and rationalization of the claim of the developing nations upon the permanent economic support of the developed ones.

Yet, while disillusionment with foreign aid for economic development is widespread among developed and developing nations alike, the competition for the privilege to proffer foreign aid, regardless of its effects upon economic development, continues among the major developed nations. They continue this costly competition for political reasons. If a nation were to drop out of the competition, it would risk losing the influence it has, or imagines it has, upon the policies of the recipient country.

Yet the result of this competition has by and large been a standoff. None of the competitors has much to show for its expenditures and efforts either in the economic development of the developing nations or in political advantage to itself. In other words, if nobody had ever entered into this competition, the situation of all concerned would not be markedly different from what it is now. A case can even be made for the proposition that at least some of the developing nations might be better off if they were not able to rely upon the availability of foreign aid competitively given. For they would then be compelled to put their economic house in order or go under.

It is probably too much to expect that the major competitors in foreign aid, heeding such rational considerations, will give up the competition altogether and by making the economic benefit for the recipient the main yardstick of foreign aid, pool their resources in multilateral efforts. However, the persistent lack of political and economic success of foreign aid, commensurate with the efforts made and the resources committed, ought to call forth a reciprocal abatement of the competitive efforts on the order of "arms control," if not of "disarmament." Thus the conclusion we shall arrive at in our discussion of intervention in general also applies to that special kind of intervention called foreign aid: Selectivity oriented toward the political advantage of the donor and, if feasible, the economic benefit of the recipient ought to be the order of the day.

5

To Intervene or Not To Intervene

THE DOCTRINE

Both the United States and the Soviet Union are officially opposed to intervention in the affairs of other nations—that is, interference in their affairs against their will. Both voted in December 1965 for a U.N. General Assembly resolution entitled *Declaration on the Inadmissibility of Intervention in the Domestic Affairs of States and the Protection of their Independence and Sovereignty*. According to this resolution, "no state has the right to intervene, directly or indirectly, for any reason whatever, in the internal or external affairs of any other state" and "no state shall organize, assist, foment, finance, incite or tolerate subversive, terrorist or armed activities directed toward the violent overthrow of another state, or interfere in civil strife in another state." Yet both the United States and the Soviet Union are at the same time in favor of intervention under certain conditions. The trouble is that the United States opposes the interventions of the Soviet Union and justifies its own interventions by that opposition, and vice versa.

The Soviet Union has qualified its policy of "peaceful coexistence of states with different social systems" by its support for "wars of national liberation." As Mr. Brezhnev put it in his report to the Twenty-third Party Congress in March 1966: "It goes without saying that there can be no peaceful coexistence where matters concern the internal processes of the class and national liberation struggle in the capitalist countries or in colonies. Peaceful coexistence is not applicable to the relations between oppressors and the oppressed, between colonialists and the victims of colonial oppression." And to quote Mr. Khrushchev's address to the graduates of the Soviet Military Academy on July 8, 1964: "There are, however, other wars, wars of national liberation, wars in which oppressed peoples rise against their oppressors, colonialists and imperialists. We regard such wars as just and sacred. We support the peoples who take up arms and uphold their independence and freedom, and we support them not only in words, but by concrete deeds."

The United States, on the other hand, is committed to intervene against any attempt to change the political status quo by outside violence. Secretary of State Rusk declared on August 25, 1966, before a Senate subcommittee that "no would-be aggressor should suppose that the absence of a defense treaty, congressional declaration, or U.S. military presence grants immunity to aggression. . . . The United States, as an important and responsible member of the U.N., may be required in the future, in accordance with established Charter procedures, to take action that cannot now be anticipated with any precision."

Yet American intervention against somebody else's intervention is opposed by the Soviet Union. Replying to President Johnson's speech of August 26, 1966, in which he called for an improvement of American-Soviet relation, *Pravda* wrote in an editorial on September 1, 1966: "But he preferred to pass over in silence the cardinal issues of principle which separate the United States from the Soviet Union. We mean specifically the police doctrine of armed interference by the United States anywhere in the world where the U.S.A. believes such interference to be in line with its interests." Yet this was exactly the position the

Soviet Union took after the occupation of Czechoslovakia in August 1968, when it not only claimed the right to intervene in the affairs of other members of the "socialist commonwealth," but also declared, according to *Pravda* of August 22, 1968, such intervention "in defense of Socialism" to be "the supreme international duty." Against this claim, the Ministerial Council of the North Atlantic Treaty Organization reaffirmed on November 16, 1968, "the inviolability of the principle which has been invoked on numerous occasions by every country including the U.S.S.R. that all nations are independent and that consequently any intervention by one state in the affairs of another is unlawful."

What is interesting and, as we shall see, illuminating in these doctrinal arguments is their intellectual similarity in spite of their contradictory practical consequences. Both the United States and the Soviet Union are opposed to intervention as a matter of general principle. Both envisage an ideal world from which intervention in the affairs of other nations will have been banished. But both admit that, considering the world as it is, they have the right and even the duty to intervene in the affairs of other nations on behalf of an overriding moral principle. For the Soviet Union, that overriding principle requires the support of nations subjected to colonial or neo-colonial rule and the preservation and, if need be, restoration of governments subservient to it in Eastern Europe. For the United States, it requires the defense of nations threatened by Communist aggression or subversion. In short, both superpowers are committed to the principle of nonintervention, provided no overriding principle justifies intervention.

Their doctrinal position is similar to that developed by writers on international law during the nineteenth and the beginning of the twentieth centuries. These writers stipulated the principle of nonintervention, derived from the principle of the sovereign equality of all nations and their consequent independence from each other. Yet, according to a count by one of these writers, the principle of nonintervention was qualified at one time or another by more than forty exceptions justifying intervention. The sweeping character of these exceptions is indicated by one that gained general acceptance and was formulated by one of the most eminent authorities on international law in the nineteenth century, Professor William Edward Hall, in these terms: "If a government is too weak to prevent actual attacks upon a neighbor by its subjects, if it foments revolution abroad, or if it threatens hostilities which may be averted by its overthrow, a menaced state may adopt such measures as are necessary to obtain substantial guarantees for its own security." [1] According to another more recent authority, Professor Percy H. Winfield, "Intervention is justifiable if its aim is to check or to undo the effects of an illegal intervention on the part of another state." [2]

The pervasive contrast between the principle of nonintervention in the abstract and other principles negating it in practice is nowhere more strikingly and also more naïvely revealed than in the essay John Stuart Mill wrote in 1859 with the title "A Few Words on Non-Intervention." Referring of course to Great Britain, Mill starts by saying:

> There is a country in Europe, equal to the greatest in extent of dominion, far exceeding any other in wealth, and in the power that wealth bestows, the declared principle of whose foreign policy is to let other nations alone. . . . It will hold its own, it will not submit to encroachment, but if other nations do not meddle with it, it will not meddle with them. Any attempt it makes to exert influence over them, even by persuasion, is rather in the service of others, than of itself: to mediate in the quarrels which break out between foreign States, to arrest obstinate civil wars, to reconcile belligerents, to intercede for mild treatment of the vanquished, or finally to procure the abandonment of some national crime and scandal to humanity, such as the slave-trade. . . . If the aggressions of barbarians force it to a successful war, and its victorious arms put it in a position to command liberty of trade, whatever it demands for itself it demands for all mankind. The cost of war is its own;

[1] William Edward Hall, *A Treatise on International Law* (7th ed.; London: Oxford University Press, 1917), p. 295.

[2] Percy H. Winfield, "The Grounds of Intervention in International Law," *British Yearbook of International Law* (London: Oxford University Press, 1924), p. 154.

the fruits it shares in fraternal equality with the whole human race.

This argument, which is obviously in support not so much of nonintervention as of selfless intervention, is virtually invalidated by two sweeping qualifications. On the one hand, Mill stipulates the right to intervene "when England's safety is threatened, or any of her interests hostilely or unfairly endangered." On the other hand, searching for "some rule or criterion whereby the justifiableness of intervening in the affairs of other countries, and (what is sometimes fully as questionable) the justifiableness of refraining from intervention, may be brought to a definite test," Mill argues that "there is a great difference (for example) between the case in which the nations concerned are of the same, or something like the same, degree of civilization, and that in which one of the parties to the situation is of a high, and the other of a very low grade of social improvement. To suppose that the same international customs, and the same rules of international morality, can obtain between one civilized nation and another, and between civilized nations and barbarians, is a grave error." This is so for two reasons. "In the first place, the rules of ordinary international morality imply reciprocity. But barbarians will not reciprocate. . . . In the next place, nations which are still barbarous have not got beyond the period during which it is likely to be for their benefit that they should be conquered and held in subjection by foreigners. . . . The sacred duties which civilized nations owe to the independence and nationality of each other, are not binding toward those to whom nationality and independence are either a certain evil, or at best a questionable good." Hence intervention is here justified, and Mill points to the Roman Empire, the French in Algeria, and the British in India in support of his case.

Thirdly, Mill considers the case of a "protracted civil war, in which the contending parties are so equally balanced that there is no probability of a speedy issue; or if there is, the victorious side cannot hope to keep down the vanquished but by severities repugnant to humanity and injurious to the permanent welfare of the country. In this exceptional case it seems now to be an admitted doctrine, that the neighboring nations, or one powerful neighbor with the acquiescence of the rest, are warranted in demanding that the contest shall cease, and a reconciliation take place on equitable terms of compromise."

Finally, Mill considers the case of a people fighting for its freedom against an oppressive government. He finds intervention here justified on two grounds. On the one hand, if England, "on account of its freedom . . . should find itself menaced with attack by a coalition of Continental despots, it ought to consider the popular party in every nation of the Continent as its natural ally: the Liberals should be to it what the Protestants of Europe were to the Government of Queen Elizabeth." On the other hand, intervention is justified on behalf of "a people struggling against a foreign yoke or against a native tyranny upheld by foreign arms. . . . The doctrine of non-intervention, to be a legitimate principle of morality, must be accepted by all governments. The despots must consent to be bound by it as well as the free States. Unless they do, the profession of it by free countries comes but to this miserable issue, that the wrong side may help the wrong, but the right must not help the right. Intervention to enforce non-intervention is always rightful, always moral, if not always prudent."

Having started by praising England for its policy of nonintervention, Mill ends by imploring England to embark upon a policy of intervention on behalf of freedom:

The first nation which, being powerful enough to make its voice effectual, has the spirit and courage to say that not a gun shall be fired in Europe by the soldiers of one Power against the revolted subjects of another, will be the idol of the friends of freedom throughout Europe. That declaration alone will ensure the almost immediate emancipation of every people which desires liberty sufficiently to be capable of maintaining it: and the nation which gives the word will soon find itself at the head of an alliance of free peoples, so strong as to defy the efforts of any number of confederated despots to bring it down. The prize is too glorious not to be snatched sooner or later by some free country; and the time may not be distant when England, if she does not take this heroic part because of its heroism, will be compelled to take it from consideration for her own safety."

I have dwelt upon John Stuart Mill's arguments at some length because they appear to show conclusively the impossibility of developing a coherent doctrine of nonintervention. If one of the noblest and most brilliant minds of modern times, in the attempt to square his country's foreign policies with certain abstract principles, can entangle himself unknowingly in such blatant contradictions, it stands to reason that there must be something incurably wrong with the attempt itself. For a century and a half, statesmen, lawyers, and political writers have tried in vain to formulate objective criteria by which to distinguish between legitimate and illegitimate intervention. They have only succeeded in clothing the interests and policies of their respective nations with the appearance of legitimacy. For from the time of the ancient Greeks to this day, some states have found it advantageous to intervene in the affairs of other states on behalf of their own interests. And other states, in view of their interests, have opposed such interventions and have intervened on behalf of theirs. Yet it was only concomitant with the rise of the modern nation-state that an explicit doctrine of nonintervention was developed. Its purpose was to protect the new nation-states from interference by the traditional monarchies of Europe. After the Napoleonic Wars, these monarchies established the Holy Alliance, whose purpose it was to protect the conservative status quo against the rising national and liberal movements. The main instrument of the Holy Alliance, openly proclaimed in the treaty establishing it, was intervention. Thus, to give only two examples among many, Russia tried to intervene in Spain in 1820, and actually intervened in Hungary in 1848, in order to oppose liberal revolutions. Great Britain opposed these interventions because it was opposed to the expansion of Russian power. Yet it intervened on behalf of nationalism in Greece and on behalf of the conservative status quo in Portugal because its interests seemed to require it.

CONTEMPORARY PRACTICE

What we have witnessed since the end of the Second World War appears, then, as a mere continuation of a tradition that was well established in the nineteenth century. There appears to be nothing new either in the contemporary confusion of doctrine or in the pragmatic use of intervention on behalf of the interests of individual nations. What Great Britain and Russia were doing in the nineteenth century, the United States and the Soviet Union seem to be doing today. Thus, to cite again two spectacular examples among many, the Soviet Union intervened in Hungary in 1956 as Russia had done in 1848, and the United States intervened in Cuba at the beginning of the 1960s as it had done in the first decades of the century. Yet there are fundamental differences between the interventions of the past and those of the present. Five such differences exert an important influence upon the techniques of contemporary intervention as well as upon the peace and order of the world.

First, the process of decolonization, which started after the Second World War and is now almost completed, has more than doubled the number of sovereign nations. Many, if not most of these new nations are not viable political, military, and economic entities; they are lacking in some, if not all of the prerequisites of nationhood. Their governments need regular outside support. Thus France subsidizes its former colonies in Africa; all the major industrial nations extend economic and financial aid to the new ones, and the United States, the Soviet Union, and China do so on a competitive basis.

What makes this aid a lever for intervention is the fact that in most cases it is not just an advantage the new nations can afford to take or leave, but a condition for their survival. The Indian economy, for example, would collapse without outside support and in consequence the Indian state itself would probably disintegrate. Large masses of Egyptians would starve without the outside supply of food. What is true of these two ancient and relatively well-developed nations is of course true of most of the new nations, which are nations within their present boundaries only by virtue of the accidents of colonial policy: The supplier of foreign aid holds the power of life and death over them. If a foreign nation supplies aid, it intervenes; if it does not supply aid, it also intervenes. In the measure that the government must depend on foreign aid for its own and its nation's survival, it is inevitably exposed to political pressures from the supplying government. Many of the recipient governments have been able to minimize or even neutralize these political pressures by keeping open alternative sources of foreign aid and by playing one supplying government against the other. Some nations have developed this technique into a fine and highly successful art.

Second, our age resembles the period of history after the Napoleonic Wars, when the theory of nonintervention and the practice of intervention flourished, in that it is a revolutionary age. Many nations, new and old, are threatened by revolution or are at one time or other in the throes of it. A successful revolution frequently portends a new orientation in the country's foreign policy, as it did in the Congo, Cuba, and Indonesia. Thus the great powers, expecting gains or fearing disadvantages from the revolution, are tempted to intervene on the side of the faction favoring them. The temptation is particularly acute when the revolution is committed to a Communist or anti-Communist position. Thus the United States and the Soviet Union often oppose each other surreptitiously through the intermediary of governments and political movements. It is at this point that the third new factor comes into play.

Of all the revolutionary changes that have occurred in world politics since the end of the Second World War, none has exerted a greater influence upon the conduct of foreign policy than the recognition on the part of the two superpowers, armed with a large arsenal of nuclear weapons, that a direct confrontation between them would entail unacceptable risks, for it could lead to their mutual destruction. Thus they have decided that they must avoid such a confrontation. This is the real political and military meaning of the slogan "peaceful coexistence."

Instead of confronting each other openly and directly, the United States and the Soviet Union have chosen to oppose and compete with each other through third parties. The internal weakness of most new and emerging nations, requiring foreign support, and the revolutionary situation in many of them give them the opportunity of doing so. Thus, aside from competing for influence upon a particular government in the traditional ways, the United States and the Soviet Union have interjected their power into the domestic conflicts of weak nations, supporting the government or the opposition as the case may be. While one might think that on ideological grounds the United States, a status-quo power, would always intervene on the side of the government and the Soviet Union, a revolutionary power, on the side of the opposition, it is characteristic for the interplay between ideology and power politics (to which we turn in a moment) that this has not always been so. Thus the Soviet Union intervened in Hungary in 1956 on the side of the government, and the United States has been intervening in Cuba on the side of the opposition. The Soviet slogan of support for "wars of national liberation" is in truth an ideological justification of Soviet support for that side in a civil conflict in which the Soviet Union happens to have an interest. In the Congo, the United States and the Soviet Union have switched their support from the government to the opposition and back again according to the fortunes of a succession of civil wars.

While contemporary interventions, serving national power interests, have sometimes been masked by the ideologies of Communism and anti-Communism, these ideologies have been an independent motivating force. This is the fourth factor we must consider. The United States and the Soviet Union face each other not only as two great powers competing for the advantage in the traditional ways. They face each other also as the fountainheads of two hostile and incompatible ideologies, systems of government, and ways of life, trying to expand the reach of their respective political values and institutions and to prevent the expansion of the other's. Thus the Cold War has been a conflict not only between two world powers but also between two secular religions. And like the religious wars of the seventeenth century, the war between Communism and democracy does not respect national boundaries. It finds enemies and allies in all countries, opposing the one and supporting the other regardless of the niceties of international law. Here is the dynamic force that has led the two superpowers to intervene all over the globe, sometimes surreptitiously, sometimes openly, sometimes with the accepted methods of diplomatic pressure and propaganda, sometimes with the frowned-upon instruments of covert subversion and open force.

These four factors favoring intervention in our time are counteracted by a fifth one, which is in a sense a counterpart to the weakness of the nations intervened in. These nations have just emerged from a colonial status or are in the process of emerging from a semicolonial one. They compensate their need for outside support with a fierce resistance to the threat of "neo-colonialism." While they cannot exist without support from stronger nations, they refuse to exchange their newly won independence for a new dependency. Hence their ambivalent reaction to outside intervention. They need it and they resent it. This ambivalence compels them to choose among several different courses of action. They can seek support from multiple outside sources, thereby canceling out dependence on one by dependence on the other. They can alternate among different sources of support, at one time relying on one, and at another time relying on another. Finally, they can choose between complete dependence and complete independence, by either becoming a client of one of the major powers or by renouncing outside support altogether.

This ambivalence of the weak nations imposes new techniques upon the intervening ones. Intervention must either be brutally direct in order to overcome resistance, or it must be surreptitious in order to be acceptable, or the two extremes may be combined. Thus the United States intervened in Cuba in 1961 through the proxy of a refugee force, and the Soviet Union intervened in Hungary in 1956 by appointing a government that asked for its intervention.

U.S. POLICY OF INTERVENTION

What follows from this condition of intervention in our time for the foreign policies of the United States? Four basic conclusions can be drawn: the futility of the search for abstract principles, the error of anti-Communist intervention *per se*, the self-defeating character of antirevolutionary intervention per se, and the requirement of prudence.

First, it is futile to search for an abstract principle that would allow us to distinguish in a concrete case between legitimate and illegitimate intervention. This was so even in the nineteenth century, when intervention for the purpose of colonial expansion was generally regarded to be legitimate and when the active players on the political stage were relatively self-sufficient nation-states, opposed to intervention as a threat to their existence. If this was so, then, it stands to reason that in an age where large segments of whole continents must choose between anarchy and intervention, intervention cannot be limited by abstract principles, let alone effectively outlawed by a United Nations resolution.

Let us suppose that nation *A* intervenes on behalf of the government of nation *B* by giving it military, economic, and technical aid on the latter's request, and that the government of *B* becomes so completely dependent upon *A* as to act as the latter's satellite. Let us further suppose that the opposition calls upon *C* for support against the agents of a foreign oppressor and that *C* heeds that call. Which one of these interventions is legitimate? *A* will of course say that its own is and *C*'s is not, and vice versa, and the ideologues on both sides will be kept busy justifying the one and damning the other. This ideological shadow-boxing cannot affect the incidence of interventions. All nations will continue to be guided in their decisions to intervene and their choice of the means of intervention by what they regard as their respective national interests. There is indeed an urgent need for the governments of the great powers to abide by certain rules according to which the game of intervention is to be played. But these rules must be deduced not from abstract principles which are incapable of controlling the actions of governments, but from the interests of the nations concerned and from their practice of foreign policy reflecting those interests.

The failure to understand this distinction between abstract principles and national interests as guidance for a policy of intervention was in good measure responsible for the fiasco of the Bay of Pigs in 1961. The United States was resolved to intervene on behalf of its interests, but it was also resolved to intervene in such a way as not openly to violate the principle of nonintervention. Both resolutions were legitimate in terms of American interests. The United States had an interest in eliminating the political and military power of the Soviet Union, which used Cuba as a base from which to threaten the security of the United States in the Western Hemisphere. It was also an interest of the United States to avoid jeopardizing its prestige in the uncommitted nations through intervention in Cuba. The United States failed to assign priorities to these two interests. In order to minimize the loss of prestige, the United States jeopardized the success of the intervention. Instead of using concern for prestige as just one interest among others in the political equation, it submitted to it as though it were an abstract principle imposing absolute limits upon the actions necessary to achieve success. In consequence, the United States failed thrice. The intervention did not succeed, and in the attempt we suffered a temporary loss of prestige as the friend of the uncommitted nations, as well as much of our prestige as a great nation able to use its power successfully on behalf of its interests.

Had the United States approached the problem of intervening in Cuba in a rational fashion, it would have asked itself which was more important: to succeed in the intervention or to prevent a temporary loss of prestige among the uncommitted nations. Had it settled upon the latter alternative, it would have refrained from intervening altogether; had it chosen the former alternative, it would have taken all the measures necessary to make the intervention a success, regardless of unfavorable reactions in the rest of the world. Instead, it sought the best of both alternatives and got the worst.

The Soviet Union's interventions in Hungary in 1956 and in Czechoslovakia in 1968 are instructive in this respect. The Soviet Union put the success of the interventions above all other considerations, and succeeded. Hungary and Czechoslovakia are today Communist states within the orbit of the Soviet Union. However, while Soviet prestige did recover from the damage it suffered in 1956, it was dealt an apparently irreparable blow in 1968.

The interventions of the United States in Cuba, the Dominican Republic, and Vietnam, and other less spectacular ones, have been justified as reactions to Communist intervention. This argument derives from the assumption that Communism everywhere in the world is not only morally unacceptable and philosophically hostile to the United States, but also detrimental to the national interests of the United States and must therefore be opposed on political and military as well as moral and philosophic grounds. I shall assume for the purposes of this discussion that, as a matter of fact, Communist intervention actually preceded ours in all these instances, and shall raise the question as to whether our national interest required our intervention against the Communist one.

Ten or twenty years ago, this question could have been answered in the positive without further examination. For then Communism anywhere in the world was a mere extension of Soviet power, controlled and used for the purposes of that power. Since we were committed to the containment of the Soviet Union, we were also committed to the containment of Communism anywhere in the world. Today however, we are faced not with one monolithic Communist bloc controlled and used by the Soviet Union, but with a variety of Communisms, whose relations with the Soviet Union and China change from country to country and from time to time and whose bearing upon the interests of the United States requires empirical examination in each instance. Communism has become polycentric, with each Communist government and movement, to a greater or lesser extent, pursuing its own national interests within the common framework of Communist ideology and institutions. The bearing which the pursuit of those interests has upon the policies of the United States must be determined in terms not of Communist ideology but of their compatibility with the interests of the United States.

Subjecting our interventions in Cuba, the Dominican Republic, and Vietnam to this empirical test, one realizes the inadequacy of the simple slogan "Stop Communism" as the rationale of our interventions. While this slogan is popular at home and makes only minimal demands upon discriminating judgment, it inspires policies that do either too much or too little in opposing Communism, and can provide no yardstick for a policy that measures the degree of its opposition to the degree of the Communist threat. Thus, on the one hand, as part of the settlement of the missile crisis of 1962, we pledged ourselves not to intervene in Cuba, which is today a military and political client of the Soviet Union and seeks to become the fountainhead of subversion and military intervention in the Western Hemisphere, and as such directly affects the interests of the United States. On the other hand, we have intervened massively in Vietnam, even at the risk of a major war, although the Communist threat to American interests emanating from Vietnam is at best remote, and in any event infinitely more remote than the Communist threat emanating from Cuba.

As concerns the intervention in the Dominican Republic, even if one takes at face value the official assessment of the facts that the revolution of April 1965 was controlled by Cuban Communists, it appears incongruous that we intervened there in a revolution that was, according to that same assessment, a mere symptom of the disease, while the disease itself—Cuban Communism —remained exempt from effective intervention.

This type of intervention against Communism per se naturally tends to blend into intervention against revolution per se. We tend to intervene against all radical revolutionary movements because we are afraid lest they be taken over by Communists, and conversely we tend to intervene on behalf of all governments and movements opposed to radical revolution, because they are also opposed to Communism. Such a policy of intervention is unsound on intellectual grounds for the reasons mentioned in our discussion of contemporary Communism; it is also bound to fail in practice.

Many nations of Asia, Africa, and Latin America are today objectively in a prerevolutionary stage, and it is likely to be only a matter of time until actual revolution breaks out in one or the other of these nations. The revolutionary movements that will then come to the fore are bound to have, to a greater or lesser degree, a Communist component—that is, they run the risk of being taken over by Communism. Nothing is simpler, in terms of both intellectual effort and, at least initially, practical execution, than to trace all these revolutions to a common conspiratorial source, to equate all revolutionary movements with world Communism, and to oppose them with indiscriminate fervor as uniformly hostile to the interests of the United States. Under this rationale, the United States would be forced to intervene against revolutions throughout the world because of the ever-present threat of a Communist take-over and would transform itself, in spite of its better insight and intentions, into an antirevolutionary power per se.

Such a policy of intervention might succeed if it had to deal with nothing more than isolated revolutionary movements that could be smothered by force of arms. But it cannot succeed, since it is faced with revolutionary situations all over the world; for even the militarily most powerful nation does not have sufficient usable resources to deal simultaneously with a number of acute revolutions. Such a policy of indiscriminate intervention is bound to fail not only with regard to the individual revolution to which it is applied, but also in terms of its own indiscriminate anti-Communism. For the very logic that would make us appear as the antirevolutionary power per se would surrender to Communism the sponsorship of revolution everywhere. Thus indiscriminate anti-Communist intervention achieves what it aims to prevent: the exploitation of the revolutions of the age by Communism.

If this analysis of our policy of intervention is correct, then we have intervened not wisely but too well. Our policy of intervention has been under the ideological spell of our opposition to Communism and to potentially Communist-led revolutions. While this ideological orientation has continued to determine our policy of intervention, the Soviet Union has continued to pay lip service to the support of "wars of national liberation" but has in practice relegated these wars to a secondary place in the struggle for the world. This softening of the Soviet ideological position has become one of the points of contention in the ideological dispute between the Soviet Union and China. In a statement of June 14, 1963, the Chinese Communist Party declared that "the whole cause of the international proletarian revolution hinges on the outcome of revolutionary struggles" in the "vast areas of Asia, Africa, and Latin America" that are today the "storm centers of world revolution dealing direct blows at imperialism." Conforming to this doctrine, China has almost indiscriminately intervened throughout the world on behalf of subversive movements, very much in the manner in which the Bolshevist government under Lenin and Trotsky tried to promote world revolution. In their reply of July 14th of the same year, the Soviet leaders opposed the " 'new theory' according to which the decisive force in the struggle against imperialism . . . is not the world system of socialism, not the struggle of the international working class, but . . . the national liberation movement." The Soviet Union's recent practice of restraint in fomenting and supporting revolution has matched this theoretical position. This ideological "revisionism" has of course not prevented the Soviet Union from intervening—as in Egypt, Somalia, and Czechoslovakia—when its national interest appeared to require intervention.

One factor that cannot have failed to influence the Soviet Union in toning down its ideological commitment to intervention has been the relative failure of ideological intervention. The United States, China, and Cuba have joined the Soviet Union in the experience of that failure. The uncommitted nations have been eager to reap the benefits of intervention, but have also been very anxious not to be tied with ideological strings to the intervening nation. After making great efforts, expending considerable resources, and running serious risks, the participants in this world-wide ideological competition are still approximately at the point from which they started: Measured against their ambitions and expectations, the uncommitted third of the world is still by and large an ideological no man's land.

This experience of failure is particularly painful, and ought to be particularly instructive, for the United States. For since the end of the Second World War we have intervened in the political, military, and economic affairs of other countries at a cost far in excess of $100 billion, and we have for some time been involved in a costly, risky war in order to build a nation in South Vietnam. Only the enemies of the United States will question the generosity of these efforts, which have no parallel in history. But have these efforts been wise? Have the commitments made and risks taken been commensurate with the results to be expected and actually achieved? The answer must be in the negative. Our economic aid has been successful in supporting economies that were already in the process of development; it has been by and large unsuccessful in creating economic development where none existed before because the moral and national preconditions for such development were lacking. Learning from this failure, we have established the principle of giving aid only to the few nations who can use it rather than to the many who need it. While this principle of selectivity is sound in theory, its consistent practical application has been thwarted by the harsh political and military realities that sometimes make it necessary to give aid when it is not economically justified, as well as by political and military considerations derived from the ideological concerns discussed above.

This principle of selectivity must be extended to the political and military sphere as well. We have come to overrate enormously what a nation can do for another nation by intervening in its affairs even with the latter's consent. This overestimation of our power to intervene is only a counterfoil to our ideological commitment, which by its very nature has no limit. Committed to intervening against Communist aggression and subversion anywhere, we have come to assume that we have the power to do so successfully. But in truth, both the need for intervention and the chances for successful intervention are much more limited than we have been led to believe. Intervene we must where our national interest requires it and where our power gives us a chance to succeed. The choice of these occasions will be determined not by sweeping **ideological commitments** or by blind reliance upon American power, but by a careful calculation of the interests involved and the power available. If the United States applies this standard, it will intervene less and succeed more.

THE INTERVENTION IN VIETNAM

The policies the United States is pursuing in Vietnam are open to criticism on three grounds: They do not serve the interests of the United States, they even run counter to these interests, and the objectives we have set ourselves are not attainable, if they are attainable at all, without unreasonable moral liabilities and military risks.

In order to understand the rationale underlying our involvement in Southeast Asia, one must again revert to the year 1947, when the postwar policies of the United States in the form of the policy of containment, the Truman Doctrine, and the Marshall Plan were formulated and put into practice. These policies pursued one single aim by different means: the containment of Communism. That aim derived from two assumptions: the unlimited expansionism of the Soviet Union as a revolutionary power and the monolithic direction and control the Soviet Union exerted over the world Communist movement. These assumptions, in turn, were based upon the empirical evidence of the policies pursued by the Soviet Union during the last phase and the immediate aftermath of the Second World War. The Red Army had advanced to a distance of a hundred miles east of the Rhine, and behind that line of military demarcation the Soviet Union had reduced the nations of Eastern Europe to the status of satellites. Nothing by way of material power stood in the path of the Red Army if it was intent upon taking over the nations of Western Europe, all of which had been drastically weakened by the war and in some of which, such as France and Italy, large Communist parties were ready to make common cause with the "liberators" from the East.

It was against this essentially traditional military threat that the policy of containment was devised. Thus it partook of the rationale that, since the beginning of the Republic, has formed the policies of the United States with regard to Europe: the maintenance or, if need be, the restoration of the balance of power. It was for this reason that we intervened in two world wars on the seemingly weaker side, and it was for the same reason that we embarked upon the policy of containing the Soviet Union. The Truman Doctrine, itself originally applied to a specific, geographically limited emergency concerning Greece and Turkey, erected this traditional and geographically limited commitment into a general principle of universal application by stipulating that the United States would come to the assistance of any nation threatened by Communist aggression or subversion.

The Marshall Plan served the purpose of the policy of containment in that it tried to make the nations of Western Europe immune from Communist subversion and strong enough collectively to withstand Soviet aggression by restoring them to economic health. The spectacular success of the Marshall Plan had intellectual and political consequences similar to those of the policy of containment. The rationale underlying the Marshall Plan also was transformed into a general principle of American statecraft to be applied anywhere in the form of foreign aid.

It is against this background that one must consider the involvement of the United States in Southeast Asia. For the modes of thought and action growing from the specific European experiences of the postwar period still dominate today the foreign policies of the United States, paradoxically enough not so much in Europe as elsewhere throughout the world. The Administration has consistently justified its Asian policies by analogy with our European experiences. We think of Asia in the late 1960s as we thought of Europe in 1947, and the successes of our European policies have become the curse of the policies we have been pursuing in Asia. For the problems we are facing in Asia are utterly different from those we successfully dealt with in Europe two decades ago, and the political world we were facing in Europe two decades ago has been radically transformed.

The active involvement of the United States in Southeast Asia is a response to the Korean War. That war was interpreted by our government as the opening shot in a military campaign for world conquest under the auspices of the Soviet Union. In view of this interpretation, it was consistent for the United States to defend South Korea against the North Korean Communists, as it would have defended Western Europe had the Red Army stepped over the line of demarcation of 1945. Similarly, it was consistent for the United States to support with massive financial and material aid the French military effort to defeat the Vietnamese Communists. When in 1954 France was threatened with defeat, it was also consistent for Secretary of State Dulles and Admiral Radford, then Chairman of the Joint Chiefs of Staff, to recommend to President Eisenhower intervention with American airpower on the side of France. Finally, after the partition of 1954, it was a logical application of this policy of containing Communism in Asia to establish and support an anti-Communist regime in South Vietnam. When the disintegration of this regime became acute, roughly from 1960 onward, we continued the policy of containment as though the nature of world Communism had not changed since 1950 and as though the political disintegration of South Vietnam posed for us an issue similar to the North Korean invasion of South Korea. It was at this point that our policy went astray.

While it was plausible, even though it has proven to be historically incorrect, to attribute the outbreak of the Korean War to a world-wide Communist conspiracy, there is no historic evidence whatsoever to interpret what has happened in Vietnam since 1960 in that manner. The period of history since Khrushchev's denunciation of Stalin in 1956 has been characterized by the disintegration of the Communist bloc into its national components, pursuing to a greater or lesser degree their own particular national policies within a common framework of Communist ideology and institutions. The influence that the Soviet Union and China still are able to exert over Communist governments and movements is not the automatic result of their common Communist character, but of the convergence of national interests and of particular power relations. This has always been true of the Vietnamese Communists. Many of them were nationalists before they became Communists, and it was partly in response to the indifference or hostility of the West that they embraced Communism as the only alternative. Even under the most unfavorable conditions of war with the United States, the government of North Vietnam has been able to retain a considerable measure of independence vis-à-vis both the Soviet Union and China by playing one off against the other. The Vietnamese Communists are not mere agents of either the Soviet Union or China. Both the sources of their strength and their aims are indigenous and must be judged on their own merits.

This being the case, our professed war aim to "Stop Communism" in South Vietnam reveals itself as an empty slogan. It must be made concrete by raising such questions as what kind of Communism it is that we are trying to stop in South Vietnam and what bearing that Communism has upon the interest of the United States in containing the Soviet Union and China. The answers to these questions reveal the unsoundness of our policy. Communism in South Vietnam is irrelevant to the containment of Soviet or Chinese Communism since Vietnamese Communism is not controlled by either of them. Our fight against the South Vietnamese Communists is relevant only to our relations with South Vietnam, which, even if it were governed by Communists, is unlikely to affect the balance of power in Asia.

Not only does the containment of Vietnamese Communism not further the interests of the United States; but, paradoxical as it may sound, it is even detrimental to them. We have a legitimate interest in the containment of China, and our involvement in Vietnam is frequently justified by this interest. But Vietnamese nationalism has been for a millennium a barrier to the expansion of Chinese power into Southeast Asia. There is no patriotic Vietnamese, North or South, Communist or non-Communist, Buddhist or Catholic, who does not regard China as the hereditary enemy of Vietnam. Yet, in the measure that we have weakened Vietnam as a national entity through the destruction of its human and material resources, we have created a political military, and social vacuum into which either we must move or the Soviet Union or China will move.

The instruments we have been using to achieve our aim in

Vietnam are three: "counterinsurgency" and "nation-building" in the South and the bombing of the North. These instruments have failed, as they were bound to fail.

It can be held as an axiom, derived from the experience of many such situations, that a guerrilla war supported or at least not actively opposed by the indigenous population cannot be won, short of the physical destruction of that population. In the nature of things, the guerrilla is indistinguishable from the rest of the population, and in truth the very distinction is tenuous in a situation where the guerrilla is an organic element of the social and political structure. In such a situation, everyone is in a sense a potential guerrilla. The whole population is composed of full-time guerrillas, part-time guerrillas, auxiliaries who feed, clothe, and hide the combatants, make arms, build hide-outs, and carry ammunition, and only a minority is permanently passive or sur-reptitiously hostile. What we have been facing in South Vietnam is a primitive nation-in-arms, the war of a total population which can be won only by incapacitating the total population.

It is for this reason that "pacification," repeated time and again for almost a decade under different names and auspices, has been a consistent failure. For it is based upon the misconception that the guerrillas are an alien element within the indige-nous population, as we thought the Nazis were among the German people, who therefore could be separated from the popula-tion by an appropriate technique. Many a Vietnamese village is pacified only when all the men capable of bearing arms are either dead or driven away and prevented from returning. The last condition is impossible to achieve. Thus many villages have been "pacified" time and again, only to fall back under guerrilla con-trol when the military occupation was relaxed.

What makes "counterinsurgency" so futile an undertaking is the difference between the motivation of the guerrillas and that of the professional army fighting them. No professional army could have withstood the punishment inflicted upon the South Viet-namese guerrillas since the beginning of 1965. It is for this reason that our military leaders have assured us time and again that the Viet Cong were at the verge of collapse, as they would have been if they were professional soldiers. But they are, like the Spanish and Tyrolean guerrillas fighting the armies of Napoleon, fanatical protagonists of an ideal—social revolution or national survival or both—and they would rather die than admit defeat. Against them fights a professional army that does its duty efficiently and courageously and uses "counterinsurgency" as a mechanical contrivance, a particular kind of military tactic with which to fight an "unorthodox" war. However, guerrilla war is not just "unorthodox" in the technical, tactical sense, but different in quality from traditional war, and hence it cannot be "won" in the traditional sense.

Our government has recognized implicitly the truth of that analysis when it has maintained that we were fighting two wars in South Vietnam, a military and a political one—and that victory in the latter would be decisive. In order to win the political war, we have embarked upon a massive program for the political, social, and economic reconstruction of South Vietnam. The purpose of the program is to establish the government of South Vietnam as a new focus that will attract the loyalties of the large mass of South Vietnamese who are indifferent to either side, as well as the disenchanted supporters of the Viet Cong. This program is up against three obstacles which, in the aggregate, appear to be insurmountable.

First, the government of South Vietnam is a military government and has remained so in spite of the democratic gloss which carefully circumscribed and managed elections have tried to put on it. The foundation of the government's power is the army, in terms of both the administrative structure and what there is of loyal support. Yet the army is regarded by large masses of the population not as the expression of the popular will but as their enemy; for the army oppresses the peasants and, more particularly, there is reportedly no officer in the South Vietnamese army above the rank of lieutenant colonel who did not take the side of the French against his own people.

Second, this impression of an army fighting against its own people is reinforced by the massive presence of foreign armed forces without whose support neither the army nor the government based on it could survive. Regardless of our professed and actual intentions, our military presence, with its destructive economic, social, and moral results for South Vietnam, appears to an ever increasing number of South Vietnamese as an evil to be removed at any price. Thus our massive visible support for the government of South Vietnam, largely because it is indispensable, discredits that government in the eyes of the people of South Vietnam.

Finally, the radical change in political loyalties we are striving for requires radical social, economic, and political reforms, especially with regard to the distribution of land. The achievement of such reforms has indeed earned the Viet Cong the allegiance of large masses of peasants. What the government of South Vietnam represents, both in its composition and policies, is the interests of a small group of absentee land owners and members of the urban upper middle class who would lose their economic, social, and political privileges were that government really trying to counter the social revolution of the Viet Cong with radical social reforms of its own. We are facing here the same dilemma which has frustrated our foreign-aid policies throughout the world (e.g., the Alliance for Progress): We are trying to achieve radical social reforms through the instrumentality of governments that have a vital interest in the preservation of the status quo.

The universally recognized weaknesses of the government of South Vietnam—corruption, inefficiency, apathy, lack of public spirit, low military performance, a staggering military desertion rate—result irremediably from the nature of that government. They are not to be remedied by American appeals to the South Vietnamese government to do more for the country or to let the South Vietnamese army take over a large share of the fighting and of pacification. A government imposed upon an unwilling or at best indifferent people by a foreign power in order to defend the status quo against a national and social revolution is by its very nature precluded from doing what we expect it to do. That nature dooms our efforts at politically effective reconstruction.

The third policy we have been pursuing in Vietnam, the bombing of the North, has had two major goals: to win the war in the South by interdicting the influx of men and matériel from the North, and to force the government of North Vietnam to the conference table by making it too costly for it to continue the war. Both purposes derived from a faulty perception of reality. Our government assumed that what we were facing in South Vietnam was the result of foreign aggression and that there would be no unmanageable trouble in the South if only, in Secretary of State Rusk's often-repeated phrase, North Vietnam would leave its neighbor alone. It follows logically from this assumption that internal peace could be restored to South Vietnam if one could insulate it from the North or compel the North to cease its assistance to the insurgents in the South. However, this assumption does not square with historic reality.

The roots of the trouble are in the South. They were deeply embedded in the nature of the Diem regime, which combined a fierce nationalism with a totalitarian defense of the economic and social status quo. Nobody can doubt that the government of North Vietnam welcomed and aided and abetted the progressive disintegration of the Diem regime. But it did not cause that disintegration, nor was its support responsible for the Viet Cong's success. When, at the beginning of 1965, the government of South Vietnam was close to being defeated by the Viet Cong, 90 per cent of the Viet Cong weapons were of American origin, according to official estimates, and the annual infiltration from the North amounted to no more than a few thousand men, most of them originally Southerners. Only a total of a few hundred were regulars of the North Vietnamese army.

Consequently, the war could not be won by bombing the North even if the bombing were more effective than it actually has been. To quote General Maxwell Taylor:

> What would happen if Hanoi were suddenly to disappear? Suppose everything of value in the North were destroyed; we would still have over 200,000 armed guerrillas in South Vietnam who would have to be accounted for in some way. For food they could live off the land without supplies from the North. If they avoided contact with large military forces, they could husband their weapons and ammunition stocks and maintain for a long time a low level of

sustained depredations and terrorist activity. If they were determined to carry on the war, if their morale did not collapse at this disaster in the North, they could conceivably remain in action for the next ten years, or the next twenty years, and we might still be tied down by this vast guerrilla force.[3]

The situation would be no different if the government of North Vietnam were suddenly to sign our peace terms on the dotted line. Who would impose these terms on the Viet Cong, who have not been defeated in the field and continue to draw upon the support or at least the indifference of large masses of the indigenous population?

Precisely because we have been unable to win the war in the South, we continued to assume that the source of the war was in the North and that it could be won by bombing the North. However, most targets that appeared to be worth bombing were bombed and the war in the South was still not being won. From the assumption that the war could be won through action against the North, it followed logically to advocate the invasion of North Vietnam; for if North Vietnam was responsible for the war, then the conquest of North Vietnam could make an end to the war. That logical step was not taken because it would have conjured up the likelihood of a direct military confrontation with the Soviet Union or China or both. The Soviet Union assured us that it would not stand idly by while we destroyed the government of North Vietnam, and China made it clear that it would intervene, as it did in the Korean War, if a hostile army approached its frontiers.

However, if the war in the South were to last long enough, we would have a good chance of winning it. We were not likely to win it in the traditional way by breaking the enemy's will to resist, but rather by killing so many of the enemy that there is nobody left to resist. Killing in war has traditionally been a means to a psychological end. Here killing becomes an end in itself. The physical elimination of the enemy and victory become synonomous. Hence, the "body count," however fictitious in itself, was the sole measure of our success.

[3] Maxwell D. Taylor, *Responsibility and Response* (New York: Harper & Row, 1967), p. 38,

No civilized nation can wage such a war without suffering incalculable moral damage. The damage is particularly grave since the nation can see no plausible military or political benefit that could justify killing for killing's sake. And it is particularly painful for a nation like the United States, which was founded as a novel experiment in government, morally superior to those that went before it, and which has throughout its history thought of itself, and was regarded by the other nations of the world, as performing a uniquely beneficial mission not only for itself but for all mankind.

Why, then, in the fall of 1968, were we still resolved to continue fighting a war which appears politically aimless, militarily unpromising, and morally dubious? The answer is to be found in the concern for our prestige. If we should leave Vietnam without having won a victory, so it is argued, the credibility of our commitments throughout the world would suffer, Communist revolutions everywhere would be encouraged, and the reputation for invincibility of the most powerful nation on earth would be impaired.

In order to assess the validity of these arguments, it is first necessary to keep in mind that we are embarked upon a profitless enterprise. We are in the position of a businessman, say, the operator of a chain of stores, one of which consistently loses money. Since he is not going to come out of that misadventure with a net gain, the issue before him is how to minimize his losses. If he insists upon getting a profit out of the losing enterprise by throwing good money after bad, he will only maximize his losses. This is the course we have been following in Vietnam.

The decline of American prestige in consequence of the liquidation of our involvement in Vietnam is a matter for speculation; its drastic decline by virtue of our involvement is a matter of fact. Here is the most powerful nation on earth trying to force a primitive nation of peasants into submission by the massive use of all the modern means of mass destruction, with the exception of biological and nuclear weapons, and it is unable either to win or to liquidate the war. Here is the champion of the "free world" which protects the people of South Vietnam from Communism by the method of destroying them. Here is the last best hope of the downtrodden and the enslaved, to which men of good will throughout the world have looked as a shining example, relieving its frustration in blind ideological fury and aimless destructiveness upon a helpless people. Here is the other nuclear superpower which, in the process of trying to win the war, moves the world closer and closer to an unwinnable war with China, if not to the cataclysm of nuclear war. This is the image the United States presented in 1968 to most of the outside world; in consequence its prestige was never lower.

If the United States were to liquidate the war, the damage to its prestige would at least in a certain measure be repaired. The United States would show that it is wise and strong enough to admit a mistake and correct it. Nothing would follow from the liquidation of this misadventure for the kind of policies we and other nations might pursue in the future. Commitments are not entered into and honored by way of precedent, nor are revolutions started that way. For better or for worse, history does not operate like the Supreme Court of the United States (and even the Supreme Court has been known to disregard precedent for reasons of principle or prudence).

What the argument from prestige really amounts to is concern for the prestige not of the United States but of those who are responsible for its involvement in Vietnam. But those who are responsible for the straits in which the nation finds itself today must bear the consequences of their ideological blindness and political and military miscalculations. They ought not ask the nation to suffer for their false pride.

THE LESSONS OF VIETNAM

When a government composed of intelligent and responsible men embarks upon a course of action that is utterly at variance with what the national interest requires and is bound to end in failure, it is impossible to attribute such persistence in error to an accident of personality or circumstance. Nor is it possible to make such an attribution when the preponderance of public opinion—political, expert, and lay—for years supports such a mistaken course of action. When a nation allows itself to be misgoverned in such a flagrant fashion, there must be something essentially wrong in its intellectual, moral, and political constitution. To lay bare what is wrong is not an idle exercise in *ex-post-facto* fault-finding. Rather it is an act of public purification and rectification. If it is not performed and accepted by government and people alike, faults undiscovered and uncorrected are bound to call forth new disasters—perhaps different from the one we have experienced in Vietnam, but just as detrimental to the interests of the nation.

What accounts for the failure of a nation so amply endowed with human and material resources? The roots of our failure in Vietnam are to be looked for in three areas: intellectual understanding, political judgment, and moral standards.

Failures of intellectual understanding have led us into four far-reaching errors: the mechanistic approach to politics, reasoning by historic analogy, belief in the transferability of Western political institutions to Asia, and confidence in the unlimited perfectibility of governments.

I have argued elsewhere at length against the pseudo science of politics which endeavors to reduce the political sphere to an interplay of quantitative factors and which ends up by banishing politics altogether. The new theories, in so far as they are new in more than terminology, are in truth not so much theories as dogmas. They do not so much try to reflect reality as it actually is, as to superimpose upon a recalcitrant reality a theoretical scheme that satisfies the desire for thorough rationalization. Their practicality is specious since it substitutes what is desirable for what is possible.

What characterizes the most spectacular contemporary theories of politics is the attempt to use the tools of modern economic analysis in a modified form in order to understand their subject matter. Their mainstay is quantification. The use of terms such as "systems analysis," "feedback," "input," and "output" (to mention only a few common and easily accessible ones) is revealing; for these concepts were first developed by economic theory.

Even more revealing is the mode of thought that dominates many of the contemporary theories of politics. Whether they deal with the strategy of conflict or diplomatic bargaining or nuclear escalation, they visualize international conflict as a special case of social conflict in general (which is correct if one does not neglect the paramount distinctive factor that the parties to international conflict are sovereign nations with a monopoly of organized force), whose paradigm is economic conflict (which, as we shall see, is incorrect). In such a theoretical scheme, nations confront each other not as living historic entities with all their complexities but as rational abstractions, after the model of "economic man," playing games of military and diplomatic chess according to a rational calculus that exists nowhere but in the theoretician's mind.

It is widely recognized by economists that this rationalistic, quantitative approach is of limited applicability even to economics; for even here it neglects psychological forces that interfere with the smooth operation of the rational calculus. Its applicability is established by the nature of the central concept of economics: wealth. Conversely, its inapplicability to politics is established by the nature of the central concept of politics: power. Wealth is a measurable quantity that an individual aspires to, competes or fights for, controls, possesses, or loses. Power is a quality of interpersonal relations that can be experienced, evaluated, guessed at, but that is not susceptible to quantification. What can be quantified are certain elements that go into the making of power, individual or collective, and it is a common error to equate such a quantifiable element of power with power as such. It is certainly possible and necessary to determine how many votes a politician controls, how many divisions or nuclear warheads a government disposes of; but if I want to know how much power this politician or that government has, I must leave the adding machine and the computer for historic and necessarily qualitative judgment.

Modern theorists of politics are repelled by history; for history is the realm of the accidental, the contingent, the unpredictable. They are instead fascinated by the rational model of the natural sciences, which appears to be free of these blemishes that stand in the way of the thorough rationalization of politics. I tried to show more than twenty years ago that this model of the natural sciences harks back to a Newtonian universe that the contemporary natural sciences have left far behind. This rational model is a Utopia that reflects the desires of theoreticians but not the real physical world, dominated as that world is by the principle of indeterminacy, and predictable as it is, at least as microcosmos, only by way of statistical probability.

I have also tried to show that politics, domestic and international, is susceptible to a radically different kind of understanding from that which is appropriate to the world of nature. When we try to understand politics, we are dealing, it is true, with men in the aggregate, but with men per se—that is, as spiritual and moral beings—whose actions and reactions can be rationalized and quantitatively understood only on the lowest level of their existence. Thus what the contemporary theories of politics endeavor to exorcise as deficiencies in view of an ideal, pervasively rational theory are in truth only the ineradicable qualities of the subject matter itself. A theory that does not take them into account transforms itself into a dogma, a kind of metaphysics, regardless in what empirical or mathematical garb it is clothed.

This dogmatic outlook of modern political science has greatly contributed to our failure in Vietnam. It has prevented us from understanding the true nature of the issues we were facing and, more particularly, their complexity and imponderable qualities. Thus we reduced what was actually a national and social revolution dominated by a national Communism to the simplicity of foreign aggression under the auspices of Chinese Communism. Success or failure in resisting foreign aggression can easily be ascertained by the standard of the relative geographic position of the contesting armies; thus we resisted foreign aggression in Korea by holding the 38th parallel. No such standard is available when one is engaged in a counterrevolution, as we have been in Vietnam, against a genuine popular revolution. Success in such a case is to be achieved by a combination of military and political measures, culminating in giving satisfaction to the revolutionary aspirations; it is to be determined by a qualitative political judgment, which is bound to be tentative and precarious while the struggle is going on.

The prevailing dogmatic presuppositions have precluded us from making such qualitative judgments. These presuppositions compel us to search for quantitative measurements which will determine the success or failure of our enterprise. Thus we have been reduced to making the "body count" the main evidence of our achievements. I shall not dwell upon the self-evident fictitious character of this quantitative measurement, especially in the conditions of a jungle war of movement, which invariably has favored our side. I shall only raise the question as to what the "body count" would prove for our success or failure, provided it were technically feasible. It would prove only that the number of enemy soldiers killed is greater or smaller than our losses. Given the actual and potential reserves of manpower of which the enemy disposes, this measurement would be irrelevant even in conventional warfare, since it leaves out of account all strategic and tactical considerations. It is doubly irrelevant for the kind of counterrevolutionary warfare in which we have been engaged in Vietnam.

The determinant of the success or failure of a counterrevolutionary war is not the number killed but the conditions of life and the state of mind of those who stay alive. That is what we mean by "pacification" as the ultimate goal of our efforts. The answer to the question as to whether a man or a village has been "pacified" in the sense of not only being protected from enemy action but also of having been weaned away from the revolutionary movement is a matter of political judgment. Yet having been disabused of such "inexact" intellectual operations, we sought the answer in quantitative computation. We have isolated a number of quantitative criteria, such as whether or not the village chief sleeps in the village, according to which we distinguish different degrees of pacification. We fed these factors into a computer that could determine at a glance to what extent that village had been pacified.

However, this mechanistic, quantitative operation cannot tell us where the loyalties of the villagers lie, which side they will choose when the chips are down, and in whose hands effective political and administrative control rests. But these are the questions to which the policy-maker needs answers, and only qualitative political judgment can try to answer them. The computer can provide only the illusion of an answer. This is not to say that the computerization of quantitative criteria is worthless in itself. It has its proper place as one datum among others upon which a political judgment must be based. What makes it an intellectual error is its substitution for a qualitative political judgment. The inevitable consequence of this intellectual error is the failure of political judgment. In Vietnam, this failure has manifested itself in the consistent illusion of military and political success, derived from the delusion that the "body count" and the quantitative criteria of physical control are the determinants of that success.

This mechanistic approach to politics is duplicated, perhaps less crudely and simplistically, by the approach to history that has dominated official thinking on Vietnam: reasoning by analogy without awareness of the unique character of historic events. When we try to draw lessons from history, it is indeed inevitable that we reason by analogy; for we have nothing else to go on but past events similar to those we must deal with in the present. Yet this is only half the story. While the historic events are similar in certain respects in so far as they are the typical manifestations of basic social and psychological forces, they are in other respects unique events which happened only once in that way. The typicality of historic events enables us to understand history as an unfolding objective process which has a rational meaning. The uniqueness of historic events precludes us from drawing unambiguous lessons from historic experience. What is required of the circumspect observer who consults history as a teacher for action, then, is a sharp distinction between what is typical and what is unique in two historic situations. If the typical elements coincide and are relevant to the issue at hand, the lesson of the past can indeed be applied to the present.

It is characteristic of the official mode of thought to be oblivious to that distinction. It takes the coincidence and relevance of the typical elements in the historic and the present situation for granted. Thus it equates without investigation Nazism and Communism because they are both totalitarian; Vietnam in 1968 and Czechoslovakia in 1938 because they are both threatened with a totalitarian takeover; retreat from Vietnam and appeasement preceding the Second World War because both constitute territorial concessions to totalitarianism. These equations serve the purpose of justifying policies which, since they would have been appropriate to the historic situation, must also be appropriate to the contemporary one.

These unqualified analogies obliterate the unique elements in the historic situations that are being compared. The policies recommended for the present may or may not be justified, but they cannot be justified through the invocation of these analogies. However, while that invocation is without intellectual value, it performs an important political function. It makes it appear that today's policy-makers have learned the lessons history teaches. We have been assured that President Johnson has not made and will not make Neville Chamberlain's mistake. But that assurance does not cover the possibility that Mr. Johnson, thinking in false historic analogies, has not made other mistakes, perhaps worse than that of which Mr. Chamberlain stands accused.

An analogy of a different kind is responsible for the almost universal insistence upon free elections as the way out of the political impasse in Vietnam. That insistence derives from the assumption that free elections are able to perform in Vietnam, and for that matter anywhere else, the same functions for the distribution of political power they perform in Western democracies. However, the very essence of Chinese political culture, of which Vietnam forms a part, militates against the correctness of that assumption.

Elections in the Western sense have two roots: a political pluralism which allows different individuals, philosophies, and policies to compete for political power on the basis of equality; and a political individualism which allows the individual citizen to choose among these competitors. These two interconnected concepts are completely alien to Chinese political culture. That culture postulates an objective order from the compliance with which the government derives its legitimacy. That order allows the citizen no choice among political competitors but demands his obedience to the legitimate government, which can claim that obedience as long as it governs in accord with the objective order. When it visibly ceases to do so, having lost the "mandate of heaven," the citizen is absolved of the duty to obey and can and must transfer his allegiance to another government representative of the objective order.

It ought to be obvious that in such a cultural context national elections—in contrast to those on the village level where personal choice may come into play—perform a function utterly different from that performed in a relativistic and individualistic society of the West. In a country such as Vietnam, elections are in the nature of a plebiscite in support of the government rather than a choice among several competitors for the powers of the government. This is obviously the case in North Vietnam and in the part of South Vietnam controlled by the Viet Cong. But it is also so in the part of South Vietnam controlled by the Saigon government; for the freedom of choice among different parties and individuals which obviously exists there is strictly limited to parties and individuals who have essentially the same outlook and agree on basic policies.

Considering the present situation in Vietnam in which two governments are controlling different parts of the country, both claiming legitimacy for the whole, elections are likely to confirm the status quo without resolving the conflict. That is to say, people will vote for the government that happens to control them, for both philosophic and practical reasons. For an individual living under the control of the Saigon government who voted for the Viet Cong, and an individual controlled by the Viet Cong who voted for the Saigon government, would each take very considerable risks for his livelihood, freedom, and life. Thus elections are not likely to settle the fundamental issue over which the war is being fought: whether South Vietnam is to be governed by a Communist or non-Communist government. That issue can be decided only by a political settlement that reflects the actual distribution of military and political power between the Communist and non-Communist factions.

Finally, another ethnocentrism, projected from the American experience onto the Vietnam scene, has led us into an intellectual error—the assumption that all defects of a government are susceptible to remedial efforts. Imbued with this belief in the unlimited perfectibility of governments, we have been urging a succession of South Vietnamese governments to institute land reforms, to stamp out corruption, and in particular to shift the main burden of the war from the American armed forces to the South Vietnamese army. While these urgings have been well-nigh universal, amounting to a veritable consensus among supporters and critics of the war, they have been fruitless. It could not have been otherwise.

One does not need to be a Marxist in order to realize that individual and collective interests set limits to the ability of governments to reform themselves. That is as true of the government of the United States as it is of all governments past and present. The stringency of these limits may change from country to country and from one historic situation to another. But in view of the interests of its members and supporters, no government can do by way of reforms everything it ought to do on rational grounds. The limits within which a government is able to reform itself are particularly narrow when that government has been imposed upon a hostile or indifferent population by a foreign power and can keep itself in office only through the instrumentality of a large foreign army of occupation. A government's ability to reform itself is first of all predicated upon its willingness to do so. That willingness, in turn, depends upon incentives of a moral, political, or material nature, not only for the leaders but for the main body of the administration as well. But why should a government institute land reforms when its principal supporters derive their economic and political power from the unequal distribution of land? Why should a South Vietnamese soldier risk his life in a war that is ever more intensely and widely experienced by the people of South Vietnam as being waged by a foreign power on Vietnamese soil for foreign purposes? How can a government thus constituted be expected to stamp out corruption, which in a country such as South Vietnam is not a deviation from the norm but is bound to be the norm itself? For a government so precariously and in all likelihood temporarily placed as that of South Vietnam can have only two main incentives: to ensure the survival of its members and to draw as much material gain as possible from an advantageous situation which is not likely to last. For such a government, corruption is not a vice but a necessity. To expect such a government to rid itself of corruption is tantamount to expecting it to act against its very nature.

Errors in the way of thinking about foreign policy lead of necessity to wrong political judgments. There are, however, wrong political judgments which are not so occasioned but can result from a variety of intellectual errors. Three such misjudgments have had a deleterious effect upon policies in Vietnam. They concern the nature of Communism, of revolution, and of limited war.

It is one of the great ironies of history that we have tended to take Communism more seriously as a political ideology than have the major Communist governments. For Stalin and his successors in particular, Communism was first of all an ideological means to the traditional ends of imperial Russia. By contrast, we have tended to take the Communist postulates and prophecies at their face value and in consequence have been unable to divorce our political judgments from the assumption of the monolithic, conspiratorial character of Communism. Thus we have been unable to judge Vietnamese Communism on its own national merits, as an indigenous phenomenon resulting from the peculiar circumstances of time and place. Instead, Vietnamese Communism has appeared to us as a special instance of a general phenomenon which is not by accident the same regardless of time and place; for it has been created by a world-wide conspiracy whose headquarters are assumed to be in Moscow or Peking or both, and whose aim is to Communize the world. In this view, what happens in Vietnam is just an episode in that international struggle between Communism and the "free world," and consequently the outcome of the Vietnamese War has world-wide significance.

The misjudgment of revolution fits organically into this largely fictitious picture of the political world. Revolution, too, must not be understood on its own terms but must be traced to a conspiracy of foreign origin imposed upon an unwilling people. That concept of revolution is in good measure responsible for the fiasco of the Bay of Pigs. We thought of Castro as a dictator imposed by the Communist conspiracy of Moscow upon the unwilling Cubans, who, at the sight of a thousand anti-Castro refugees, would rise *en masse* against their oppressor. Similarly, the revolution in South Vietnam must be traced to a foreign conspiracy located in Hanoi and, at one remove, in Moscow and Peking. What looks like revolution, then, is really foreign aggression, and the revolution can be suppressed by thwarting that aggression.

What is inadmissible to us is the recognition that in large parts of the world there exists today an objective revolutionary situation. This revolutionary situation would exist even if Communism had never been heard of, and is in good measure a response to the Western teachings and examples of national self-determination and radical social reform. That these national and social revolutions are largely identified with Communism is primarily the result of the West's failure to identify with them morally and to support them materially. The Vietnamese revolution is a case in point. In Vietnam as elsewhere, particularly in Latin America, the Communist and anti-American orientation of revolutionary movements is directly related to the American misunderstanding of the nature both of Communism and of revolution.

While our misjudgments of Communism and revolution are organically related, our reliance upon limited war to combat them is a spectacular *non sequitur.* For if we are combating in Vietnam foreign aggression inspired and supported by the centers of world Communism, particularly Peking, and if we are serious about getting rid of the trouble, then we must strike at the source and not only at one of its outward manifestations. But for perfectly good reasons we shy away from a direct military confrontation with China, let alone the Soviet Union. Thus the means we have been employing in Vietnam are divorced from our conception of the nature of the conflict. While we conceive of the conflict as a particular manifestation of a world-wide struggle, we have tried to win that struggle through victory in a localized war.

That discrepancy also determines the nature of the localized war we have been fighting. Not only have we been fighting North Vietnam in order to suppress a South Vietnamese revolution inspired and supported by either China or the Soviet Union or both, but we have also imposed limitations upon this war against North Vietnam in order to avoid a direct military confrontation with either the Soviet Union or China or both. But these limitations have at the very least been a factor that has made military victory more difficult to attain. Thus our political misjudgments have put us into the doubly paradoxical situation in which we respond to what we consider to be the world-wide challenge of Communist revolution with a local war which is itself subject to limitations making a military victory more difficult, if not impossible, to attain. Thus we have been engaged in a war which we can neither win on the battlefield without risking a direct military confrontation with the two major Communist powers nor liquidate without giving the lie to the political assumptions on which our involvement is based.

What accounts for the persistence of these intellectual errors and political misjudgments in the face of unmistakable evidence to the contrary? It is hardly surprising that we can make such errors, but it is extraordinary that intelligent and honest men, drawing upon the best expert advice and ample sources of information, have been unable for so long to renounce a course of action that should have been recognized as unpromising and potentially disastrous from the very outset and is now so recognized by almost all concerned. The issue we are here facing is neither intellectual nor political but moral. Defects of moral standards are responsible for this persistence in a losing undertaking.

The conduct of foreign policy under democratic conditions inevitably puts the moral stamina of the makers of the policy to the test. A democratic government must accomplish two tasks: On the one hand, it must pursue foreign policies which maximize the chances for success; on the other, it must secure the approval of its people for these foreign policies as well as for the domestic ones designed to support them. The necessity to perform these tasks simultaneously faces a democratic government with a dilemma; for the conditions under which popular support can be obtained for a foreign policy are not necessarily identical with the conditions under which such a policy can be successfully pursued. A popular foreign policy is not necessarily a good one. As de Tocqueville put it, with special reference to the United States: "Foreign politics demand scarcely any of those qualities which are peculiar to a democracy; they require, on the contrary, the perfect use of almost all those in which it is deficient."

Faced with this dilemma, a government is naturally tempted to sacrifice the sound policy upon the altar of public opinion, abdicating leadership and exchanging short-lived political advantage for the permanent interest of the country. This temptation will become well-nigh irresistible if the government has persuaded itself that the foreign policy it pursues is sound just because it has popular support. The policy-maker who points to the latest public-opinion poll as proof of the soundness of his policy is no longer even aware of the existence of the dilemma. He escapes it by identifying standards of foreign policy with what appear to be the preferences of the people. He is no longer called upon to make a moral choice since his frame of reference precludes it. His unawareness of the existential dilemma and of the moral choice it requires is morally worse than yielding to the temptation to make the wrong choice. We are here in the presence not of moral corruption, which still presupposes the awareness of moral standards, but of moral decay: "What the crowd wants," to quote Mr. Justice Holmes, "becomes the ultimate standard by which the soundness of a policy is judged."

Since, however, what the crowd wants is in good measure determined by what the government and the molders of public opinion which are at its service suggest it ought to want, the government is here caught in a vicious circle of its own making. It molds public opinion in support of a foreign policy upon which it has decided, and then invokes public opinion in justification of that policy. "The competition of the market," to quote Holmes again, from which the truth is supposed to emerge, is here replaced by a quasi-monopoly, which does not allow the truth—that is, the correct policy—to be discovered through the free interplay of diverse opinions and divergent interests. Rather the truth is assumed to be exclusively owned by a government supported by public opinion. The issue is thus settled before it is really joined.

In such a situation, the dissenter fulfills no function useful for the government. Quite to the contrary, he becomes the disturber of a pre-established consensus, endowed with the attributes of truth and virtue. He must be silenced, and if he does not allow himself to be silenced, he must at least be discredited. Having thus pre-established the correctness of its policies, the government has morally incapacitated itself to put the correctness of its policies in question. Thus the simple-minded persistence in error, which has been characteristic of our policies in Vietnam, results from the government's destruction of the dynamics of pluralistic debate through which errors can be corrected and wrong policies set right. It is quite in character that the Johnson administration has changed its policies when it became obvious that the continuation of its futile efforts on an escalating scale would have required a reallocation of resources threatening its domestic support.

This tendency, common to all democratic governments, to compromise the quality of foreign policy for the sake of popular support is strengthened by the tendency, common to all bureaucracies, to support and execute government policies regardless of individual views of the merits. Within broad limits, this is as it should be. For no government could function if subordinate officials were to substitute their own views for those of the government with regard to the merits of the policy to be put into practice. However, from time to time, a government will embark upon policies which raise basic issues, such as our involvement in Vietnam. In such a case, the public official charged with the execution of a policy with which he fundamentally disagrees on political, military, or moral grounds is faced with a dilemma. By opposing policies which he deems to be detrimental to the national interest, he risks jeopardizing his public career. By supporting and executing such a foreign policy, he will remain a team worker in good standing at the sacrifice of his convictions and of the national interest.

As the government faced with a choice between a sound foreign policy and popular support is likely to sacrifice the former for the sake of the latter, so the public official having to choose between his career and his convictions is likely to choose the former over the latter. Human nature being what it is, powerfully supported by the specific intensity of America's conformism, these choices are not surprising. What is disquieting is the virtual absence of an exception to the rule of conformity In talking to high government officials, I have time and again been startled, and sometimes confounded, by the contrast between their public positions and private convictions. This contrast, I should add, concerned not only subjective estimates of the political and military situation but hard facts and figures ascertainable by objective calculations.

While many high-ranking officials who are opposed to our policies in Vietnam have resigned their positions since 1965, not one of them has justified his resignation with his opposition to these policies. If some of the more illustrious of them had made their opposition a matter of public record, they might well have rendered a great service to the national interest. But they would have risked the premature termination of their public careers, and none of them was evidently willing to face that dire prospect. As in the case of government policy as a collective enterprise discussed above, the issue of a moral choice does not even seem to have arisen. Here again, the issue was settled before it could have been raised, and it was settled in favor of private concerns and to the detriment of the national interest. And here again, what is ominous is not so much that moral judgment has been corrupted as that it has disappeared.

As bureaucratic conformism supports the government's substitution of popular support for sound foreign policies, so academic conformism creates a climate of expert opinion favorable to both.

The fact that most academic experts in international relations and Asian politics either actively supported the government policies in Vietnam or cast no public judgment on them greatly contributed to giving these policies at least a temporary respectability. Rereading the transcripts of the televised Washington teach-in of May 15, 1965, of *Meet the Press* of May 16, 1965, and of the confrontation on CBS on June 21, 1965, I have been struck by the almost comic effect of the statements made by eminent scholars in defense of government policy and in disparagement of its critics. Hardly any of these statements were correct then or were proven to be correct by subsequent events.

This subservience of scholars to the government performs the same sociological function as does the conformity of the bureaucracy. Many of these scholars were, or expect to be again, members of the bureaucracy, or part-time members of it, or to entertain contractual relations with it. The same psychological pressures that keep the bureaucracy in line operate in generally attenuated form on the scholars. As an eminent academic put it in private after he had given a public lecture defending the government policy: "We are approaching a catastrophe in Vietnam, but I cannot say so in public without losing my connections with the government."

This sector of the academic community thus transforms itself into a mere extension of the government bureaucracy, defending and implementing government policies regardless of their objective merits. While performing this function, it maintains its claim that its judgments are arrived at through a detached search for the objective truth. The result of this contrast between the function actually performed and the function claimed is moral ambiguity. When does a scholar speak as scholar, and when as servant of the government? When does he search for the truth regardless of what it may be, and when does he try to validate government policies by investing them with the appearance of objective truth? These distinctions, vital for the autonomy and validity of scholarship, are blurred, and in the end even the scholar concerned is incapable of making them. This outcome is no doubt advantageous to the government of the day, but it is also destructive of the long-term function political scholarship ought to perform for the nation, the government included.

There are only three ways in which a government can be induced to change wrong policies: through the brutal language of the facts indicating failure, through the erosion of political support, and through the rational demonstration of error. It is that last function which political scholarship is called upon to perform. By speaking truth to power, it serves not only truth but also power. For it provides the powers-that-be as well as the public at large with the intellectual standards with which to distinguish between success and failure. If it is taken seriously, it shortens the interval necessary for the correction of unsound policies.

Scholarship has not been able to perform that vital function because it has not taken itself seriously, nor has it been taken seriously by the government, except as the provider of ideological rationalizations and justifications of the government's policies. It has been only too eager to accept that ideological function assigned to it by the government and has thereby disqualified itself to perform its vital role for the government and society at large: to provide a corrective to the errors of government, born of a disinterested search for the truth. By investing the errors of government with the appearance of truth, it has encouraged the continuation of error.

This moral collapse of a large section of the academic community would not have been possible without its encouragement and the concomitant disparagement of academic dissent by the government. The last question we must raise, then, concerns the government's motives for the a priori rejection of responsible dissent. Here we are not dealing with a typical failure of moral sensitivity, but with personality traits in the highest policy-makers which, in such extreme manifestations at least, are unique. We are referring to the sin of pride.

All men naturally identify themselves with their work, and a maker of policy has a personal stake in the soundness and success of that policy. He will not easily admit that it is unsound and doomed to failure. This universal human tendency, however, differs from the stubborn pursuit of a wrong course of action in the face of all the evidence and all the arguments pointing to its unsoundness and the inevitability of failure. This persistence in error does not stem from a man's pride in his work but from a man's awareness of his insufficiency and his fear lest patent failure might give him away. Mr. Johnson's statement to Mr. Lodge, then our Ambassador to South Vietnam, immediately after President Kennedy's death that he was not going to be the first American president to lose a war expresses something of that mood.

Policies here are less related to objective reality than to the impression of the policy-maker's manly qualities they convey, and objective reality is replaced by an artificial one which is attuned to the policy. Thus policy moves in a wonderland of the policy-maker's creation, and the invulnerability of that creation is vitally important to the policy-maker's ego and the policy reflecting it. Thus the dissenter who opposes the real world to the fictitious one of the policy-maker constitutes a mortal threat not only to the policy but to the person of the policy-maker. He does not limit himself to suggesting a different policy from the official one, but threatens to expose the fictitious character of the reality from which the policy is derived and upon which it is intended to act.

The policy-maker might tolerate the former function, since he must be prepared to consider different policy proposals; he cannot countenance the latter, which threatens with destruction the very world within which he moves and puts into doubt his competence to understand and act upon it. Thus it is the very extremity of the defects responsible for our failure in Vietnam which in the last analysis accounts for the unwillingness of the policy-makers to change their course of action. To do so would be an admission not only of the failure of a particular policy but of the invalidity of the perception of reality and of the intellectual, political, and moral standards of the persons who have initiated and sustained the policy. Only great men, who are sure of themselves and think they are sure of their place in history, are capable of such an admission.

6

The United States and Europe

THE HISTORICAL BACKGROUND

Throughout its history, the United States has consistently pursued three interconnected interests with regard to Europe: not to get involved in the conflicts of European powers; to prevent European powers from interfering in the affairs of the Western Hemisphere; and to maintain or, if need be, to restore the balance of power in Europe. These three interests serve the most elemental of the national interests of the United States: the security of the United States in the Western Hemisphere through the preservation of its unique position as a hegemonial power without rival.

It was obvious from the outset that the privileged position of the United States in the Western Hemisphere could not be effectively challenged from within the Hemisphere. It could only be so challenged from the outside—that is, if a European power were to make common cause with an American one or to acquire territory in the Americas. Hence, the United States had to deprive the powers of Europe of both the incentive and the opportunity to challenge the United States in the Western Hemisphere. The Monroe Doctrine and the policies implementing it have served both purposes.

Of the policies implementing the Monroe Doctrine, the support of the European balance of power has been the one requiring an active American foreign policy beyond the limits of the Western Hemisphere. It has been the purpose of that policy to prevent conditions in Europe from arising which would provide incentives for a European power to intervene in the affairs of the Western Hemisphere or to contemplate a direct attack upon the United States. Such conditions would be most likely to arise if a European power, its predominance unchallenged within Europe, looked across the ocean for new conquests without needing to fear a challenge at the center of its power—that is, in Europe itself.

It is for this reason that the United States has consistently—the War of 1812 is the sole major exception—pursued policies aimed at the maintenance or, if need be, the restoration of the balance of power in Europe. It has opposed any European nation—be it Great Britain, France, Germany, or Russia—that seemed likely to gain ascendancy over its European competitors and thereby jeopardize the hemispheric predominance and eventually the very security of the United States. Conversely, it has supported whatever European nation appeared capable of restoring the balance of power by offering successful resistance to the would-be conqueror. While it is hard to imagine a greater contrast in ways of thinking about matters political than that between Alexander Hamilton and Woodrow Wilson, in their concern for the maintenance of the balance of power in Europe—for whatever different reasons—they were one. It is with this concern that the United States has intervened in both World Wars on the side of the initially weaker coalition and has pursued European policies largely paralleling those of Great Britain.

There is an apparent contradiction between the isolationism of Washington's Farewell Address and the abstentionism of the Monroe Doctrine, on the one hand, and the interventionism of our balance-of-power policies, on the other. This contradiction is logically resolved by the qualification implicit in the policies of isolationism and abstentionism. The Farewell Address warns against American implication "in the *ordinary* vicissitudes of her [Europe's] politics, or the *ordinary* combinations and collisions of her friendships or enmities [italics added]." That is to say, the injunction against involvement was predicated upon the continuing operation of the European balance of power; it did not apply to "extraordinary" vicissitudes and "extraordinary" combinations and collisions. It did not apply to those fundamental conflicts which put into question the very existence of the European balance of power.

This apparent contradiction has posed a practical issue for the conduct of American foreign policy. When was it necessary for the United States to intervene in order to maintain or restore the European balance of power, and when should the United States abstain because intervention would amount to meddling in "ordinary" conflicts and would therefore not be justified by the American interest in the European balance of power? The issue became acute at the very beginning of American history, culminating in Washington's Neutrality Proclamation of 1793. It remained dormant until the First World War because there was no occasion for it to be raised. From 1917 onward, it has remained a constant concern of American foreign policy, and it has posed itself in the aftermath of the Second World War with unprecedented acuteness and radically modified under the impact of the new technologies of communication, transportation, and warfare.

In 1793, Washington was urged by a preponderant public opinion to enter the War of the First Coalition on the side of France. This course of action was urged not in support of the European balance of power but in terms of treaty commitments, moral obligations, and political ideology. Calculations of interests and power, as presented by Hamilton in the "Americanus" and "Pacificus" articles, carried the day against these arguments.

Between April 22, 1793, and April 6, 1917, Europe did not present the United States with such a clear-cut choice between abstention and intervention, putting to the test of policy the American understanding of its interest in the European balance of power. And yet during that long period of actual isolation, awareness of that vital interest remained alive in both theory and practice. Two historic episodes illuminate the point: the changes in Jefferson's preferences from Great Britain to France and back according to the fortunes of the Napoleonic wars during their concluding decade, and American diplomacy during the Crimean War.

In 1806, Jefferson favored "an English ascendancy on the ocean" as being "safer for us than that of France." In 1807, he was forced by the logic of events to admit:

> I never expected to be under the necessity of wishing success to Buonaparte. But the English being equally tyrannical at sea as he is on land, and that tyranny bearing on us in every point of either honor or interest, I say "down with England" and as for what Buonaparte is then to do to us, let us trust to the chapter of accidents, I cannot, with the Anglomen, prefer a certain present evil to a future hypothetical one.[1]

However, in 1812, when Napoleon was at the pinnacle of his power, Jefferson hoped for the restoration of the balance. Speaking of England, he said:

> It is for the general interest that she should be a sensible and independent weight in the scale of nations, and be able to contribute, when a favorable moment presents itself, to reduce under the same order, her great rival in flagitiousness. We especially ought to pray that the powers of Europe may be so poised and counterpoised among themselves, that their own security may require the presence of all their forces at home, leaving the other quarters of the globe in undisturbed tranquility.[2]

In 1814, again compelled by the logic of events, he came out clearly against Napoleon and in favor of a balance of power that would leave the power of Napoleon and of England limited but intact:

> Surely none of us wish to see Buonaparte conquer Russia, and lay thus at his feet the whole continent of Europe. This done, England

[1] Letter to Thomas Leiper, August 21, 1807, *The Writings of Thomas Jefferson,* collected and edited by P. L. Ford (New York: G. P. Putnam's and Sons, 1892–99), IX, p. 130.

[2] Letter to Dr. Crawford, January 2, 1812, *Writings of Thomas Jefferson,* edited by H. A. Washington (New York: H. W. Derby and Co., 1861), VI, p. 33.

would be but a breakfast; and, although I am free from the vision-
ary fears which the votaries of England have effected to entertain,
because I believe he cannot effect the conquest of Europe; yet put
all Europe into his hands, and he might spare such a force to be
sent in British ships, as I would as leave not have to encounter,
when I see how much trouble a handful of British soldiers in
Canada has given us. No. It cannot be to our interest that all
Europe should be reduced to a single monarchy. The true line of
interest for us, is, that Buonaparte should be able to effect the
complete exclusion of England and from the whole continent of
Europe, in order, as the same letter said, "by this peaceable engine
of constraint, to make her renounce her views of dominion over
the ocean, of permitting no other nation to navigate it but with her
license, and on tribute to her, and her aggressions on the persons
of our citizens who may choose to exercise their right of passing
over that element." And this would be effected by Buonaparte's
succeeding so far as to close the Baltic against her. This success I
wished him the last year; but were he again advanced to Moscow,
I should again wish him such disasters as would prevent his reach-
ing Petersburg. And were the consequences even to be the longer
continuance of our war, I would rather meet them than see the
whole force of Europe wielded by a single hand.[3]

Similarly, in 1815, Jefferson wrote:

For my part, I wish that all nations may recover and retain their
independence; that those which are overgrown may not advance
beyond safe measures of power, that a salutary balance may be
ever maintained among nations, and that our peace, commerce,
and friendship, may be sought and cultivated by all.[4]

The concrete issues of the Crimean War were of no concern to
the United States, and thus the United States declared its neutrality in that war. Yet the United States was concerned with the
preservation of the European balance of power, and its diplomacy reflected that concern. The Crimean War coincided with a
particularly active phase of American expansionist agitation.
Great Britain, France, and Spain tried to contain the territorial
expansion of the United States. The United States had an interest in preventing the Anglo-French combination from surviving

[3] Letter to Thomas Leiper, January 1, 1814, Ford, IX, p. 445.
[4] Letter to Thomas Leiper, June 12, 1815, Ford, IX, p. 520.

the war and emerging from it with hegemonial power. Since Spain was too weak to contain the United States without Anglo-French support, the United States also had an interest in gaining advantages at the expense of Spain as long as the war lasted. Thus it supported Russia against Great Britain and France, and it took advantage of the military preoccupation of the latter powers and the resulting isolation of Spain by exerting pressure upon Spain. As a contemporary writer, Francis I. Grund, put it:

> If the map of Europe is to be changed—if Turkey is to be divided, and the nations to Europe are to extend their power and influence into Asia, we may consider how far this great historical movement of the people of the old world may affect the conditions of the new; and what steps it may be prudent for us to take, to balance the account. . . .
>
> If it be contended that we must remain indifferent to the affairs of Europe—that the changes wrought in the institutions and mutual relations of European governments do not merit our consideration and challenge our watchfulness, then, assuredly, our neutrality doctrine would amount to an injunction on ourselves, and condemn us, in our foreign relations, to absolute political inaction. It would insure all other nations against harm from our growing energy and power; while it would not protect us from *their* intermeddling with *our* affairs.[5]

The American intervention in the two World Wars made explicit in terms of policy what throughout American history had been recognized in theory and, however inconspicuously, translated into practice: the vital interest of the United States in the European balance of power. The official documents have made clear that Wilson was moved to intervene not only by his concern for the rights of neutrals but also by the anticipation of the consequences of a German victory, as foreshadowed by the German policies immediately preceding the American declaration of war. Wilson's subsequent policy of "peace without victory" was similarly inspired by the rationale of the balance of power. Wilson went to war in order to prevent a German hegemony; while

[5] Francis I. Grund, *Thoughts and Reflections on the Present Position of Europe* (Philadelphia: Childs & Peterson, 1860), pp. 225, 233.

during the war and at the peace table he proclaimed as his purpose to put an end to the balance of power, he actually tried to prevent the hegemony of the Allies.

Similarly, the United States intervened in the Second World War on the side of the Allies in order to prevent a German victory. From the very outset of hostilities in 1939, while remaining legally neutral, we took the side of Great Britain and France against Germany, the would-be hegemonial power, and took measures—such as lend-lease, the destroyer deal, the defense of Iceland, the order to the Navy to "shoot on sight"—that were incompatible with the status of a neutral. When Germany's defeat appeared assured, the United States tried unsuccessfully at Yalta to prevent the expansion of Russian power into Eastern and Central Europe. After a period of fumbling and hesitation following the end of the European War—what Churchill called the "deadly hiatus"—the United States embarked from 1947 onward upon a consistent policy based on the balance of power.

This policy differed radically from preceding ones. The rationale of preventing any European power or combination of powers from gaining a hegemonial position remained the same. Yet the policies serving this rationale had to be adapted to a new distribution of power and a new technology of war. At the beginning of each of the two World Wars, the distribution of power, while it might have favored one or the other side, did not make the victory of one side a foregone conclusion. Furthermore, neither side had at its disposal technological means for achieving a sudden victory which would have been irremediable or remediable only at prohibitive costs and risks for the United States. In both respects, the conditions prevailing in Europe in the aftermath of the Second World War were utterly different. With respect to the distribution of power in Europe, the Soviet Union had already become the hegemonial power; no counterweight existed in Europe that could stop the Red Army or prevent Communist subversion on behalf of the Soviet Union after the model of the Communist take-over in Czechoslovakia in 1948. Furthermore, the Soviet Union had the quantitative and qualitative technological superiority in communication, transportation, and weaponry to make the submission of Western Europe an accomplished fact before the United States had the opportunity to intervene.

Thus the United States was then faced with the task not of maintaining an existing balance of power or of shoring up one that was in danger of being disturbed, but of restoring a balance of power that was in acute disarray and could not be restored from within Europe alone. In order to be able to support this balance, the United States had to become a European power by adding its resources in virtual permanence to those of the European nations threatened by Soviet hegemony. These were the factors of interest and power that led to the formation of the Atlantic Alliance.

As concerns the political, military, and institutional arrangements within the Alliance, one fact stood out in the aftermath of the Second World War: the great discrepancy between the resources of the United States and those of its European allies. For the latter, the political, military, and economic support of the United States was a matter not of choice but of life or death. Without that support, the very survival of the nations of Western Europe as independent national entities would have been in jeopardy. The preponderance and elemental indispensability of American power put its stamp upon the policies and institutions of the Atlantic Alliance.

This discrepancy between the power of the United States and of the Soviet Union, on the one hand, and that of the nations of Western Europe, on the other, caused the United States to view Western Europe as a whole rather than, as it had done in the past, as a haphazard conglomeration of sovereign nation-states. In order to maximize the ability of the nations of Western Europe to provide a counterweight to Soviet power, the United States promoted the economic unification of Western Europe through the Marshall Plan and support for the European Communities, and its military unification through NATO, while entertaining the hope that functional unification would culminate in political unity.

THE CRISIS

The crisis of the Atlantic Alliance results from three drastic changes that have occurred in the international situation since the immediate aftermath of the Second World War: a change in the perception of the danger against which the Alliance was formed; a change in the relations within the hostile alliance—that is, the Communist bloc; and most important, a change in the relations within the Atlantic Alliance itself.

When the Alliance was founded, its members had one interest, overriding all others, in common: protection from Communist aggression and subversion. This was the common ground on which Greece and Turkey, the United States and France, Great Britain and Italy met. Today, neither Communist subversion nor Communist aggression is experienced by the members of the Atlantic Alliance as an acute threat to their existence. It is irrelevant for the purposes of this discussion whether the fear on which the Atlantic Alliance was founded was justified, or whether the abatement of that fear today, to the detriment of the vitality of the Alliance, is without justification. Both the fear then and the abatement of it now are simply facts of life that political analysis must take into account.

The common fear of Communist aggression and subversion neutralized the separate and divergent interests of the members of the Alliance and prevented them from obstructing the common policies of the Alliance. That fear having receded, divisive interests have again come to the fore. There is not a single outstanding issue of world politics today on which all members of the Alliance see eye to eye. The United States stands virtually alone in its policies vis-à-vis China, Vietnam, and Cuba, as well as in its policies concerning trade with the Communist nations. With regard to the German question and the over-all relations between the West and the Soviet Union, irreconcilable divergences of interests have resulted in the loss of initiative and a passive commitment to the status quo. Greece and Turkey have been on the brink of war over Cyprus. In Africa and in the Middle East, the allies go their separate ways. The policies of the

United States and France toward the United Nations are diametrically opposed. A similar cleavage separates France from the United States and Great Britain in the field of disarmament.

These divergent interests and policies have had a chance to emerge because developments within the Communist bloc have given the members of the Atlantic Alliance a chance to pursue their particular interests with new policies. The Alliance was originally conceived as an instrument for the containment of the Communist bloc, which was viewed as a monolithic colossus bent upon territorial expansion by military means. Against this expansionist urge, a wall had to be erected in the form of a military shield, which the Atlantic Alliance was to provide.

The simple, clear-cut military purpose of the Atlantic Alliance, aimed at a simple, clear-cut military danger, has proven to be inadequate to the complex and varied dangers with which the members of the Alliance are confronted today. The monolithic structure of the Communist bloc has been replaced by polycentrism—that is, a reassertion of diverse national interests and distinct policies serving them. Thus the members of the Alliance must now deal with some Communist nations subservient to the Soviet Union, with others subservient to China, and with an increasing number of others subservient to neither; moreover, all these nations are seeking to increase their freedom from outside control. In their relations with the non-Communist world, the Communist nations do not seek primarily territorial aggrandizement in the traditional manner of military expansion, but aim at strengthening and expanding Communism through the complex and subtle methods of foreign aid and trade, propaganda, subversion, and support for so-called wars of national liberation. This new variety of Communist foreign policy has provided the members of the Atlantic Alliance with opportunities for maneuver and for the realignment of interests which the simple military orientation of the Alliance impedes and for which it is in any case irrelevant.

These stirrings in Eastern Europe have brought home at least to the European members of the Atlantic Alliance the artificiality of the wall of containment cutting Europe in two, which the

Atlantic Alliance and the Warsaw Pact had erected. If Turkey belongs to Europe, so does Poland; if Greece does, so does Romania; if Italy does, so does Czechoslovakia. To travel in Eastern Europe today is to be forcefully reminded of the underlying essential unity of Europe, East and West, which the westward expansion of Soviet Communism has obscured. The Atlantic Alliance and the Warsaw Pact, both implying that Europe ends at the Elbe, stand in the way of the political realization of that new sense of European community, whose eastern frontiers may not be at the Urals but are certainly not at the Elbe either.

Finally and most important, the third element in the crisis of the Atlantic Alliance came into existence at the very moment the Alliance was founded. When President Truman announced on September 23, 1949, that the Soviet Union had exploded an atomic device, it should have been obvious that it was only a question of time until one of the foundation stones of the Alliance would crumble. That foundation stone was the atomic monopoly of the United States—the instrument of "massive retaliation," which would contain the Red Army within the territorial limits it had reached at the end of the Second World War. Thus the atomic monopoly of the United States, committed to the defense of Western Europe, was for the European members of the Alliance the main guarantee of peace and security.

President Truman's announcement of the first Soviet atomic explosion indicated implicitly that the American monopoly had become a wasting asset and was bound to disappear within the span of a few years.[6] By the mid- or late 1950s, the American monopoly had indeed been replaced by Churchill's "balance of terror"— that is, the ability of both the United States and the Soviet Union to destroy each other with nuclear weapons. The Soviet Union's acquisition of this capability changed the nature of the Alliance in two respects.

On the one hand, Western Europe was now within the range of Soviet intermediate ballistic missiles, and this technical possibility of atomic destruction, as Mr. Khrushchev did not tire of

[6] See the chapter "The Precarious State of the Atlantic Alliance," in Hans J. Morgenthau, *In Defense of the National Interest* (New York: Alfred A. Knopf, 1951), pp. 195 ff.

emphasizing, was transformed into an acute threat by the alliance of the nations of Western Europe with the United States. The Soviet Union holds the nations of Western Europe as hostages: In a war between it and the United States, in which the vital interests of Western Europe may or may not be at stake, these nations will be destroyed. That possibility was brought home during the Cuban crisis of 1962. It has powerfully supported the trend toward nationalism in Western Europe, toward less than complete identification with the United States, which has been noticeable since the mid-1950s.

On the other hand, the United States was now within the range of Soviet intercontinental ballistic missiles. Could it be assumed as a matter of course that the United States would risk its own destruction on behalf of interests that were those of one or the other or even all its European allies but not its own? Spokesmen for our successive administrations have emphatically asserted that it would. But as the Europeans see it, our policies during the Suez crisis of 1956 answered that question in the negative.

This divergence of interests not only affects American and European attitudes toward the risk of nuclear war, but also leads to different conceptions of military strategy once war has broken out. The United States is committed to a strategy of "flexible response," which would provide the belligerents with a series of "pauses" or "firebreaks" before they plunge into an all-out nuclear exchange. In a war of "flexible response" the United States might have a chance to escape nuclear destruction, while Europe would in all likelihood be annihilated. Consequently, while most of the European members of the Alliance have paid lip service to the American strategy, they have been reluctant to implement it by increasing their conventional forces in accordance with the goals set by NATO.

The European members of the Alliance have no interest in fighting a conventional or limited nuclear war which would destroy them almost as thoroughly as an all-out nuclear war. Knowing that they will be doomed if war should break out, they have a vital interest in avoiding any kind of war. For this reason, they advocate the strategy of "massive retaliation," which seeks to prevent the outbreak of war by threatening an all-out nuclear response against any kind of military provocation. If the strategy succeeds, it will save both the European members of the Alliance and the United States; if it fails, it will doom both.

Germany only seemingly diverges from this position. Germany is officially committed to a "forward strategy" with conventional forces, which is supposed to offer her protection from invasion and destruction, but this strategy has always been of dubious value in view of the Soviet strength on land and the modern technology of war. Yet the defection of France from the Alliance and the reduction of American and British forces, if and when it takes place, is likely to reduce the "forward strategy" to a mere variant of the policy of "massive retaliation." In other words, the impossibility of a successful implementation of the "forward strategy" will very quickly confront the Western forces with a choice between the cessation of hostilities or resort to nuclear war.

THE REACTIONS TO THE CRISIS

How have the members of the Alliance reacted to these existential incompatibilities? Three patterns can be distinguished: the French, the German, and the American.

French policy derives from three propositions, First, in an alliance of a nuclear and a non-nuclear power, the protection of the latter's vital interests and very existence depends upon the decision of the former; such a relationship deprives the non-nuclear power of true independence. Second, such dependence becomes intolerable for the non-nuclear power if its vital interests diverge from those of the nuclear one. Third, alliances between nuclear and non-nuclear powers having thus become problematic, a nation that wants to pursue an independent foreign policy must possess the means with which to support such a foreign policy— that is, nuclear weapons.

It is worthy of note that these aspirations for an independent nuclear deterrent have by no means been limited to France. In his speech at Liverpool on January 21, 1963, Harold Macmillan, then British Prime Minister, called for a Europe "great and

strong enough to build a more equal and worthy partnership"
with the United States; and in his broadcast of January 30, 1963,
he foresaw the end of the Alliance if the United States were
allowed "for all times the sole authority" over the nuclear deterrent. German leaders have voiced their misgivings, mostly in private, about the exclusive American control of the nuclear deterrent. Dependence upon the United States, declared Chancellor
Adenauer in September 1956, "must not become a permanent
condition. . . . The vital necessities of the European countries
need not always be identical with the vital necessities of the
United States and vice versa." From this general mood of dissatis-
faction and uneasiness only France has drawn radical political
and military conclusions, destructive of the cohesion of the Atlantic Alliance.

West Germany has drawn the opposite conclusions from the
same objective situation. Far from seeking independence on the
French model, she is most anxious to assure herself of the support
of her allies in order to be protected from the Soviet Union and
to achieve her main national aspiration: reunification. The
Adenauer policy of close association with France and the Erhard
policy of close association with the United States stemmed from
that same anxiety. Both policies differed only in the emphasis
they put upon the two connections. The German "Gaullists,"
while stressing Franco-German cooperation, consider the American connection to be indispensable, and the "Atlanticists," while
considering American support the cornerstone of German foreign
policy, likewise wish to avoid a choice between the United States
and France.

The main purpose of the Alliance policy of the United States
has been the maintenance of the status quo, in terms both of
exclusive American control over the nuclear deterrent and of
close military cooperation among the allies. We have sought to
reconcile the European members of the Alliance with the status
quo by conceding to them the appearance but not the substance
of participation in nuclear decisions. The multilateral seaborne
nuclear force (MLF), the main instrument of that policy, was
intended to give the European members of the Alliance a sense

of participation by making the planning and execution of nuclear strategy a collective undertaking. In one form or other, however, the United States would have retained the ultimate responsibility for the use of nuclear weapons. While the MLF was promoted at home and abroad by a small group within our government with a fanaticism and ingenuity worthy of a better cause, it was received by our European allies with indifference or open hostility; the sole exception was Germany, which supported the MLF primarily as an additional means with which to strengthen its ties with the United States. This failure was inevitable since the MLF was an attempt not to meet the fundamental issues that face the Atlantic Alliance but to evade them through an all too clever scheme that deceived nobody. Its elimination from the active agenda of American foreign policy has left a vacuum which must be filled. If the United States does not fill it in view of its interests, somebody else will, serving interests that may be at variance with those of the United States. Yet the United States has reacted to this challenge with a policy of drift.

Of the choices at the disposal of the United States, the policy of drift is the easiest and also the most dangerous. It is easy because it consists, now that the maintenance of the status quo has failed, in keeping the legal façade of the Atlantic Alliance intact and leaving the crucial political and military problems unattended. It is dangerous because it combines in an incompatible interconnection the legal commitments of a traditional alliance with nuclear proliferation. It gives those of our allies who possess nuclear weapons the power to reduce drastically our freedom of choice with regard to nuclear war.

Both France and Great Britain see the main purpose of the national nuclear deterrent in their ability to use it as a trigger with which to activate the nuclear deterrent of the United States. As the British White Paper on defense concluded on February 13, 1964: "If there were no power in Europe capable of inflicting unacceptable damage on a potential enemy," the enemy might be tempted "to attack in the mistaken belief that the United States would not act unless America herself were attacked." Or as the London *Economist* said on February 15 in commenting on the White Paper: "The bombers also give Britain the ability to involve the United States in a nuclear war for which the Americans have no stomach, the argument being that the Russians would be led to loose off an attack on the United States if any foreign nuclear bombs went off on their territory, since they would not have time to see the Union Jack painted on its warhead." In other words, proliferation combined with traditional alliance commitments turns the obsolescence of the Western Alliance, as presently constituted, against the survival of the United States. Allies of the United States armed with nuclear weapons could virtually decide whether the United States shall live or die.

To escape this danger and at the same time restore the vitality of the Atlantic Alliance requires of the United States an effort at creative statesmanship, the like of which it has not achieved since 1947, when it created a new American foreign policy through the Truman Doctrine, the Marshall Plan, and the policy of containment. Any rational and constructive consideration of the future course of American policy must start with the recognition that the crisis of the Atlantic Alliance is political and not military in nature. The crisis goes to the very core of the political life of its members. It has been said of politics that it is concerned with "who gets what, when, how," which is undoubtedly an accurate description of the politics of bargaining and spoils in established political communities. Yet where the very existence and nature of a political community are in question, the fundamental issue is who shall die for what on whose orders. It is the measure of the inevitability and gravity of the crisis of the Atlantic Alliance that this is the issue rending it asunder. Soothing official statements about the essential unity of purpose of the Alliance, about interdependence, nuclear "partnership," and nuclear "sharing" may obscure this issue. Clever technical devices, such as the MLF, may divert attention from it. Belligerent statements addressed to the Soviet Union may create a temporary euphoria suggesting that the issue no longer exists. But the issue of life and death, arising from the objective conditions in which the members of the Alliance exist, will not be stilled by inattention.

The American Interests

In order to be able to develop a rationale for a new American foreign policy with regard to Europe we must first make clear the interests that tie the United States to Europe. Our foreign policy is faced here with the continuing task of reformulating perennial interests in the light of changed circumstances. Thus the U.S. interest in the European balance of power remains intact, but it presents itself now in a setting of unprecedented novelty.

From the begining of American history to the Second World War, as we have seen, the rationale of that interest has been the ability of a hegemonial European power, unrestrained from within Europe, to endanger the hegemonial position and security of the United States in the Western Hemisphere. This rationale remains valid at present, as far as conventional war is concerned. Its weight has been vastly increased by the modern technologies of transportation, communications, and weaponry, which expose the United States directly to attack by a hegemonial European power. It is of course obvious that such a conventional attack, extremely hypothetical in itself, would, in view of the vital interests at stake, in all likelihood not remain conventional for long. A conventional war brought to the shores of the United States would almost certainly transform itself into a nuclear one.

As concerns nuclear war waged by a hegemonial European power against the United States, the American interest in the European balance of power presents itself in a new and different light. It must be assumed that there exists today a strategic nuclear balance between the United States and the Soviet Union, the potential hegemonial power in Europe. This balance exists in spite of the present American advantage in terms of the quantity and variety of nuclear weapons and delivery vehicles; for the Soviet nuclear force must be assumed to be capable of inflicting unacceptable damage on the United States even in a second strike. In consequence, the existence of a European balance of power affects the modalities of nuclear war but not necessarily— in contrast with conventional war—the over-all strategic equation. This would be true in differing degrees under the two contingencies that can be logically anticipated.,

In the first contingency, if there were no European conventional or nuclear counterweight to Soviet power, the geographic, material, and human resources of all of Europe would be at the service of the nuclear power of the Soviet Union. Three major consequences would follow. The Soviet Union would greatly increase, both quantitatively and qualitatively, its nuclear capability; the United States would lose bases from which to conduct nuclear war; and the United States would have to cover an increased number of targets. In sum, the relative position of the United States and the Soviet Union within the over-all strategic balance would be reversed; the relative advantage enjoyed by the United States today would accrue to the Soviet Union.

The other contingency—namely, if there were a conventional but no nuclear counterweight to Soviet power from within Europe under a scheme of denuclearization, such as the Rapacki Plan—would initially have only the consequence of depriving the United States of European bases from which to counter the nuclear power of the Soviet Union. In view of the distribution of conventional forces within Europe, however, the second contingency would in all likelihood quickly revert to the first. That is to say, a conventional counterweight without nuclear support from within Europe would not be sufficient to prevent the conquest of the Continent by the Soviet Union.

The American interest in the European balance of power transcends today the traditional concern with the preservation of the hegemony and security of the United States in the Western Hemisphere. The United States has become a superpower whose success or failure anywhere in the world impinges to a greater or lesser degree upon its position throughout the world. This is especially so when we deal with a commitment that is so deeply rooted in tradition and vital interest as is the commitment to the European balance of power. Even if a drastic change in the distribution of power in Europe in favor of the Soviet Union did not decisively affect the U.S. position in the Western Hemisphere, it could not help but drastically affect the position of the United States in the world.

In so far as the contest between the United States, on the one hand, and the Soviet Union and China, on the other, is carried on in terms of the attractiveness and effectiveness of their respective governmental systems, so spectacular a defeat for the United States and so spectacular a victory for the Soviet Union would of necessity make both the committed and the uncommitted nations of the world dubious about the ability of the United States to compete successfully with its adversaries on all levels of social and governmental endeavor. That doubt would touch the very core of American influence and power, which from the very beginning of our history has consisted in our ability to serve as a model for other nations to emulate.

The United States has still another interest in Europe, less tangible than the other two, but in a profound sense no less important. Europe is the fountainhead of Western civilization, and America is part of that civilization. From Europe we have received most of our people, our institutions, our ideas and values. We have created our own identity as a nation and society through a creative differentiation from Europe. The European store of men and ideas upon which this nation was founded has during the nineteenth and the beginning of the twentieth centuries been replenished by Europe, especially through successive waves of immigration, while since 1917 there has been an ever increasing flow of influence in the opposite direction. Thus, as the European immigrants have been transformed by the American environment, so Europe is being transformed through the American presence.

To deny the importance of this profound and intimate relationship for the political interests of the United States and, in consequence, to equate the American interest in Europe with that in other parts of the world is to commit two fundamental errors. The beginning of foreign policy is to establish priorities among a number of interests, all worth pursuing but not all susceptible of being pursued with equal commitments; for the resources even of a world power fall short of its interests. Furthermore, while military strength and political power are the preconditions for lasting national greatness, the substance of that greatness springs from the hidden sources of intellect and morale, from ideas and values, which we call civilization. Nobody can say what would happen to American civilization if it were suddenly cut off from its European source, the latter being destroyed by a blow that would also be a blow against the former. But one can and must say that America has a vital interest in the survival of Europe as a center of Western civilization.

THE AMERICAN POLICIES

Any consideration of the policies to be pursued by the United States in Europe must start from the assumption that the issue which led the United States in 1947 to intervene in the affairs of Europe poses itself today in novel terms, but that it has not disappeared. The Soviet Union is still today, as it was two decades ago, the potential hegemonial power on the continent of Europe. Regardless of the policies the Soviet Union is pursuing now in contrast to those it pursued then, this is so by virtue of the objective distribution of power on the European continent. Concretely, the issue of Europe continues to center upon the issue of Germany. Shall the line of division between the two Europes continue to run where it does now, dividing Germany, or shall it run at the Eastern or Western boundaries of Germany, or shall it stop running at all?

To say, then, that the Cold War has come to an end is to indulge in imprecise and overly sanguine language. The question over which the Cold War arose—Who shall control Germany and, through it, Europe?—remains unanswered, or, at best, the answer remains provisional, subject to change by the policies of the major interested parties. In truth, therefore, the Cold War has not come to an end but has only lost its intensity which in the past has threatened an armed conflagration on the occasion of every major crisis. What a Polish scholar, Dr. Longin Pastusiak, said recently of the policies of West Germany applies to the policies of all interested parties: "The main aims of this policy

remain unchanged in principle, only the tactics have been altered, and adapted to the present alignment of forces in the
world." [7]

It follows that the strategic military posture the United States
has taken during the last two decades has not been invalidated
by recent developments. This position consists in the functional
relationship between its commitment of conventional forces in
Europe and the commitment of its nuclear power to Europe's
defense. It is a matter for historic argument but no longer for
political choice whether, as I was inclined to think in the late
1940s, a unilateral military guarantee by the United States, without the elaborate arrangements for conventional forces through
NATO, would have been sufficient to protect Western Europe.
The organic connection between the American conventional
presence on the European continent and its nuclear commitments is a matter of historic fact, and one's rational doubts as to
the quantitative and organizational aspects of that presence must
yield to one's awareness of the effects that drastic changes in
those aspects might have upon the credibility of the nuclear commitment. It is obvious that this credibility must be maintained
vis-à-vis the Soviet Union since the deterrent function of our
nuclear commitment depends on it. It must also be maintained
vis-à-vis West Germany, for whose political relations with the
United States it performs a vital function.

The German policy of the United States must come to terms
with two interconnected constants. Next to the Soviet Union,
West Germany is the most powerful nation on the European
continent, and it is also the foremost potential source of trouble
because it nurtures an unfulfilled national aspiration at whose
service its power could be put. During the Adenauer era, the
foreign policies of the United States and West Germany were
identical, derived as they were from the assumption that the
integration of the Federal Republic into the West was the road
to the fulfillment of the goal of unification. It hardly needs to be
pointed out again that this policy was based upon an illusion

[7] "Dangerous Bonn-Washington Deal," *International Affairs*, July, 1966,
p. 48.

and that, far from opening the door to unification, the military integration of West Germany with the West contributed to closing it. What is important for American policy is the fact that the illusory character of this policy, of which German leaders had been aware from the outset, has now begun to dawn upon the German public at large. In consequence, the search for alternative policies has begun. Six such policies are theoretically available to West Germany, not necessarily as alternatives but in good measure supplementing each other. We shall discuss them in descending order of practicality and, hence, urgency for American foreign policy.

West Germany seeks to mitigate its position of political and military subordination to the United States. On the one hand, it recognizes the inevitability of that subordination and has shown itself to be most anxious about even the slightest indication, as a rule purely imaginary, that American political and military support might no longer be as staunch as it used to be. On the other hand, West Germany, increasingly conscious of its power, has begun to tire of its role as a mere echo and instrument of American policy. These contradictory moods have been translated into demands, addressed to the United States, for a greater measure of information and consultation before decisions are taken. As a prominent German politican, a leader of the "Gaullist faction," told me: "We don't want a national nuclear deterrent because we remember the Second World War. What we want to know is the targets you have selected in case of nuclear war. Is it Moscow, Leipzig, or Bremen?"

The second new strain in West German foreign policy affects the relations with the nations of Eastern Europe, East Germany included. Behind the façade of the Hallstein Doctrine, denying diplomatic relations to any government recognizing the government of East Germany, West Germany has established surprisingly close relations with a number of nations of Eastern Europe, primarily on the cultural and economic plane and frequently on the latter's initiative. What is remarkable in the relations between West Germany and the nations of Eastern Europe (Poland and East Germany excluded) is the normalization not so much of the explicit political relations as of the psychological outlook of the parties concerned.

These new relationships point toward political normalization in terms of the implicit or explicit recognition of the territorial status quo. As concerns East Germany, an entirely new element has entered the picture. In the past, it was taken for granted by all concerned—by Moscow and Washington, Pankow and Bonn —that unification would of necessity mean the absorption of East Germany by a more powerful, economically more attractive, and politically healthier West. For the first time, voices can be heard in Bonn which no longer take this for granted. In the measure that, on the one hand, East Germany becomes the other great industrial power on the European continent, continues to improve its standard of living, and mitigates its totalitarian rule, and, on the other, the prestige of the Bonn regime continues to falter, West Germans might ask themselves, so it is feared, what the ideological fuss about the lack of legitimacy of the East German regime was all about.

Third, the French example of a new nationalistic foreign policy has had a stimulating effect upon hitherto dormant tendencies of a similar kind in West Germany. To the extent that this trend feeds upon the example of French nationalism, its strength will depend upon the success of the new French foreign policies as well as upon the support these policies can lend to the foreign policies of West Germany. The deeper and more widespread the recognition of the failure of the Adenauer policy of reunification becomes, the stronger will be the temptation for West Germany to strike out on its own.

This temptation is held in check by the ideal of a unified Europe as a "third force," comprising all the nations of Western Europe under common political leadership and with integrated military forces and equally independent of the Soviet Union and the United States. But this fourth alternative policy, embodied in the political goals of the European Common Market, is in turn relegated to the status of a mere ideal by the nationalistic policies which France has pursued within the Common Market and outside it.

Fifth, such an independent West German foreign policy, in conjunction with the progressive disintegration of the Eastern bloc, could restore even to a truncated Germany the same pivotal position in Central Europe that a united Germany occupied under Bismarck and his successors and then again under Hitler. That position is the result of the distribution of power in Central and Eastern Europe. The nations located between Germany and Russia, because of their weakness relative to their two neighbors, have had to lean upon one or the other of their neighbors to find protection and support. For almost two decades following the First World War, France was able to take over that protective function because of the temporary weakness of Germany and Russia. In the measure that the latter two nations regained their traditional power position, the relative power of France declined, and the Munich settlement of 1938 put the seal on its decline. The ineffectiveness of the military support France tried to extend to Poland when attacked by Germany in September 1939 testified to the inability of France to perform the protective function against a strong Germany and Russia; and de Gaulle's attempts to revive at least the idea of that protective function were rebuffed by Poland.

In the aftermath of the Second World War the Soviet Union became the effective protector of the nations of Central and Eastern Europe, as the result of military conquest and the subservience of local Communist parties to the Soviet Union. However inevitable the Soviet monopoly of effective power in Central and Eastern Europe has been, it has been popular neither with the peoples concerned nor with most governments of the region. In the measure that these governments should regain their freedom of action in the conduct of their foreign policies and Germany, truncated or united, pursues a European policy of its own, Germany will again be available as the alternative protector of these nations and, as such, would become a competitor of the Soviet Union.

Sixth, the alternative culmination of such an independent West German foreign policy (purely hypothetical at present) would be a reversal of its alliances—that is, a change from its present Western to an Eastern orientation. In other words, if this were the price the Soviet Union would ask in exchange for unification, West Germany would pay it; for it stands to reason that the unification of Germany can only come about through the willing or unwilling cooperation of the Soviet Union. The Adenauer policy maintained the pretense that somehow the Soviet Union could be compelled to agree to unification. What in the 1950s was obvious to only a few ineffective critics has now become clear for all to see: The Soviet Union must be offered inducements in exchange for its agreement to German unification. Certain tentative proposals advanced by the West German government and politicians point in this direction. Yet the uncompromisingly negative reaction these proposals have received from the Soviet Union and Poland must have dispelled any doubt about the possibility of inducing the Soviet Union under present conditions to agree to German unification.

The Soviet Union's rigidly negative attitude, which is surreptitiously shared by many other governments and politicians, including strong elements within West Germany, narrowly circumscribes the freedom of maneuver West German foreign policy enjoys. A pro-Russian orientation of West Germany, against which the critics mentioned above warned and which Khrushchev repeatedly declared to be inevitable, requires a receptivity on the part of the Soviet government that thus far has been completely wanting. Thus, while it would be improvident to rule out such a reorientation of West German policy altogether, it is not an eventuality that is acute today or likely to be so tomorrow.

Alternatives five and six imply a radical change in the political and economic, if not the military, status quo in Central and Eastern Europe, and it is exactly because of this implication that their viability today is remote. For they could only be put into practice at the price of the termination of the Soviet monopoly of protective power in the region. This would clearly be the case under the fourth alternative, where Germany and the Soviet Union are assumed to be competitors. It would also be the case under the fifth alternative, where Germany and the Soviet Union are assumed to cooperate; for such cooperation presupposes the legitimization of the West German government and of its policies by the Soviet Union. The Soviet Union has withheld that legitimization by representing the West German government as imbued with the Nazi spirit, and thus it legitimizes the Soviet role as the protector of the nations of Central and Eastern Europe. And as long as the interest of the Soviet Union in the preservation of the status quo in Central and Eastern Europe determines Soviet foreign policy, that policy must confine West Germany's freedom of action within relatively narrow limits.

In considering American policy in the light of these trends and possibilities, it is first of all necessary to recognize that not all of them are clearly defined alternative policies, but that some of them are moods coexisting with each other and in good measure contradictory within themselves and with each other. These moods ebb and flow, amorphously blending into each other. It must be the purpose of American policy to strengthen those moods that serve American interests, and to weaken those that run counter to them. This is a delicate task, requiring a great deal of psychological flexibility and diplomatic finesse. What it does not require is the commitment to a rigid formula, such as the MLF, which responds to what is actually a vague and inchoate mood as though it were a clearly defined and irresistible political demand. What West Germany wants in the main of the United States is psychological satisfaction and not substantive political and military advantage. The United States is capable of providing that satisfaction in three principal areas. It can do so by narrowing the gap between appearance and reality in its policies regarding Germany, its relations with the nations of Eastern Europe, and the issue of unification.

While the United States is inevitably the predominant partner in its alliance with West Germany, it can deal with West Germany in such a way as to minimize the appearances of that predominance. This task requires consultation and information, institutionalized and informal, more particularly the latter, prior to American decision. In 1965, on a visit to Japan and on repeated recent visits to Germany, I have asked political personalities what their main complaint about American policy was. I was struck by the uniformity of the response: The United States is in the habit of making decisions affecting its allies and telling them about them after the fact. The Japanese pointed to the equalization tax on foreign investments, the Germans to American military and political strategy in Europe. Sensitivity for the feelings of our allies does not require a sacrifice of our interests or changes in the substance of our policies. It only requires a change in the style of our foreign policy.

As concerns unification and the eastern boundaries of a united Germany, it must be primarily the task of the West Germans to narrow the gap between expectation and reality which their and our pronouncements have created. But the United States can at least lend a tactfully helping hand. It must refrain from raising these issues in the unrealistic formulas of the past and support those German voices and trends which try to bring policy and reality into harmony.

Such a policy is likely to strengthen the ties between the United States and West Germany and thereby minimize the opportunities for the revival of West German nationalism and a reorientation of West German foreign policy—eventualities feared by all concerned, the West German government included. It was from the very outset one of the major political purposes of the military integration of West Germany in NATO to limit the freedom of action of the West German government. That purpose is served by an American policy which makes West Germany psychologically more comfortable as a junior partner of the United States while maintaining the paramountcy of American power and policy in the relationship. Such a result cannot be displeasing to the Soviet Union, regardless of what it may feel constrained to declare for public consumption; for it tends to preserve the status quo. Thus such a policy will also contribute to the normalization of the relations between the Soviet Union and the nations of Eastern Europe, on the one hand, and the United States and West Germany, on the other.

Such a policy is perfectly compatible with the policies the United States has pursued vis-à-vis the Soviet Union, seeking to avoid a direct military confrontation, to bring the nuclear arms race under control, and to stop nuclear proliferation. The United States does not need to choose between a European policy whose cornerstone is close relations with West Germany, and a policy toward the Soviet Union the purpose of which is the definition and realization of common interests in the nuclear field. Not only are the two policies compatible with each other, but they appear also to be organically connected. They serve the same purpose of preserving the status quo and thereby minimizing the risk of war arising from unsettled political issues.

While the problem of Germany is crucial in terms of American interests and policies, the issues that de Gaulle has raised also require rational attention rather than emotional reaction, both in their own terms and in view of their bearing on the German problem. Three major issues require such attention: the independent French nuclear force, the position of France in case of a conventional war in Europe, and the relations between France and Germany. All these issues, in view of their import for the interests of the United States, call for a normalization of our relations with France.

The main rational purpose of the French nuclear deterrent is, as we have seen, to force the hand of the United States. It is obviously in the vital interest of the United States to prevent or at least to minimize such a possibility. We have tended to approach this issue in terms of a simple choice between cooperation with France and its political and military isolation. More realistically, we ought to combine the two approaches: We ought to restore as far as possible our political and military cooperation with France and reduce our legal commitments to the level of that cooperation.

France has withdrawn from the integrated institutions of the Atlantic Alliance but not from the Alliance itself. The availability of French territory, facilities, and troops in case of a conventional war increases the chances for such a war to remain conventional. France continues to cooperate in certain military activities of the Alliance. American policy ought to seek to maintain and expand that sphere of cooperation.

We have seen that the two West German schools of thought, the Atlantic and the "Gaullist," try to avoid a clear-cut choice between the two orientations. We can strengthen this position, which conforms to our own interests and policies as outlined above, by blunting the sharp edges of that choice. West Germany will lose its ability tó choose in the measure that our relations with France loose their bipolar character and approach that of a common front, of which West Germany forms a part.

These short-term policies, unspectacular in themselves, serve the long-range purposes the United States pursues in Europe: political stability and the avoidance of nuclear war. These purposes are put in jeopardy by the revival of nationalism in Western Europe and the concommitant trend toward nuclear proliferation. The revival of nationalism presents a paradox in an age whose technological conditions require political, military, and economic institutions transcending the nation-state. But that revival is a universal fact which, however paradoxical it may appear to our rational judgment, must form the empirical starting point for long-range planning. The trend toward nuclear proliferation is a mere symptom of that universal tendency.

Nuclear proliferation expresses the desire of the major European nations to decide for themselves the issue of life and death. The policy of proliferation is likely to be futile and dangerous for the nations pursuing it. But it is equally futile to oppose it dogmatically, however much one may deplore the fact of proliferation on rational grounds. What is necessary is to create political conditions likely to minimize the risk of proliferation and in the end to deprive the members of the Western Alliance of any motive for proliferation. These political conditions were presented in a vague, idealized form by the grand design of Atlantic Partnership which John F. Kennedy formulated on July 4, 1962, in his "Declaration of Interdependence." That design has remained in the realm of political rhetoric, but it contains a political concept that alone promises to combine Western unity with nuclear power. In order to understand the concept's import, we must first remind ourselves again of the political character of the crisis of the Western Alliance.

The Alliance is in disarray not because the United States has monopolistic control over the nuclear deterrent, but because the members pursue different and sometimes incompatible policies, on behalf of which they might want to use the nuclear deterrent. If the members' policies were in harmony, the issue of the locus of the nuclear decision would lose its present political sting and de Gaulle would have had no need to raise the issue of the national nuclear deterrent. For the nations of Western Europe, either severally or united, would then consider using nuclear weapons for the same purposes as the United States, and vice versa, and the locus of the decision would be a technical issue, but no longer one of substantive importance. This is, then, the crucial question: How can the different policies of the members of the Western Alliance be brought into harmony? Can an Atlantic Union, uniting the United States and the nations of Western Europe in common policies, be brought into being?

However deeply one may be convinced of the rational need for such a union, the evidence does not allow a positive answer to that question. The task of harmonizing highly complex and diverse policies cannot be achieved, as de Gaulle recognized in 1958 when he suggested a political triumvirate for the Alliance, through the ordinary processes of diplomacy. It requires a virtual fusion of the foreign policies of the members of the Alliance under centralized direction. In the 1950s, in the heyday of NATO, the United States had the chance, and was urged by its allies, to assume the leadership in creating an Atlantic Union as a permanent political foundation for the military alliance. But then the United States lacked the will to avail itself of that opportunity. In the midst of a revived nationalism, the leading members of the Alliance, short of being faced with a direct military threat against them all, are not likely to bring forth simultaneously the political vision, determination, and skill necessary to achieve this rationally required goal.

The United States cannot afford to lose sight of Atlantic Union as the ultimate goal; for nuclear proliferation, inevitable as it has proven to be for the time being in Western Europe, can be rendered tolerable only if its centrifugal and anarchic consequences are counterbalanced by the politically unified use of proliferated nuclear weapons. As long as political union is unobtainable and since traditional Alliance commitments joined with nuclear proliferation, as pointed out above, are intolerable, the United States must strive for three goals: to mitigate the consequences of proliferation by limiting the number of independent nuclear deterrents, to bring its Alliance commitments for the time being into harmony with the interests it has actually or potentially in common with its allies, and in the end to render proliferation innocuous or obsolete through unified political control.

The first goal requires of the United States active support of the political unification of Europe. For since proliferation is an accomplished fact and Atlantic Union is in the short run unattainable, a European nuclear deterrent controlled by a European political authority is the best attainable alternative. The issue of nuclear proliferation adds to the conventional balance-of-power arguments referred to above yet another reason for American support of European unification. Such support implies a radical change in our present policies, which, by trying to isolate France, have stood in the way of the political unification of Europe and have sought in vain to restore the vitality of the Atlantic Alliance on foundations that no longer exist.

The second goal, similarly, requires a radical change from the dogmatic insistence upon the restoration of an unrestorable status quo to the pragmatic adaptation to circumstances which for the time being are not subject to our control. What we have seen to be true of our relations with France is true in general: we must narrow the gap between our comprehensive legal commitments and the limited sphere within which our interests and policies still coincide with those of our allies. Otherwise we shall run a risk to which improvident great powers (e.g., Germany in 1914) have succumbed in the past—that is, getting involved in a war not of our making and on behalf of interests not our own.

The legal basis for such an adaptation of our commitments to changing circumstances is to be found in Article V of the NATO Treaty, which requires each signatory to take "such action as it

deems necessary." In its report on June 6, 1949, the Senate
Foreign Relations Committee declared that this article makes it
"absolutely clear that each party remains free to exercise its honest judgment in deciding upon the measures it will take," and
that in the event of "an attack upon Paris or Copenhagen" the
President did not have "the power to take any action, without
specific Congressional authorization."

Finally, we must look to the ultimate goal not only of our
Alliance policy but of our over-all foreign policies as well: the
minimization of the risk of nuclear war. The substitution of a
European nuclear deterrent for a multiplicity of national ones is
a step in this direction. The realization on the part of France and
Great Britain that a national nuclear deterrent is both costly and
useless and therefore ought to be abandoned would be another
step. Political Atlantic Union would be still another step, although impossible to achieve at present. As important as changes
in substantive policies and a prerequisite for their sound formulation and success is a change in our general attitude toward the
Atlantic Alliance and Europe at large. While the disparity of
power and responsibility between the United States and its allies
is a fact of life which one may welcome or deplore but which is
not subject to change, it is possible for the United States, as
indicated above, to mitigate that discrepancy by dealing with its
allies as though they were its equals in power and responsibility.

These changes in our general attitude toward the Atlantic
Alliance must culminate in a change in our attitude toward
Europe itself. We must reconcile ourselves to the fact that the
simple rigidity of the policy of containment, which in the 1950s
became a shibboleth for American foreign policy, has been left
behind by history. The trend toward national disintegration of
the two Europes, east and west of the iron curtain, is likely to
continue either with or without our support, calling forth the
prospects of new combinations. What the United States needs
is a new European policy that is prepared for these prospects,
promoting those that serve its perennial interest in Europe and
opposing those that stand in the way of that interest: the balance
of power.

7

The United States and China

THE INTERESTS AND POLICIES OF CHINA

China poses three fundamental issues for the United States. For purposes of analysis, these can be separated, but in practice they blend into each other. First, China is the most powerful nation on the Asian mainland and potentially the most powerful nation in the world. Second, China has been for at least a millennium a great power of a peculiar kind in that her outlook upon, and relations with, the outside world have been different from those of other great powers. Third, China is today the fountainhead of the most virulent kind of Communism, proclaiming the inevitability of armed conflict and instigating and supporting Communist subversion throughout the world.

China as a Great Power

As a great Asian power, China seeks to restore the position it had before it was reduced to a semicolonial status in the middle of the nineteenth century. That goal has been proclaimed by the Chinese leaders, and the policies actually pursued by them with regard to the offshore islands and Taiwan, Korea, Vietnam, Burma, Cambodia, Tibet, and India follow a consistent pattern: restoration of the territorial boundaries and influence the Chinese empire possessed before its modern decline. These boundaries are likely to include Taiwan and the offshore islands, Outer Mongolia, and the Asian territories claimed by China and annexed by the Soviet Union during the nineteenth century. Physically, in view of the distribution of power in South and Southeast Asia, China could go much farther—in fact, virtually as far as it wants to. But it has never done so in the past, and is not likely to do so in the future. The reasons are to be found, aside from the possible military reaction on the part of the United States and the Soviet Union, in the peculiar Chinese outlook upon the world.

According to Professor C. P. FitzGerald, "Rather more than a thousand years ago, the T'ang dynasty thus fixed the geographic limits in which the Chinese people were to live until modern times." [1] Instead of conquering neighboring states, which it could have done without undue risk, China has been traditionally satisfied with the establishment of governments at her southern and southwestern borders whose political identity was left intact and whose friendliness was assured and symbolized through tributary relationships of different kinds and degrees.

These subtle and indirect relationships are the result of the traditional Chinese conception of China as the center of the political universe, the only sovereign power worthy of the name, to which all other nations owe tribute. This extreme ethnocentrism goes hand in hand with contempt for, and ignorance of, the outside world, which from the Chinese point of view really does not need to be understood and dealt with on terms of equality with China. As the present relations between China, on the one hand, and Cambodia and Burma, on the other, can be regarded as a modern version of the tributary relations of old, so the present ignorance of the Chinese leaders of the outside world,

[1] C. P. FitzGerald, *The Chinese View of Their Place in the World* (London: Oxford University Press, 1964), p. 19. See also John K. Fairbank, *China: The People's Middle Kingdom and the U.S.A.* (Cambridge, Mass.: The Balknap Press of Harvard University Press, 1967), p. 8.

their verbal assaults upon it, and their ineffective policies with regard to it can be understood as a modern version of China's traditional ethnocentrism.

China as a Communist Power

The quandary the United States faces in its relations with China is created by the addition to these traditional elements of Chinese foreign policy of a new and unprecedented one: the sponsorship of a militant world Communism. That quandary, as we have seen, is similar to the one the United States dealt with successfully in the immediate aftermath of the Second World War when it had to distinguish between the great-power and the world-revolutionary aspirations of the Soviet Union. The Soviet Union modified and mitigated its world revolutionary fervor when it began to realize, starting in the 1920s, that the risks it ran for its own survival on behalf of world revolution were out of all proportion to the chances of achieving that revolution. It is at least possible, if not likely, that China will undergo a similar process of adapting its world-revolutionary aims to political and military realities. The chances for such a development exist, provided China has a rational government, and they are enhanced by the nature of the foreign policies China has pursued in Asia since 1949. These policies are characterized by two main interrelated qualities; caution and limitation to the traditional national objectives of China—qualities that stand in stark contrast to the militant rhetoric of the Chinese leaders, which reveal an ethnocentric disregard for the realities, and contempt for the interests, of the outside world.

Minister of National Defense Lin Piao's famous manifesto of September 3, 1965, provides a particularly impressive but by no means unique example of this ethnocentrism, which is intellectually absurd and politically impractical. Lin Piao tries to apply the lessons of the Communist revolution in China to the world scene. Just as the Communists conquered the countryside, isolating, surrounding, and finally conquering the cities, so, he suggests, the Communists will conquer the rural areas of the world, and then isolate and finally conquer the cities of the world, by which he means the capitalist nations of the West. To consider these geopolitical metaphors as a program for political and military action, as many observers in the United States do, is to fail to understand their ethnocentric source. Lin Piao's manifesto is not the Chinese equivalent of *Mein Kampf*, for the simple reason that even a Chinese Hitler would be incapable of putting it into practice. Completely lacking in even the most elementary understanding of the outside world, it rather reminds one, if one needs a historic analogy, of the eccentricities of German geopolitics.

The Future Policies of China

Provided China has a rational government, it can thus be expected that both the present and the coming generation of Chinese leaders will continue to learn from experience and adapt their policies to the real world. Under the same proviso, it is also conceivable that the coming generation will be less given to militant Marxist-Leninist rhetoric and to the instigation and support of subversion throughout the world. But it would be futile to expect that the new generation will be more accommodating than is the old one when it comes to the restoration of China's traditional domain in Asia. In this respect, Mao Tse-tung and Chiang Kai-shek see eye to eye, and so must Mao Tse-tung and his successor, whoever he may be.

To mention only the most crucial issue where the traditional Chinese national interest is at stake: Both Mao Tse-tung and Chiang Kai-shek consider Taiwan to be an integral part of China. They disagree only as to who shall rule China. Regardless of its ideological commitment, no patriotic government of China can be expected to give up this claim to Taiwan, and any Chinese government that believes it has the power will try to recover the island. The issue of Taiwan has indeed proven the main stumbling block in the Geneva and Warsaw negotiations between the United States and China, and it is bound to do so in the future. That it has proven to be no more is due to China's temporary military weakness. If and when China has realized its military potential through the acquisition of the modern technologies of transportation, communication, and weaponry, the issue of Taiwan, if it has not been settled in the meantime, will be the most likely *casus belli* between the United States and China.

One cannot rule out the possibility that the foreign policies of a powerful China, fully armed with nuclear weapons, will be oriented not toward the achievement of China's traditional national objectives but toward world conquest. The combination of traditional ethnocentrism with the ability to destroy the world might well call forth utterly irrational policies. However, while the possibility of such policies must be taken into account, their probability is small in view of the extreme caution Chinese foreign policy has shown thus far.

THE INTERESTS AND POLICIES OF THE UNITED STATES

What are the interests of the United States with regard to China, and what are the policies most likely to serve those interests? The United States has two such interests: the maintenance or, if need be, the restoration of a viable balance of power in Asia, and the maintenance of a world-wide balance of power. Thus the United States has pursued in Asia the same basic interest it has tried to realize in Europe since the beginning of its history. For in both Europe and Asia the United States has consistently opposed the power that threatened to make itself master of the Continent and thus gain a position that would endanger the security of the United States from across the ocean. After Russia's defeat by Japan, President Theodore Roosevelt wrote to Senator Henry Cabot Lodge on June 16, 1905: "While . . . Russia's triumph would have been a blow to civilization, her destruction as an eastern Asiatic power would also in my opinion be unfortunate. It is best that she should be left face to face with Japan so that each may have a moderating action on the other." [2]

As far as Europe is concerned, this interest has always existed

[2] Selections from the *Correspondence of Theodore Roosevelt and Henry Cabot Lodge 1884–1918* (New York, London: Charles Scribner's Sons, 1925), II, p. 153.

even though it has not always been recognized for what it was. It has remained throughout the persistent rationale of our European policies. The active interest of the United States in Asia dates only from the turn of the century. Its first expression was the Open Door policy with regard to China, which at the outset had an exclusively commercial purpose: It sought to maintain freedom of competition for all interested parties in the semicolonial exploitation of China. But very soon it took on a political and military connotation as well; for the United States recognized that any great power, European or Asian, which added the enormous power potential of China to its own would thereby make itself the master of its own continent, if not of the world. Thus the policy of the Open Door for China transformed itself organically into a policy of the balance of power for Asia, of which the independence of China was the cornerstone.

It was for this reason that the United States opposed from the very beginning Japan's attempts at creating an Asian empire, primarily at China's expense. Its opposition started out ineffectually in the form of the Stimson Doctrine—that is, the refusal to recognize territorial acquisitions realized by force. Yet from the late 1930s onward, ever more stringent actions implemented that verbal expression of this country's opposition until in the fall of 1941 it confronted Japan with the choice between giving up any further territorial expansion or going to war with the United States.

During and immediately after the Second World War, the United States tried to make China into a counterweight to Japan, thus restoring the Asian balance of power. In anticipation and furtherance of this development, the United States endowed China both legally and politically with the status of a great power. When the Communists defeated Chiang Kai-shek and took over China in 1949, they also destroyed the foundations of our Asian policy. Suddenly, China, instead of serving as a counterweight to a power inimical to the United States, became the ally of one of them. Japan, disarmed and occupied, could not serve as a counterweight to the emergent power of China. That function could be performed by only one power, the United States itself.

The policies through which the United States has implemented this function have been decisively determined by the Chinese intervention in the Korean War. Before that intervention, the United States moved toward recognition of the Communist government of China and away from complete military and political identification with Chiang Kai-shek's regime on Taiwan. The policy the United States then intended to pursue vis-à-vis China was clearly formulated in the famous and often misquoted speech that Secretary of State Dean Acheson gave at the National Press Club in Washington on January 12, 1950. Acheson's speech did not envisage a unilateral military commitment of the United States on the mainland of Asia, but identified the island chain adjacent to the Asian mainland from Japan to the Philippines as the outer limits of America's military presence.

China's intervention in the Korean War radically transformed the Asian policies of the United States. The United States responded to that intervention with two policies: the policy of isolating China and the policy of peripheral military containment.

The Policy of Isolating China

The policy of isolating China sought the downfall of the Communist government. It was intimately connected with the recognition of the Chiang Kai-shek government as the legitimate government of China and anticipated that government's return to the mainland. By maintaining close relations with the Chiang Kai-shek government and none with the Communist government, a policy in which the United States expected its allies to participate, this country tried to destroy the legitimacy of the Communist government. By interdicting all personal and commercial relations with mainland China, the United States expected to make it impossible for the Communist regime to govern. This policy has obviously failed. Chiang Kai-shek will not return to the mainland, and his government survives only by virtue of the presence of the U.S. Seventh Fleet in the Strait of Taiwan. The Communist government of China enjoys diplomatic, cultural, and commercial relations with many nations, including numerous allies of the United States, and it is the United States rather than Communist China which has been isolated in consequence of its policy of isolation. In so far as China is isolated, as it is particularly in the Communist world, that isolation is in good measure self-inflicted, and our policy has had little to do with it.

This failure of the policy of isolating China has been particularly striking in the field of trade. That policy is sound in its rationale; but it has failed in application. Communist governments have consistently laid the greatest stress upon the expansion of foreign trade. They have evoked memories of Cobden and Bright, the leaders of the Manchester liberals of a century ago, as well as of our own former Secretary of State, Cordell Hull, with their emphasis on what foreign trade could do for private profits and international peace. They have consistently shown a particular interest in whole industrial plants rather than manufactured goods. But the Communist leaders are not Manchester liberals. They have wanted foreign trade not for the commercial purposes our businessmen want it for, but in order to gain the political strength necessary to achieve the universal triumph of Communism. As Lenin put it: "We welcomed Genoa [the International Economic Conference at Genoa in April 1922], we understood perfectly well, and did not conceal it that we were going there as merchants because trade with capitalistic countries is absolutely essential for us (so long as they have not yet collapsed)." Khrushchev was even more explicit when he said in 1957: "We declare war upon you . . . in the peaceful field of peaceful production. We are relentless in this, and it will prove the superiority of our system." And in 1952, Stalin also voiced his confidence in the profit motive of Western businessmen as an instrument through which the Soviet Union would be made strong enough for its final triumph.

I am not arguing here against Western trade with Communist nations per se. I am only arguing in favor of the proposition that foreign trade has a different meaning for Communist nations than it has for us. Trade with Communist nations is a political act which has political consequences. It is folly to trade, or fc̄ that matter to refuse to trade, with Communist nations without concern for these political consequences. There is no reason to object to our selling a Communist country goods it needs in exchange for goods we need. There is no reason to object to trading with Communist countries like Yugoslavia, if such trade promises economic gains and political results favorable to our interests. But it is a folly, comparable to the sale of scrap iron to Japan in the 1930s, to equip the Soviet Union and China with industrial plants and transportation systems which will then be used as weapons in the political, military, and economic offensives of Communism against the West.

That folly is compounded in the case of trade with China. The Soviet Union terminated its economic relations with China at the beginning of the 1960s because it did not find it in its interest to supply the economic foundations for the power of a hostile China. An industrially developed China, whose population might then approach a billion, would be the most powerful nation on earth, more powerful than either the Soviet Union or the United States. It is extremely doubtful that China, in view of the numbers and poverty of its population, could find within its own borders the resources for such industrial development if it were not supplied with capital and goods from abroad. China would then remain for the foreseeable future a weak and fragile giant, a threat to its immediate neighbors but not to the two superpowers.

The Soviet Union has understood this prospect and has left China to its own economic devices. Yet Western governments and businessmen have been rushing into the gap left by the Russian withdrawal, replacing the Soviet Union as a source of capital and goods for China. But is China less hostile, and will it be less dangerous, to the West if and when it has become an advanced industrial nation, than it is, and will be, to the Soviet Union? Obviously, the West has at least as good reason as the Soviet Union to fear a powerful China. If it is in the interest of the

Soviet Union not to help China become a modern industrial nation, it is by the very same token in the interest of the West.

Yet, while the Soviet Union knows its interest and acts upon it, the West does not know it, and in so far as it does, is unable to act upon it. Marx said that the capitalists would be their own gravediggers. Western businessmen, so staunchly anti-Communist when it costs nothing, except perhaps freedom of speech for others, seem bent upon proving that Marx was right.

It is, of course, obvious that a politically oriented, rational foreign trade policy can be pursued by the United States only in close cooperation with its allies. For if the United States were to follow such a policy while its allies traded indiscriminately with the Soviet Union and China, it would simply eliminate itself from commercial competition without achieving its political aim. If, on the other hand, the United States were to compete freely with its allies for Communist markets, it would sacrifice the public interest at the altar of private economic gain.

Hence, the United States finds itself today in a real dilemma. It can, and appears to be trying to, mitigate this dilemma in the case of the Soviet Union by competing with its allies, maintaining as far as possible the distinction between politically innocuous and politically damaging foreign trade. In the case of China, it has left the field to its allies by maintaining a strict boycott which the allies disregard. Yet, while the dilemma can be mitigated, it can be resolved only through the creation of a common front among the Western nations which would put their common political interests ahead of their individual commercial gain.

Thus the problem of East-West trade is at bottom a problem of the relations between the United States and its allies. In the absence of a common front between them, it is impossible to develop a rational American policy of East-West trade. Yet even in the absence of such a common front, the United States cannot afford to lose sight of the political nature of East-West trade and of the vital distinction between that East-West trade which is politically innocuous and that which politically and militarily strengthens one or the other of the major Communist powers.

Thus from China's point of view, our policy of isolation is no longer an important issue, and hence no favorable response can be expected from China if the United States should give up this policy. However, even in the absence of a favorable Chinese response, a new American policy of establishing contacts with China through trade, cultural exchanges, and China's admission to the United Nations would at least be in tune with the policies pursued by most other nations and would thereby relieve the United States of its present isolation. To avail itself of the opportunities thus presented, even without giving up its hostility to the United States, China might learn a great deal about the outside world and thereby overcome its own isolation from, and hostility to, that world.

Yet, aside from these secondary and imponderable considerations, the real issue is not isolation but containment. This is the crucial point at which the traditional national interests of China and the policy of the United States clash. The slogan "containment without isolation" obscures that crucial issue. It is a formula for continuing the policy of military containment at the periphery of China by making it appear that the abandonment of the policy of isolation portends a significant change in American policy. It tends to make the policy of peripheral military containment palatable by tying it to an apparently real and benevolent change in our China policy. It also carries a suggestion of condescension—"We are going to be nice to you from now on"—which is not likely to impress a China that is mindful of its humiliations, past and present.

Similar considerations apply to the proposal to end the isolation of China by engaging in trade with it. Trade relations between the United States and China, which might possibly have the secondary and imponderable effects mentioned above, would be irrelevant to the basic political and military issues that divide the two nations. Furthermore, to engage in indiscriminate trade with China, apart from an over-all political settlement, would be self-defeating; for such trade would strengthen China politically and militarily without giving an equivalent political or military advantage to the other partner.

Finally, the seating of the Communist government as the representative of China in the United Nations is not likely to be feasible if it is conceived merely as the liquidation of the policy of isolation and not also and primarily as a settlement of the issue of Taiwan. It is virtually inconceivable that a representative of the Communist government should set foot in the United Nations while a representative of the Chiang Kai-shek government is present; for the idea of "two Chinas" is as repellent to Mao Tse-tung as it is to Chiang Kai-shek. If the General Assembly should vote that the representative of the Communist government replace the representative of the Chiang Kai-shek government, the latter would no longer be represented in the General Assembly but would still occupy the seat of China as a permanent member of the Security Council—where the issue would then be joined.

If the Security Council should decide to emulate the General Assembly and install the representative of the Communist government in the permanent seat of China—a decision the United States could prevent by vetoing it—the Chiang Kai-shek government would be deprived of any representation in the United Nations. In consequence, its claim to be the legitimate government of China would be destroyed, and its claim to be the legitimate government of Taiwan would be considerably impaired. Thus our policy of containing Communist China, which we could continue behind the military shield of the Seventh Fleet, would be politically undermined. For by weakening Chiang Kai-shek's claim, Communist China would have taken the first step toward achieving the recognition of its own. Thus it becomes obvious again that the real issue is not isolation but containment.

The Policy of Peripheral Military Containment

Convinced that the policy of military containment which worked so well against the Soviet Union in Europe would work equally well elsewhere, the United States applied it to the Middle East through the Baghdad Pact and to Asia through SEATO. Yet what succeeded in Europe was bound to fail elsewhere. The reasons for that failure are twofold.

First, the threat that faced the nations of Western Europe in the aftermath of the Second World War was primarily military. It was the threat of the Red Army marching westward. Behind the line of military demarcation of 1945 which the policy of containment declared to be the westernmost limits of the Soviet empire, there was a highly developed civilization, only temporarily weakened and able to maintain itself against the threat of Communist subversion. The situation is different in the Middle East and Asia. The threat there is not primarily military but political in nature, and weak governments and societies provide opportunities for Communist subversion. Military containment is irrelevant to that threat and may even be counterproductive. Thus the Baghdad Pact did not shield Egypt from Soviet influence, and SEATO has had no bearing on Chinese influence in Indonesia and Pakistan.

The sole exception has been the Korean War. For here the threat was indeed primarily military and could be successfully countered by military means. However, the attempt at transforming military containment into military "liberation" was frustrated by Chinese intervention. That failure, restoring the prewar boundary at the 38th parallel, points to a balance of power on the conventional level, as does the stalemate in the Vietnam War.

China is, even in its present underdeveloped state, the dominant power in Asia by virtue of the quality and quantity of its population, its geographic position, its civilization, its past power remembered and future power anticipated. Anybody who has traveled in Asia must have been impressed by the enormous impact which the resurgence of China has made upon all kinds of men, regardless of class, political conviction, and national affiliation, from Japan to Pakistan.

The issue China poses is political and cultural predominance. The United States can no more contain Chinese influence in Asia by arming Thailand and fighting in South Vietnam than China could contain American influence in the Western Hemisphere by arming, say, Nicaragua and fighting in Lower California. If we are convinced that we cannot live with a China predominant on the mainland of Asia, then we must strike at the heart of Chinese power—that is, rather than try to contain the power of China by nibbling at the periphery of its domain, we must try to destroy that power itself. Thus there is a certain logic on the side of that small group of Americans who are convinced that war between the United States and China is inevitable and that the earlier it comes, the better will be the chances for the United States to win it.

Yet, whatever the appeal of their logic, practical judgment is against them. For while China is obviously no match for the United States in over-all power, it is largely immune to the specific types of power in which the superiority of the United States consists—that is, nuclear, air, and naval power. Certainly, the United States has the power to destroy the nuclear installations and the major industrial and population centers of China, but rather than defeating China, this would only set its development back. To be defeated, China has to be conquered.

Physical conquest would require the deployment of millions of American soldiers on the mainland of Asia. No American military leader has ever advocated a course of action so fraught with incalculable risks, so uncertain of outcome, requiring sacrifices so out of proportion to the interests at stake and the benefits to be expected. President Eisenhower declared on February 10, 1954, that he "could conceive of no greater tragedy than for the United States to become involved in an all-out war in Indochina." General MacArthur, in the Congressional hearings concerning his dismissal and in personal conversation with President Kennedy,[3] emphatically warned against sending American foot soldiers to the Asian mainland to fight China.

If we do not want to set ourselves goals that cannot be attained with the means we are willing to employ, we must learn to accommodate ourselves to the political and cultural predominance of China on the Asian mainland. It is instructive to note that those Asian nations which have done so—such as Burma and

[3] Arthur M. Schlesinger, Jr., *A Thousand Days* (Boston: Houghton Mifflin, 1965), p. 339.

Cambodia—have thus far enjoyed a measure of peace and order in the shadow of the Chinese giant. On the other hand, those Asian nations which have allowed themselves to be transformed into outposts of American military power—such as Laos in the late 1950s, South Vietnam, and Thailand—have become the actual or prospective victims of Communist aggression and subversion. Thus it appears that peripheral military containment is counterproductive. Challenged at the periphery by American military power at its weakest—that is, by the proxy of client-states—China or its proxies are able to respond with locally superior military and political power.

Thus, even if the Chinese threat were primarily of a military nature—and here is the second fallacy—peripheral military containment would be ineffective in the long run in view of China's local military superiority. The contrary view derives from a misconception of the containment of the Soviet Union and of the reasons for its success. The Soviet Union has not been contained by the armed forces this country has been able to put in the field locally in Europe so much as it has been contained by the near certainty that an attack upon them would be countered by the nuclear retaliation of the United States. If we are to assume that the Chinese armies stand, or one day will stand, poised to sweep over Asia, or that irrational Chinese leadership will try to conquer the world by threatening it with nuclear destruction, they will not be contained by the armed forces we or our allies can put into the field on the mainland of Asia. They will only be deterred by the near certainty that China as an organized society will be destroyed in the process of nuclear retaliation.

China is today protected from the full measure of American nuclear retaliation by its own technological backwardness; for it does not possess the number of industrial and population centers whose nuclear destruction would spell its defeat. This explains why China today is more daring in words, and might well become more daring in action if its vital interests were sufficiently threatened, than would be justified in view of the over-all distribution of power between it and the United States. However, in the measure that China develops its nuclear capability, it also becomes vulnerable to nuclear retaliation; for if and when China has developed into a modern nation with a high technological capability, it will also have developed a large number of vital industrial and population centers and will then have become as vulnerable to nuclear attack as are the United States and the Soviet Union today. Assuming a modicum of rationality in the government which will then govern China, fear of nuclear retaliation must be assumed to have the same restraining influence upon Chinese policies as it has had upon the policies of the United States and the Soviet Union since the beginning of the nuclear age. Thus the nuclear arms race, at least as long as it is carried on among a few great powers, carries within itself its own corrective, however tenuous: Nuclear power and nuclear vulnerability go hand in hand, and so does the rational requirement of self-restraint.

The World-wide Containment of China

The peripheral military containment of China is, however, being justified not only in local terms but also, and to an ever greater extent, in world-wide terms. We are told that by containing China in South Vietnam we are containing it everywhere, and that by frustrating a "war of national liberation" in Southeast Asia, we frustrate all "wars of national liberation." This argument has the virtue of simplicity, but it is supported by no historical evidence. It brings to mind the statement William Graham Sumner made at the beginning of the century: "The amount of superstition is not much changed, but it now attaches to politics, not to religion."

The so-called domino theory is indeed an echo of the Marxist dogma of historic inevitability, which asserts that Communism will inevitably spread from country to country until in the end it will engulf the world. Nothing of the kind has actually happened. After World War II, the nations of Eastern Europe went Communist, but Finland to this day has not. After the collapse of French rule in Indochina in 1954, North Vietnam went Com-

munist, but nobody else did. By 1960, half of Laos had gone
Communist, but nobody else followed suit. For almost two decades, the fortunes of Communism in Indonesia have fluctuated
according to local conditions, not according to what happened or
did not happen elsewhere. Can anyone seriously maintain that
the fortunes of the guerrilla wars in Guatemala, Colombia, or
Venezuela will depend upon what happens or does not happen
in South Vietnam? It stands to reason that the triumph or defeat
of Communism in any particular country is not simply a by-
product of what happens or does not happen in other countries.
What will happen in Vietnam can at the very best be no more
than one factor among many, and most certainly not the decisive
one, that will influence developments in other countries.

A New China Policy for the United States

If this analysis of the interests the United States has in Asia and
of the policies it has pursued vis-à-vis China is correct, then it
follows that we ought finally to overcome the trauma of the
Chinese intervention in the Korean War and return to the principles Dean Acheson defined in his speech of 1950, referred to
above. It is worthy of note that the policy proposals that Professor Edwin Reischauer has advanced since his resignation as Ambassador to Japan appear to be inspired by the philosophy of
that speech.[4] If one applies that philosophy to the concrete issues
with which the United States must come to terms in its relations
with China, one arrives at the following five conclusions:

First, the policy of peripheral military containment on the
Asian mainland ought to be gradually liquidated. This policy is
not only irrelevant to the interests of the United States but actually runs counter to them.

Second, both the policy of isolating China and the policy of
ending that isolation are essentially irrelevant to the issue at
hand. One may aggravate, and the other ameliorate, the inter-

4 See Edwin O. Reischauer, *Beyond Vietnam: The United States and Asia*
(New York: Alfred A. Knopf, 1967).

national climate; but they have no relevance, one way or the other, to the basic issue of containment.

Third, since the expansion of Chinese power and influence, threatening the Asian and world balance of power, proceeds by political rather than by military means, it must be contained primarily by political means. To that purpose, it is necessary to strengthen politically, socially, and economically the nations of Asia that are within China's reach, especially Japan, without exacting in return political and military alignments directed against China. We ought to pursue a similar policy with regard to the uncommitted nations outside Asia in which China in the recent past has attempted to gain a foothold.

Fourth, we ought to be clear in our minds that if we should continue the present policy of the peripheral military containment of China, we will find ourselves in all likelihood, sooner or later, at war with China. If we want to avoid such a war, we must change our policy. If we do not want to change our policy, we must be ready to go to war. That is to say, either we bring the means we are willing to employ into line with our objectives, or we cut down our objectives to the measure of the means we are willing to employ.

Fifth, the ultimate instrument for containing China is the same that has contained the Soviet Union: the retaliatory nuclear capability of the United States. It must be brought home to China, as it was brought home to the Soviet Union, that in the unlikely event it should embark upon a policy of Asian or world conquest, it is bound to be at war with the United States.

8
Nuclear Power and Foreign Policy

Even if the foreign policy of the United States were to come to terms with the basic issues thus far discussed, it would still fail in the end if it were unable to master the one issue overshadowing all others: nuclear power. For nuclear weapons are not just a quantitative extension of conventional weapons, but are qualitatively different from them. Conventional weapons can be used in a rational manner as an instrument of national policy. A statesman of the pre-nuclear age could and did ask himself whether he could achieve what he had set out to achieve by the peaceful means of diplomacy or whether he had to resort to force in the form of the threat or the actuality of war. His calculations might turn out to be faulty or be brought to nought by accident, but they were in themselves perfectly rational.

These calculations have remained rational in so far as they apply to conventional force in a non-nuclear context. Thus India and Pakistan, Israel and the Arab states have acted rationally when they continued to use conventional force as an instrument of their national policies. A case can even be made for the rationality of using conventional force in a nuclear context, provided adequate precautions are taken to insulate the use of such force from the nuclear context. The Korean War is a case in point.

However, this rational relationship that existed from the beginning of history to 1945 between force as a means and the ends of foreign policy does not apply to nuclear weapons. The destructiveness of nuclear weapons is so enormous that it overwhelms all possible objectives of a rational foreign policy. If they were used as instruments of national policy, nuclear weapons would destroy the tangible objective of the policy and the belligerents as well. In consequence, they are not susceptible to rational use as instruments of national policy. Yet their availability makes it impossible for foreign policy to be conducted in a rational manner as though they did not exist. Their very existence compels us to rethink the basic issues of foreign policy. But we continue in large measure to think and act as though 1945 did not mark one of the great watersheds of history where a new age began, as distinct from the age that preceded it as the modern age has been from the Middle Ages or the Middle Ages have been from Antiquity.

A rational foreign policy in the nuclear age would have to move on two different and separate levels: the conventional and the nuclear. It would have to insist upon the radically distinct character of the nuclear sphere and upon the vital importance of its strict separation from the conventional one. Instead, we have been trying to apply conventional modes of thought and action to the nuclear sphere. Instead of emphasizing the distinctness of nuclear weapons, we have been trying to assimilate them to conventional ones. Instead of maintaining and strengthening the separation of the two spheres, we have endeavored to integrate nuclear weapons into our conventional armory.

This contradiction between our modes of thought and action, belonging to an age that has passed, and the objective to conditions of our existence has engendered four paradoxes in our nuclear strategy: the commitment to the use of force, nuclear or otherwise, paralyzed by the fear of having to use it; the search for a nuclear strategy that would avoid the predictable consequences of nuclear war; the pursuit of a nuclear armaments race joined with attempts to stop it; the pursuit of an alliance policy which the availability of nuclear weapons has rendered obsolete. All these paradoxes result from the contrast between traditional attitudes and the possibility of nuclear war and from the fruitless attempts to reconcile the two.

NUCLEAR WEAPONS AS INSTRUMENTS OF NATIONAL POLICY

It is no exaggeration to state that both the United States and the Soviet Union have ruled out the use of nuclear force as an instrument of their national policies; neither is willing to use nuclear weapons to achieve its ends. The United States is committed to the unification of Germany, but it has emphatically ruled out the use of force in any form to achieve it. Similarly, the Soviet Union is committed to the support of "wars of national liberation," but has ruled out the use of its own military force to that end.

More particularly, both nuclear powers, in pursuit of their goals, refrain from taking steps that might provoke the other side to resort to force, especially in its nuclear form. Thus the United States declared at the outset of the Hungarian revolution in 1956 that it would not intervene and gave as its reason the fear of nuclear war. The Soviet Union has repeatedly—and twice in the form of ultimatums—called for a change in the status of West Berlin, but has refrained from the use of violence for that purpose. In the Korean War, both sides refrained from committing, qualitatively or quantitatively, more than a fraction of their resources and from exploiting their strategic opportunities to the full, and thus granted "privileged sanctuaries" to each other, fearful lest one provoke the other to resort to nuclear force. Similarly, during the Cuban crisis of October 1962, both sides went as far as they dared without compelling the other side to take steps that might lead to nuclear war. For this reason, the United States was satisfied with the success of the "quarantine" in removing the so-called offensive weapons from Cuba, and did not dare to press its advantage to the point of eliminating the Russian presence from Cuba altogether; and for the same reason, the Soviet Union did not attempt to break the quarantine and yielded to the American insistence on the removal of its offensive missiles.

The same dynamic of reciprocal self-restraint has operated in Vietnam between the United States, on the one hand, and the Soviet Union and China, on the other. The United States has been careful to keep the war limited by avoiding any direct military threat or damage to the Soviet Union and China. These powers, in turn, have allowed the United States a free hand within these self-imposed limits by refraining from direct military intervention and supplying North Vietnam only with defensive weapons. Thus Russian ships and Chinese airfields, as well as the American ones, have been treated as "privileged sanctuaries" through reciprocal self-restraint.

However, this consistent restraint in action is belied by as consistent a verbal commitment to the use of violence, especially in its nuclear form, in certain contingencies. Thus the United States has time and again declared that it is resolved to defend its presence in Berlin by all means required, nuclear weapons included. In November 1956, on the occasion of the Franco-British invasion of Egypt, the Soviet Union threatened Great Britain and France with nuclear war, and the Soviet Union has time and again made similar threats against the United States and one or the other of its allies. Yet how seriously must these mutual threats be taken?

In view of what is known to both sides of the likely consequences of nuclear war, the threats obviously can not be taken at their face value. On the other hand, in view of the importance of some of the interests at stake, in view of the massive preparations for nuclear war on both sides and the military doctrines supporting them, and in view of the impossibility of responding to an armed attack upon some of these interests by any other but nuclear force, neither can these threats be dismissed as empty. Thus in the successive Berlin crises, for instance, the United States and the Soviet Union tried to convince each other that they were irrational enough to incur their own destruction by supporting their respective positions with nuclear force, assuming at the same time that the other side would be rational enough not to provoke such an irrational reaction. Here we observe the mechanics of mutual deterrence.

The threat of nuclear force has taken on a function that is novel at least in its exclusiveness. Traditional force is an instrument for breaking the will of the opponent through either successful defense or attack; its primary function lies in the effectiveness of its physical application. But the primary function of nuclear force lies in making its physical application superfluous by deterring the prospective opponent from its use. While traditional force operates psychologically through the intermediary of actual physical employment, nuclear force has a psychological function pure and simple. The prospective opponents are kept constantly aware of the inevitability of their own destruction should they resort to nuclear force, and this awareness prevents them from resorting to it.

In the pre-nuclear age the threat and the counterthreat of force could always be, and frequently were, put to the test of actual performance, and either the threat or the counterthreat was then proved to be empty. In the nuclear age, the very purpose of threat and counterthreat is to prevent the test of actual performance from taking place. The appearance of possessing both the ability and the resolution to make good the threat and counterthreat becomes, then, of paramount importance as a condition for the success of mutual deterrence.

The nature of this condition, it will be noted, is political rather than military; for what is essential is the appearance, not the reality, of possessing the ability and resolution to make good threat and counterthreat. In order to make mutual deterrence work, two nations need only create the mutual belief that they are willing and able to destroy each other in nuclear war. As long as this belief exists, it is irrelevant whether or not the reality corresponds to it. In other words, the mechanics of mutual deterrence require an element of bluff, either real or suspect.

At this point, a most serious political dilemma arises. No nation can afford to yield to a threat of nuclear war that is only a bluff; nor can it afford to stand up to a threat that turns out not to be a bluff. Miscalculation is bound to be fatal either to the interests of the nation threatened if it yields to the bluff, or to its existence if it stands up to a nuclear threat that is not a bluff. Yet—and here is the dilemma—a nation cannot determine with certainty when the other side is bluffing without the test of actual performance, a test that it is the very purpose of mutual deterrence to avoid. Deterrence has thus far worked only because there has remained in the minds of both sides a doubt as to whether the other side was really bluffing. Or, to put it the other way around, both sides were able to give the threat of nuclear war at least a certain measure of plausibility.

This plausibility is bound to be affected by repetitive threats of nuclear war and it is likely to be affected in the negative. A nation that has stopped at a certain point, far short of its goal, because it was afraid of a nuclear response that did not materialize is likely to be just a little bit less timid when it must gauge the enemy's intentions at the next confrontation. Having stopped the first time at three paces from what it thought to be the brink, it may well calculate that it can afford now to take another half-step forward and still remain at a safe distance. If its calculation turns out to be correct, it may well be tempted at the third confrontation to take another half-step forward, and so forth, so that either the margin of safety between the threat of nuclear war and its actuality will narrow with every confrontation or the likelihood of nuclear response will decrease with every retreat by the challenged nation.

This process of erosion is likely to result from the very dynamics of mutual deterrence. With every demonstration of its emptiness, the nuclear threat will lose a measure of its plausibility. In consequence, it will lose a measure of its restraining effect. Inherent in that dynamics is, then, a dual escalation, one feeding upon the other: the ever-diminishing credibility of the nuclear threat and ever bolder challenges to make good on it. The effects of deterrence are likely to decrease with the frequency of its use—to the point where, as it were, the psychological capital of deterrence has been nearly expended and the policy of deterrence will be close to bankruptcy. When they reach that point, the nations concerned can choose one of three alternatives: resort to nuclear war, retreat, or resort to conventional war.

The alternative of conventional war appears to be the only rational one. It seems to assure the nations concerned a chance both to survive and to pursue their national objectives. However, the paradox of the use of force in the nuclear age is not limited to nuclear war; rather it impedes the use of conventional force as well, even though—under certain conditions—to a lesser degree. For the neat distinction between conventional and nuclear force which the theoreticians of conventional war make and its advocates imply, is valid only on the condition that the stakes of a conventional conflict are small enough to make defeat or stalemate acceptable without recourse to nuclear weapons. Korea was a case in point, and so is Vietnam. Yet Berlin and Cuba are not, and it is doubtful whether Korea would be today and Vietnam would be tomorrow. It is relatively safe for nuclear powers to resort to conventional force only if they bring that force to bear upon an issue which is either limited by nature, such as geography, or can be limited politically by the will of the parties to the conflict. The limitation upon the use of force, then, corresponds to the limited character of the issue; and win, lose, or draw, the parties will not commit to the conflict more than a deliberately limited force.

It is not necessary to demonstrate that few issues on behalf of which the nuclear powers might resort to violence are thus limited by nature or could be kept by the belligerents indefinitely on a sufficiently low level of priorities. Most issues are either so important from the outset or acquire such importance through accidents, miscalculations, or the dynamics of the conflict itself that neither side could reconcile itself to defeat without having used a maximum of force to stave it off. Once force has been committed to such an issue on however small a scale, the risk of escalation is ever present, first quantitatively within conventional force itself and then qualitatively from conventional to nuclear force. Thus the awareness of the irrationality of nuclear war— which, as we have seen, impedes the resort to nuclear force—also stands in the way of the use of conventional force in so far as the latter might prepare resort to the former.

The immensity of the military force which the nuclear age has generated goes hand in hand with the devaluation of its practical use. The more endowed a nation is with military force, the less it is able to use it. Non-nuclear nations have shown themselves to be much less inhibited in the use of military force than nuclear powers; for the risk of escalation presented by the intervention of one of the nuclear powers with nuclear weapons is likely to be remote. The nuclear powers are inhibited in the use of force not only in relation to each other, but also in their relations to non-nuclear powers, because of the ever present risk that another nuclear power may use force on behalf of the other side.

Great Britain and France derive no substantive political or military advantage from their possession of nuclear weapons. These weapons add nothing to their ability to protect and promote their respective interests. The fact that the United States has a nuclear arsenal capable of destroying all human life on this planet in a matter of hours has been irrelevant to its military posture vis-à-vis Vietnam. If the United States had no nuclear weapons at all, its usable military power would not thereby have been diminished. Quite to the contrary, it can be plausibly argued that its usable power would thereby have been increased because the fear of nuclear escalation would then not have exerted its restraining influence upon the use of conventional military power. Thus while the discrepancy between the strong and the weak is today much more pronounced than it has ever been in history, it is exactly this disproportion which renders the powerful impotent in the fullness of their power.

NUCLEAR WEAPONS AND MILITARY CONVENTIONS

The second paradox arising from the operation of traditional policy in the nuclear age is presented by the idea of limited nuclear war. This idea has appeared in different manifestations in different periods, such as the "clean" H-bomb, which produces no significant fallout, tactical nuclear war, graduated deterrence with "firebreaks" between the stages, counterforce strategy. All these manifestations have one quality in common: the desire to reconcile the use of nuclear weapons with the admitted irrationality of all-out nuclear war and the attempt, inspired by this desire, to discover a rational way to use them. Each of these attempts has been supported by a vast body of learned and sophisticated literature dedicated to the demonstration of its rationality and feasibility, and each has been discarded after a while to be replaced by a new one. What has remained constant is the urge to reconcile the irreconcilable and to find a way of waging nuclear war without incurring one's destruction. Thus we have been in search of a method of waging nuclear war in the conventional manner so that nuclear war may produce conventional, that is, rational and tolerable, consequences.

However, the enormous destructiveness natural to nuclear weapons, upon which the dynamics of warfare is brought to bear, makes the rationalization of nuclear war, however attempted, a hopeless undertaking. Hardly anything needs to be said of the "clean" bomb, now deservedly half-forgotten, which merely introduces a modification into the over-all destructiveness of nuclear weapons, without affecting the destructiveness itself.[1]

1 *The Effects of Nuclear Weapons* (Washington, D.C.: Government Printing Office, 1962), pp. 435 ff., published under the joint auspices of the Department of Defense and the Atomic Energy Commission, has written the epitaph to this piece of science fiction:

> The terms "clean" and "dirty" are often used to describe the amount of radioactivity produced by a fusion weapon (or hydrogen bomb) relative to that from what might be described as a "normal" weapon. The latter may be defined as one in which no special effort has been made either to increase or to decrease the amount of radioactivity produced for the given explosion yield. A "clean" weapon would then be one which is designed to yield significantly less radioactivity than an equivalent normal weapon. It should be noted, however, that a clean fusion weapon would inevitably produce some radioactive species. Even if a pure fusion weapon, with no fission, should be developed, its explosion in air would still result in the formation of carbon-14 and possibly other neutron-induced activities. If special steps were taken in the design of a

Both tactical nuclear war and graduated deterrence presuppose three capabilities on the part of the belligerents: the rational ability to deduce the intentions of the enemy from his use of nuclear weapons, the rational ability to know exactly at every moment of the war what kind of nuclear weapon it is necessary and prudent to use, and the practical ability to impose the limitations so determined upon all nuclear command posts. Both tactical nuclear war and graduated deterrence require a rational and reliable interplay of the intentions and actions of the belligerents, an interplay which theoreticians may calculate in the form of "models" but which it is impossible to achieve consistently in reality. That impossibility derives from three factors: the essential ambiguity of the military act (which it of course shares with the political act), uncertainty about the enemy's intentions, and the enormous and irreparable risks, in nuclear war, of mistakes in interpretation.

When does a nuclear attack serve a tactical, and when a strategic, purpose? In the case, say, of the interruption by force of our communications with Berlin or of a civil war between East and West Germany, we would probably intend to use tactical nuclear weapons at the beginning of the conflict, escalating our nuclear commitment to the point at which the enemy would desist, and we would expect the Soviet Union to respond in kind. We would initially select strictly military targets, such as concentrations of troops and military equipment and missile sites, and try to interdict the enemy communications and logistics by aiming at civilian targets with a preponderant military significance, such as airports, railroad stations, bridges, and the like—intending to spare civilian targets, such as population and industrial centers. But how would the enemy react if we were to hit one of these civilian targets, either by accident or because of the close proximity of a military target? Would he hit a civilian target of

---

fusion device, e.g., by salting . . . so that upon detonation it generated more radioactivity than a similar normal weapon, it would be described as "dirty." By its very nature, a fission weapon must be regarded as being dirty.

ours in retaliation—and how would we react to that?—or would he continue to limit himself to the choice of military targets?

But even if he does the latter, the asymmetry of the tactical situation on both sides is bound to blur the distinction between the tactical and the strategic uses of nuclear weapons. Let us supppose, for instance, that the Soviet Union were to pursue in Central Europe tactical aims analogous to ours. Yet, although in pursuit of such aims we could afford to spare population centers because of the location of our targets, the Soviet Union might need to designate the Atlantic ports of NATO as tactical military targets, destroying in the process population and industrial centers. What interpretation would we put upon such an action, and how would we react to it? We might take out a number of Soviet or satellite cities in retaliation, and how would the Soviet Union react to that?

These choices would not be made, it must be emphasized against what seems to be the prevailing academic opinion, in the detached and rational manner in which chess players make their choices. Rather they would be made against the doubly threatening background of the enemy's uncertain intentions and the ever-increasing stakes of the war. It is not too difficult to ascertain the enemy's intentions when a war is fought after the model of the Korean War in a geographically limited area for secondary stakes and with non-nuclear weapons. But even there we utterly misjudged the Chinese intentions once our conduct of the war had greatly increased the stakes for China; and we misjudged similarly the place the Korean War occupied in the world-wide strategy of the Soviet Union when we interpreted it as the opening move in a campaign seeking the military conquest of the world.

The assessment of enemy intentions becomes a guessing game carrying extreme risks in a war, such as the one we have stipulated for Europe, which has left narrow limits of geography, stakes, and weapons behind. We have put simultaneously and successively the most divergent interpretations upon the Soviet intentions concerning Berlin, ranging all the way from mere bluff, through the consolidation of the East German regime and the testing of our intentions, to gaining control of West Germany. Soviet intentions have no doubt changed in response to the Soviet interpretation of our intentions. In the course of actual hostilities, however, both sides will try to impress each other with the firmness of certain of their intentions, real or feigned, in accordance with the requirements of deterrence and at the same time to conceal other intentions from each other, in accordance with the requirements of warfare. The intertwining of these two requirements will make the ascertainment of the enemy's intentions a hopelessly irrational game of chance.

This game would be played in a nuclear war for the highest stakes imaginable: the survival of the belligerents. In consequence, the assessment of enemy intentions would be driven by irresistible pressure, legitimate within the context of nuclear war, toward assuming the worst and avoiding the common mistake of underrating the enemy. This happened under relatively favorable conditions, as concerns the immediate stakes and pressures, when we evaluated the place of the Korean War in the over-all Russian intentions in such sweeping—and erroneous—terms, that we embarked upon a policy of massive rearmament, far in excess of what was required by the local situation in Korea. Neither side could be expected—nor would it be justified—to give the enemy the benefit of the doubt in the initial stages of limited nuclear war and thereby risk its own destruction. Both sides are likely to convince themselves that their best chance to emerge from the war without fatal damage lies in destroying the enemy's retaliatory capability, or at the least his will to continue the war, by a first strike. Thus escalation is, as it were, built into the very dynamics of nuclear war, as the maximization of violence is built into the dynamics of any war. Once a limited nuclear war has started, escalation is not a matter of choice. Short of stopping the war itself, escalation cannot be avoided. Both the logic of deterrence, in the face of the ambiguities of responses and the uncertainties of intentions, and the expanding stakes of the war require it.

These considerations apply with particular force to a specific purpose graduated deterrence is intended to serve: the provision of a "pause" or "firebreak" between conventional or tactical nuclear war, on the one hand, and all-out nuclear war, on the other. Before the belligerents plunge into self-destruction through all-out nuclear war, it is intended that they be given a chance to reflect, to pull back, and to negotiate a settlement. Yet such a pause, assuming its feasibility, is an ambiguous device. The more the belligerents will rely upon a pause between tactical and all-out nuclear war, the more readily they will make the transition from conventional to tactical nuclear war. In other words, the assumption of a pause between tactical and all-out nuclear war increases the likelihood of escalation from conventional to tactical nuclear war. However, even if one shares the optimistic assumption that a war for major stakes could develop in such rationally definable stages that the progression of the war would be determined by a succession of conscious choices, the belligerents, once they have arrived at the brink of unlimited nuclear war, would have to be absolutely certain of each other's resolution to stop there. Such resolution cannot be taken for granted in view of the very great advantages of a surprise first strike, emphasized by Russian strategic doctrine. How could such intentions be ascertained?

They can only be ascertained by facts—that is, deeds and circumstances, which, as we have seen, are even more uncertain and ambiguous in war than they are in peace. The direct teletype connection, the so-called hot-line, established in 1963 between Washington and Moscow, serves the purposes of clarifying the intentions of both sides in times of crisis. *The New York Times* of April 6, 1963, quoted Administration officials as having "expressed hope that an always ready 'hot-line would help prevent misunderstanding and accidents at a moment of peril." Yet such a technical device used for political purposes partakes of the ambiguity of the political act. A direct communications link between the White House and the Kremlin could indeed be used for the beneficial purposes indicated by official statements. But it could also be used for purposes quite different. Imagine for a moment that there had existed such a direct link between the

White House and the Imperial Palace in Tokyo on December 6, 1941. Such a link would have afforded the Japanese government a splendid opportunity to conceal its intentions from the government of the United States without having to go to the trouble of sending a special envoy to Washington for that purpose.

The fundamental problem that the attempts at rationalizing and "conventionalizing" nuclear war pose will not be solved by a technical contrivance such as the hot-line. That problem simply reappears here in a new technological setting. The hot-line does not answer the question, which in the nature of things appears to be unanswerable: Will nations already engaged in a war for high stakes and publicly committed to certain objectives have the moral courage, the intellectual assurance, and the rational control to stop short of all-out nuclear war? The best answer one can give is that it is unlikely but not impossible that they will be able to do so. But that is not a good enough answer when the existence of great nations and the fate of civilizations are at stake.

Finally, the idea of limited nuclear war is predicated upon the ability of the supreme military authorities to hold all nuclear command posts consistently to the limits decided upon. Yet, however centralized the decision to start a nuclear war might be—a moot question into which we shall not enter here—the choice of weapons and targets in the course of the war must at least to some considerable degree lie in the hands of local commanders. Their judgment will in good measure determine the limits of the nuclear war. It is certainly utopian to expect that all, without exception and always, will assess correctly the different factors discussed above, thereby preserve the limits the central authorities have decided upon, and thus prevent escalation. It is in all likelihood unduly optimistic to expect that even a considerable number will consistently make such correct assessments. It is much more probable, given the experience of previous wars and the natural tendency of the military decision toward the maximization of violence, that the decentralized choice of targets and weapons will powerfully reinforce the objective tendencies toward escalation to which we have already referred. Professor Oskar Morgenstern's proposal, rationally unexceptionable, to train local commanders in the making of correct decisions for a nuclear war [2] could at best mitigate somewhat these deficiencies; for the latter are in the last analysis the subjective manifestations of objective factors which are bound to frustrate the making of correct assessments on all levels of the political and military hierarchy.

More particularly, in view of past experience, it cannot be assumed that local commanders, even if they were intellectually equipped to make the correct assessments, will always have the will to make them. For military commanders have a natural desire to win victories by smashing the enemy rather than to maintain a stalemate by inflicting carefully measured damage. Thus their natural bias presents still another argument against the possibility of holding the military hierarchy consistently to the limits on nuclear war decided upon by the central authorities.

The most consistent attempt thus far at conceiving a nuclear war after the model of a conventional one is the conception of counterforce strategy. As former Secretary of Defense McNamara put it in his address at the University of Michigan on June 16, 1962: "The United States has come to the conclusion that to the extent feasible, basic military strategy in a possible general nuclear war should be approached in much the same way that more conventional military operations have been regarded in the past. That is to say, principal military objectives, in the event of a nuclear war stemming from a major attack on the Alliance, should be the destruction of the enemy's military forces, not of his civilian population."

It is the distinctive characteristic of counterforce strategy that it expands the sphere of attempted rationalization from tactical into strategic nuclear war. It seeks to use nuclear bombs for pinpoint attacks after the model of conventional ones and assimilate the strategic use of missiles to that of long-range artillery. An all-out nuclear war would then be fought, to quote Mr. McNamara again, "against all of the enemy's vital nuclear capabilities." The belligerents would emerge from such a war shaken and wounded

2 "How To Plan To Beat Hell," *Fortune,* Vol. 67, No. 1 (January, 1963), pp. 103 ff.

but with their societies essentially intact. If such a counterforce strategy were feasible, the belligerents at the end of a nuclear war fought on such principles would be better off than Germany was at the end of World War II, subjected as it had been to conventional saturation bombing. However, four arguments militate against the feasibility of a counterforce strategy.

First of all, World War II showed that the expansion of the list of legitimate military targets under the impact of total war has made the traditional distinction between military and non-military targets tenuous in theory and untenable in practice. Railroad stations and factories, for instance, have become legitimate military targets, and they were attacked and destroyed as such during the Second World War. Yet, as a rule, large expanses of nonmilitary targets in the surrounding areas were destroyed as well. It can of course be argued that missiles are more reliable instruments for pin-point attack than bombs dropped from airplanes by humans, who during the Second World War frequently dropped their bombs in the vicinity of, rather than on, the military target because of the hazards of the latter's anti-aircraft protection. But the greater precision of the missiles is offset by the enormously increased range of the destructiveness of their warheads. For this reason alone, counterforce strategy would be feasible only on the assumption that all military targets were isolated from population centers by the number of miles sufficient to protect the latter from the destructive effects of a nuclear attack upon the former.

Yet even if one assumes for the sake of argument that all Russian military targets are of that nature, an obvious asymmetry differentiates their location from the location of our nuclear installations. Many of our nuclear installations are in the vicinity of cities, and the Soviet Union could not attack the former without risking the destruction of the latter. It could not attack —to give only one concrete example—our missile installations in the vicinity of Cheyenne and Phoenix without for all practical purposes attacking these cities. If this should happen, we would be faced, on the level of strategic nuclear war, with the same dilemma discussed earlier in connection with tactical nuclear war.

Second, another asymmetry which renders counterforce strategy unfeasible concerns the nuclear arsenal at the disposal of the United States and the Soviet Union. Counterforce strategy is predicated upon the availability of a highly diversified nuclear arsenal, each weapon appropriate in kind and yield to its target. The United States is supposed to possess such a nuclear arsenal, while the Soviet Union is not. But the latter is supposed to have compensated for the lack of diversity and quantity of its nuclear arsenal by relying for intercontinental strategic purposes upon a relatively small number of high-yield weapons in the tens-of-megatons range. So although it may be possible to limit destruction from, say, a one-megaton weapon to an isolated military target—provided such a target is available—there is no American nuclear installation that could be made the target for a Russian ten-, twenty-, or fifty-megaton device without increasingly large civilian centers being affected. Thus, assuming we were technically able, in view of the location of our targets and the quantity and diversification of our nuclear arsenal, to pursue a counterforce strategy, the Soviet Union, because of the location of its targets and the nature of its nuclear weapons system, would be unable to do so even if it had a mind to. Since counterforce strategy is predicated upon reciprocity—in the words of Mr. McNamara, "We are giving a possible opponent the strongest imaginable incentive to refrain from striking our own cities"—this dual asymmetry makes it impossible for the Soviet Union "to refrain from striking our own cities," and, hence, makes the conduct of a counterforce strategy unprofitable on our part.

Third, apart from the asymmetry of targets and weapons, counterforce strategy is also negated by an asymmetry in fundamental strategic position. An effective counterforce strategy is inseparable from a first-strike strategy. The nuclear installations of the two major nuclear powers are composed of two types: those that are vulnerable and, hence, lend themselves as targets for the counterforce and those that are relatively invulnerable, because of their location in hardened sites or, more particularly, their mobility, and can provide but marginal targets for counterforce. Nation *A* which pursues a counterforce strategy against nation *B* through a first strike will be able to cripple, if not destroy completely, *B*'s vulnerable nuclear installations by using primarily its own vulnerable nuclear installations for that purpose. *B,* committed to a counterforce strategy against *A* through a second strike, would have to use its invulnerable nuclear installations. But against what targets of *A* could it use them? It could destroy soft launching sites without missiles, empty submarine berths, airfields, and factories. The damage it could do to *A* through a second strike would certainly be far inferior to the damage it suffered from *A*'s first strike, and it could do so only at the price of committing unilaterally at least a fraction of its remaining invulnerable nuclear reserve. Thus after the first nuclear exchange carried out within the limits of counterforce strategy, *A* has a great advantage by virtue of having been the first to strike.

The advantage of *A* results from a peculiarity of nuclear weapons. A launching installation, such as a gun, a cannon, or a missile pad, is an active element in the military equation only as long as ammunition is available for it to fire. The launching mechanism has lost its military usefulness when it runs out of ammunition, and the availability of ammunition stands in inverse ratio to its potency. At one extreme, the carrier of a pistol can fire his weapon hundreds of times with the ammunition he is able to carry. At the other extreme, a mobile missile carrier can be fired only once and must rely for each successive firing upon a fresh supply, which in case of war may at best be forthcoming only at uncertain and prolonged intervals. A Polaris submarine, after it has fired its salvo, loses its function as a weapons carrier until it has access to a fresh supply of missiles. Thus the active usefulness of a mobile nuclear weapon is enormous but limited to an instant, while the active usefulness of conventional weapons is much inferior in potency but extends over considerable spans of time. Or to put it into the language of conventional warfare: Conventional infantry or artillery may temporarily run out of ammunition under exceptional circumstances and may lose for the time being its active military usefulness; but that mobile nuclear installations will run out of ammunition instantaneously or at least after a relatively few firings is inherent in the nature of nuclear weaponry.

By virtue of this peculiarity of nuclear weapons, A gains a military advantage if it can compel B to expend unilaterally a fraction of its invulnerable deterrent. Let us suppose, to take an oversimplified but illustrative example, that A and B each possess ten Polaris submarines and that after A's first strike with land-based missiles B commits six of its submarines to counterforce retaliation. If A were to start the second nuclear exchange by committing four of its Polaris submarines to a selective countercity strategy and if B were to retaliate in kind with its remaining Polaris submarines, the quantitative relationship between A and B in terms of Polaris submarines at the end of the second round would be six to zero. In other words, the unilateral commitment of B's invulnerable deterrent would have resulted in a clear nuclear superiority for A. It would be irrelevant to this argument that B might have a nuclear stockpile quantitatively and qualitatively the equal or even superior of that of A. What is decisive is the destructive power of nuclear weapons deliverable at a particular moment. It is here that A's advantage lies, regardless of what B might be able to deliver a week or a month hence.

Since A and B must be aware of the advantage of a first strike before the war starts, both have an incentive to be the first to strike. Countercity strategy would allow A and B to wait for the other side to make the first move, secure in their possession of an invulnerable nuclear deterrent and their knowledge of the unacceptable damage it could inflict upon the other side. This countercity strategy, through the mechanics of mutual deterrence, minimizes the possibility of nuclear war. Countercity strategy, as it were, expresses the inner logic of nuclear war. On the other hand, counterforce strategy, by presuming to superimpose upon the dynamics of nuclear war a pattern appropriate to conventional war, increases the likelihood of nuclear war. For it puts a premium upon preventive war and thus stimulates not the desire to prevent a nuclear war but rather competition for starting one.

However, even if A did not have the advantage after its first strike—and this is the fourth and last argument against counterforce strategy—what would *A* and *B* do after the nuclear exchange? They have destroyed what counterforce strategy allows them to destroy and they now find themselves in a political and military blind alley. Wars are fought for the purpose of breaking the will of the opponent through victory in battle. Yet the predictable outcome of a nuclear war fought within the limits of counterforce strategy is stalemate. After the nuclear exchange the belligerents will find themselves—as to weapons—in the same relative position they occupied before the outbreak of the war, minus their vulnerable nuclear installations. They can of course make peace on the basis of the *status quo ante bellum,* and then counterforce strategy will have revealed itself as a complete waste of human and material resources. Or they can continue the war with conventional means, supplemented by tactical nuclear weapons. But then they will be up against the insoluble problems posed by tactical nuclear war, already discussed above.

There is still another, and perhaps the most likely, alternative. Even if one assumes—quite unrealistically in view of the first two arguments presented here—that counterforce strategy will work during the initial nuclear exchange, the very fact of that exchange will conjure up the possibility of escalation into countercity strategy. *A* will have an incentive to embark upon that course in order to exploit the advantage the first strike has given it. *A* may reason, rightly or wrongly, that *B*, by unilaterally committing a part of its invulnerable deterrent, has been at least temporarily weakened to such an extent as to give *A* a chance of victory. *B*, on the other hand, has an incentive to dissuade *A* from pursuing a countercity strategy by demonstrating its ability and resolution to embark upon one itself.

Thus counterforce strategy turns out to be unfeasible as a conventional and rationally limited version of nuclear war—first, because of the inherent asymmetry of targets and weapons, secondly, because of the asymmetry between the likely effects of a first and second strike, and finally, because of the impossibility of following up the initial nuclear exchange with a politically and militarily satisfactory conclusion.

Like its predecessors, this attempt at reconciling nuclear war with the conventional modes of thought and action has been abandoned. This became clear in Mr. McNamara's statement of February 23, 1966, before a joint session of the Senate Armed Services Committee and the Senate Subcommittee on Department of Defense Appropriations. This statement faced the reality of nuclear war by emphasizing the capability of the United States for the "assured destruction" of the population and industrial capacity of the Soviet Union. Yet while the strategic concept of counterforce has been abandoned, certain military policies, justifiable only in terms of that concept, linger on. The most important of them is the nuclear armaments race.

THE NUCLEAR ARMAMENTS RACE

The quantitative and qualitative competition for conventional weapons is a rational instrument of foreign policy. The greater the quantity and quality of a nation's armory, the greater obviously is its material military power. This rationale of the conventional armaments race results from the limited capacity of conventional weapons in relation to the available users and targets. Nation A which possesses, say, 10 per cent more machine guns than nation B is, everything else being equal, militarily superior to nation B. If A has x machine guns and B has y, then x minus y equals the margin of A's superiority over B.

One can of course postulate a situation in which A and B would be saturated with machine guns, so that further competition would become irrational. This condition would obtain if A and B were supplied with an abundance of machine guns in relation to the respective numbers of available arms-bearing men and required replacements. Since this condition of saturation is purely hypothetical, it is rational for A and B to compete for the quantitative and qualitative improvement of their respective supplies.

What is as a rule hypothetical with regard to conventional weapons is an established fact in the nuclear field. Both nuclear powers claim the ability to destroy the other's society regardless of what the opponent might do, and the United States has been particularly emphatic in claiming that it could do so many times over. But since the destruction of the enemy's society, primarily by destroying its industrial and population centers, is the maximum damage to be inflicted by force of arms, quantitative and qualitative improvements in those arms can at best alter the modalities of the damage, but cannot enlarge the ability to inflict that damage itself. X, regardless of how much superior it is to y, here equals y. Once a nation possesses a delivery system capable of surviving a first strike and carrying nuclear warheads to all possible targets, it has reached the rational limits of nuclear armaments. There is no rational justification for continuing the nuclear armaments race after both sides have reached that limit.

But the nuclear armaments race continues, both quantitatively and qualitatively—and here is the first element of the paradox— as though the same rules of competition applied to conventional and nuclear weapons alike. The habits of thought and action which experience has taught us from the beginning of history to the end of the Second World War are being carried over into an age for which they are no longer relevant.[3] Their continuing application is being justified on two main grounds: counterforce strategy and the prospect of technological innovations.

Indeed, the continuation of the nuclear armaments race follows logically from the commitment to a counterforce strategy. The conventional conception of nuclear war presented by counterforce strategy demands a correspondingly conventional approach to competitive armaments. Under the assumptions of that

[3] It is of interest to note that these habits of thought and action had already become obsolescent before the First World War:

> From 1872 to 1913, this rigorous competition in the building up of armies went on, every government spending as much money as it could persuade its people to pay or the national economy would support . . . without, however, any corresponding increase in security being felt. In fact, the proportionate strength of the various armies was not greatly different in 1914 from what it had been in 1872, but the feeling of insecurity was much greater than it had been forty years earlier.

(Bernadotte E. Schmitt, "The Origins of the First World War," in W. N. Medlicott [ed.], *From Metternich to Hitler* [London: Routledge & Kegan Paul, 1963], pp. 186–87.)

strategy, a dynamic relationship exists between the number of targets presented by one side and the number and quality of weapons directed at those targets by the other. Given a static number of targets, an increase in the number and quality of counterforce weapons will improve the prospects of counterforce strategy. Given a static number of counterforce weapons, an increase in the number of targets will improve the prospects of the defender. Both sides have, then, an incentive to increase targets and counterforce weapons indefinitely, and the logic and dynamics of the conventional armaments race apply of necessity to the competition for nuclear arms seen in the perspective of "conventionalized" nuclear war.

Yet, while the logic of this argument in favor of a nuclear armaments race is unassailable, its practical validity depends upon the feasibility of counterforce strategy. Both stand and fall together. The arguments we have advanced against the feasibility of counterforce strategy, then, dispose of the rationality of a nuclear armaments race as well.

The argument in favor of a nuclear armaments race, based upon the prospect of technological progress, is bound to be speculative, as is its refutation. The argument operates in three main areas: anti-missile defense, improvement of weapons, and discovery of unknown weapons technologies.

It is a peculiarity of anti-nuclear missiles defense, in contrast to conventional anti-aircraft defense, that it is hardly worth having if it is not very close to 100 per cent effective. Effective nuclear defense has a meaning radically different from that of effective conventional defense. When more than one-sixth and one-fourth, respectively, of the attacking aircraft were incapacitated by active defense in the air raids on Schweinfurt on August 17 and October 14, 1943, the defense was deemed to have been successful since the attacker could not have sustained such an attrition rate for long and his losses were out of proportion to the damage achieved. However, if, say, 90 per cent of a missile force could be destroyed by active defense, the remaining 10 per cent, especially if their warheads were in the multi-megaton range, would nullify the defense by inflicting unacceptable damage upon the defender. Yet there is at present no prospect for the development of an anti-missile defense which would come even close to being 100 per cent effective. For in view of the present state of the art, the attack will be able, through the quantitative and qualitative improvement of its weapons, to maintain that margin of effectiveness which will nullify the purpose of the defense.

Nuclear weapons, then, differ from conventional ones in that they cannot be counteracted by defensive measures. Deterrence takes the place of defense. To protect oneself from a nuclear attack one must deter it from being launched by threatening retaliation in kind. Once deterrence has failed and the nuclear attack has been launched, rational policy has come to an end and nothing is left for the victim of the first strike but the irrationality of a retaliatory reaction. Thus the competitive search for a nuclear-missile defense is rooted in an obsolete mode of thought appropriate to conventional weapons. That competition will lead to a quantitative and qualitative intensification of the nuclear armaments race in which the attack will try to maintain its margin of effectiveness and the defense will try to wipe that margin out. At best, this competition will result in a new "balance of terror" on a much higher level of nuclear armaments—a balance, however, that will still repose upon the reciprocal threat of effective retaliation and not upon the effectiveness of the defense. At worst, this new nuclear armaments race between offensive and defensive weapons will have a destabilizing effect upon the "balance of terror" if it creates in one or the other or in all participants the illusion of having gained a defensive advantage that will allow them to use nuclear weapons against each other without risking unacceptable damage by way of effective retaliation.

The search for an ever better and bigger nuclear arsenal is an obvious residue from the age of conventional warfare. For, as pointed out above, once a nation has the nuclear capability of destroying its enemy many times over, even under the worst possible conditions, it is irrelevant how numerous, varied, and sophisticated its nuclear weapons are. The search for improved nuclear weapons is from the outset rational only in so far as it is aimed at the invulnerable nuclear deterrent of the enemy. A nation that could render these installations vulnerable would have gained a decisive military advantage. It is theoretically conceivable to destroy an invulnerable deterrent by blanketing large expanses of land and sea with multi-megaton nuclear devices, and it may even be practical in so far as a distant land mass is concerned. But it is totally impractical with regard to the seaborne nuclear deterrent. For here the nuclear forces of several nations, in the nature of things, do not operate either from fixed locations or at least clearly defined separate territories, but move and intermingle in unpredictable constellations. No improved nuclear weapons system can be expected to be able to distinguish between friendly and hostile seaborne installations. Thus the seaborne nuclear deterrent is likely to remain invulnerable in the foreseeable future.

Finally, no rational weapons policy can be based upon the expectation that another revolution in the technology of war will occur, of which the present gives no indication. The present and foreseeable relation between pure science and weapons technology is quite different from that which obtained in the 1930s. Then the theoretical achievements of atomic physics foreshadowed at least the theoretical possibility of nuclear weapons. Achievements of contemporary pure science do not allow an analogous prognosis. Thus, while it is certainly legitimate for scientific research and technical experimentation to go on, preparing for the unexpected in nuclear weapons technology and trying to bring it about, it is just as certainly futile to continue the nuclear armaments race on the basis of the scientific knowledge and technological ability both major nuclear powers have achieved.

However, our thoughts and actions concerning the nuclear armaments race are at odds not only with nuclear reality, but also—and here is the other element of the paradox—with themselves. Two contradictory impulses compete for the control of our thoughts and actions. On the one hand, we embark upon a nuclear armaments race as though it were a conventional one. On the other, aware of its irrationality, we try to stop it; and sometimes an extraordinary conjunction strikingly reveals the division of our mind against itself. Thus the partial nuclear test-ban treaty of 1963 has been defended by government and private organizations alike because, on the one hand, it is supposed to be the first step toward control of the nuclear armaments race and, on the other hand, it is supposed not to interfere in any significant manner with the nuclear armaments race we are engaged in with the Soviet Union. Public discussion centered upon the effects the treaty would have upon the ability of the United States to carry on the nuclear armaments race; the supporters of the treaty claimed that it would have no adverse effects, the opponents claimed it would. As an inducement to the Senate to ratify the treaty, the Administration had to give the most solemn assurances that ratification would not prevent it from continuing the nuclear armaments race with utmost energy. It appears to have lived up to that assurance.

If the analysis of the nuclear armaments race previously given is correct, then a rational policy requires the quantitative and qualitative stabilization of the present levels of nuclear armaments. This policy generally goes by the name of arms control. It is a somewhat ambiguous term in that it covers international, mutual, and unilateral controls. What is essential to arms control is a yardstick, determining the level of one's own nuclear armaments, other than the level of the nuclear armaments of the prospective enemy. Arms control, then, signifies stopping one's nuclear armaments at the point where they provide an invulnerable, effective deterrent and cutting them back to that point in so far as they have exceeded it.

While it is doubtful under present political conditions that arms control can be achieved by formal international agreement, both the United States and the Soviet Union have at times practiced it. The Soviet Union, according to current estimates, has produced far fewer intercontinental ballistic missiles than it was capable of producing. The "missile gap" of the late 1950s was the result of our equating productive capacity with actual production. In other words, we then thought that the Soviet Union would apply to the production of intercontinental ballistic missiles the traditional principles of the conventional armaments race rather than the principles of arms control appropriate to nuclear armaments—that it would produce as many delivery vehicles as it was capable of in order to establish quantitative superiority over the United States, rather than producing only as many as were necessary to establish an invulnerable, effective deterrent. The Soviet Union, having an advantage in powerful intercontinental ballistic missiles appropriate to multi-megaton warheads, could indeed achieve an invulnerable, effective deterrent with a much smaller number of delivery vehicles than ours. The United States, on the other hand, has in 1964, 1965, and 1968, cut back the production of fissionable material and nuclear warheads to the quantity needed for the maintenance of an invulnerable, effective deterrent.

Thus the logic of nuclear weaponry, substituting unilateral arms control for the conventional armaments race, challenges, however haltingly and with very partial success, conventional modes of thought and action.

ALLIANCES, PROLIFERATION, AND GEOGRAPHY

The conflict between traditional modes of thought and action and the objective conditions of the nuclear age has nowhere had a more baffling and destructive effect than in the relations between the two major nuclear powers and their respective allies. In the pre-nuclear age, nations with certain interests in common would try to defend and promote these interests by coordinating or pooling their diplomatic and military resources. Thus nation *A* would go to war on behalf of the interests of nation *B,* or vice versa, when it thought the defense and promotion of the other nation's interests was in its own interest as well. Thereby a nation would take a double risk: It could be mistaken about the identity of the interests involved and find itself drawn into a war without its own interests being sufficiently engaged, or it could miscalculate the distribution of power on either side and allow itself to get involved in a war it would then lose. What a nation had to guard against in its relations with its allies was a diplomatic blunder or a military miscalculation. In either event, it would as a rule risk, at worst, defeat in war with the consequent loss of an army or of territory.

The availability of nuclear weapons has radically transformed these traditional relations among allies and the risks attending them. Nuclear nation *A* which enters into an alliance with nation *B*, nuclear or non-nuclear, runs a double risk different in kind from the risks facing a member of a traditional alliance. In honoring the alliance, it might have to fight a nuclear war against nuclear power *C*, thereby forfeiting its own existence. Or ally *B* may provoke a war with nuclear power *C* on behalf of interests other than those contemplated by the alliance and thereby force *A*'s hand, involving it in a nuclear war on behalf of interests other than its own. That latter risk is magnified if *B* is also a nuclear power, of however small dimensions. If *B* were to threaten or attack *C* with nuclear weapons, *C* might, rightly or wrongly, consider *B*'s military power as a mere extension of *A*'s and anticipate and partly prevent the commitment of *A* through a first strike against *A*. Or *A*, anticipating *C*'s reaction against itself or seeking to save *B* through nuclear deterrence, will commit its own nuclear arsenal against *C*. In either case, *B*, however weak as a nuclear power, has the ability to act as a trigger for a general nuclear war.

B, on the other hand, faces a double risk, too. It may forfeit its existence in a nuclear war fought by *A* on behalf of its interests. Or it may find itself abandoned by *A*, which refuses to run the risk of its own destruction on behalf of the interests of *B*.

This radical difference from the risks taken by allies in the pre-nuclear and nuclear age has led to a radical difference in the reliability of alliances. In the pre-nuclear age, ally *A* could have been expected with a very high degree of certainty to come to the aid of ally *B* at the risk of defeat in war. In the nuclear age, ally *A* cannot be expected with the same degree of certainty to come to the aid of ally *B* at the risk of its own destruction. Here we contemplate the reverse side of the mechanics of deterrence. The very same doubt that deters *C* disheartens *B*. *C* cannot be certain that *A* will not actually forfeit its existence by resorting to nuclear war and, hence, is deterred. *B*, on the other hand, cannot be certain that *A* is willing to forfeit its existence by resorting to nuclear war and, hence, is disheartened. The three-cornered relationship offers opportunities for miscalculations more extensive and complex and, hence, more dangerous than those encountered in the two-cornered relationship of deterrence.

The nuclear powers have endeavored to escape this dilemma of alliances carrying unacceptable risks by two diametrically opposed policies. President de Gaulle, in his press conference of January 14, 1963, and in subsequent statements, has declared alliances to be obsolete for all practical purposes and has proposed to replace them with independent national nuclear deterrents. In opposition to this position, both the United States and the Soviet Union seek to preserve the present combination of a virtual nuclear monopoly on their part with a traditional alliance system. Both policies in different ways call into question the survival of the nuclear powers, if not of civilization itself, and, hence, give no satisfactory answer to the question raised by the existence of alliances armed with nuclear weapons. They are incapable of giving such an answer because they search for it in the intellectual armory of an age which the availability of nuclear weapons has left behind.

De Gaulle proposes to assimilate nuclear weapons to conventional ones in that at least their deterrent function is to be controlled by national governments on behalf of traditional national interests. France would use its nuclear weapons, as it has used its army, navy, and air force in the past, for the purpose of exerting pressure upon a prospective enemy. The realization of such a threat raises no general problem, providing the enemy is a non-nuclear power or a nuclear one similar in rank to France. Such a problem is posed, however, if France confronts a nuclear power of the first rank, such as the United States or the Soviet Union.

Given the industrial resources and geographic character of a nation such as France, as compared with those of the United States and the Soviet Union, an insuperable asymmetry would always exist between the nuclear threats France could address to a nuclear power of the first rank and those the latter could address to France. France could inflict serious damage on a first-rate nuclear power without being capable, at least in the foreseeable future, of destroying it utterly; but a nuclear power of the first rank, using only a small fraction of its nuclear arsenal, could wipe France off the face of the globe. France could threaten a major nuclear power, and vice versa, but if action were to follow these threats, France could not escape death while its enemy would have the option of minimizing damage to itself through a first strike. Thus an independent national nuclear deterrent gives a major nuclear power another incentive, in addition to those mentioned above, for a first strike, while it still further diminishes the credibility of the nuclear threat emanating from a second-rank nuclear power.

However, de Gaulle's design to use nuclear weapons as instruments of national policy increases the risk not only of local nuclear war but of general war as well. For erected into a general principle of statecraft to be followed by any number of nations, it would issue in the indiscriminate proliferation of nuclear weapons and thereby destroy the very mechanics of mutual deterrence. These mechanics repose upon the bipolarity of nuclear power. Detection systems, such as radar and sonar, are capable of identifying nuclear delivery systems in action, but they cannot identify their national identity, except in a limited way through the calculation of the projectory of land-based missiles. In consequence, retaliation requires the a priori determination of national identity, which bipolarity provides. Thus an anonymous explosion, caused by a seaborne delivery vehicle and destroying parts of the East coast of the United States, would automatically be attributed to the Soviet Union, calling forth nuclear retaliation. If a multiplicity of nations possessed such devices and the United States had tense relations with only two of them, such an anonymous explosion could with certainty be attributed to no one nation, however much suspicion might point to a particular one. And a new nuclear diplomacy would try its best to deflect suspicion and retaliation from the guilty to an innocent nation.

Of the three courses of action open to a nuclear power—retaliation, inaction, first strike—retaliation in the strict sense appears here to be technically impossible; for in the absence of an identifiable originator of the first strike, it would have to be indiscriminate either with regard to the geographic region whence the first strike is supposed to have originated or with regard to the political entity that is supposed to have originated it. Not to retaliate in kind at all would be a rational course of action only if it were preparatory to some kind of nuclear response. Such a response would be technically a preventive first strike against a nation which, if it was not responsible for the original first strike, is deemed likely to originate one in the future.

Under such circumstances, retaliation and prevention tend to become indistinguishable, and the distinction between first and second strike becomes blurred. If *A* has actually originated a first strike against *B*, then *B*'s nuclear response is a retaliatory second strike. But if *A* is only suspect, then *B*'s action is a preventive first strike. Since all nuclear powers would have to calculate and operate in this fashion, the proliferation of nuclear weapons, implicit in de Gaulle's design, would result in a political anarchy of unimaginable proportions, followed by total nuclear destruction either piecemeal or in one single catastrophe through the coincidence of a series of preventive-retaliatory blows.

Viewed against this prospect, the attempts of the United States and the Soviet Union to preserve the status quo of virtual nuclear bipolarity cannot but evoke sympathy. The United States and the Soviet Union have embarked upon policies which are significantly similar in that they seek to mitigate the paradox of the nuclear alliance without being able to transcend it. They risk the disintegration of their respective alliances rather than cooperate with their respective allies in nuclear proliferation. Both have strained their respective alliances to the breaking point by refusing to support France and China respectively in their attempts to acquire nuclear weapons. Both have been instrumental in achieving a partial test-ban treaty intended to slow down the process of nuclear proliferation, as well as in formulating a nonproliferation treaty acceptable to the non-nuclear nations. The United States in addition proposed to the members of NATO the formation of a multilateral seaborne nuclear force, which would have given the participants the illusion of proliferation while leaving the decision on the use of the force in American hands.

In strictly nuclear terms, these policies move on a higher level of intellectual awareness and practical sophistication than de Gaulle's design. But in strictly political terms, de Gaulle has the better of the argument. Here indeed is the nub of the paradox. The use of nuclear weapons as instruments of national policies is militarily anachronistic and self-destructive. But a traditional alliance armed with nuclear weapons is politically obsolescent; for either it cannot be relied upon when the chips are down, or it gives one member power over the life and death of another member. An alliance preserving the status quo of virtual nuclear bipolarity cannot be accepted by any other member also armed with nuclear weapons; and the proliferation of nuclear weapons among isolated nations is likely to end in universal catastrophe. Thus the paradox remains unresolved, and the modes of thought and action which the nuclear powers have brought to bear upon it can at best do no more than delay its destructive effects.

The reluctance to adapt alliance relations to the conditions created by the availability of nuclear weapons is strengthened by the survival of a conception of geography that is appropriate only to a pre-nuclear, conventional setting. The nuclear age has modified the geographic factor in two different respects. On the one hand, it has increased the protective function of geography; on the other, it has drastically reduced it.

The vulnerability of industrial and population centers and military installations to nuclear attack has given an advantage— however limited and perhaps dubious—to nations with large territories. Nations such as the United States, the Soviet Union, and China may have a chance to escape mortal damage from a less than all-out nuclear attack because their continental or semi-continental character allows them to disperse and thereby multiply the targets presented in the form of industrial and population centers and military installations. Nations with a high concentration of such centers and installations in a relatively small territory—e.g., France, Great Britain, West Germany, Japan, and Israel—are bound to receive mortal damage even from a low-level nuclear attack, while a nation with a large territory may have a chance to survive such an attack.

In the pre-nuclear age, it was rational for nations to seek control over additional territory through annexation, buffer states, or alliances; for the closer a nation could come to the frontier of a prospective enemy, the greater a military threat it could present, and the farther away from its frontiers a nation could keep a prospective enemy, the more advantageous was its defensive posture. This dual military advantage has been virtually wiped out by the availability of intercontinental nuclear missiles. Because of the availability of these missiles, additional territory provides only one military advantage: the multiplication of targets, which, as we have seen, might be important for the blunting of a low-level nuclear attack.

Yet both the United States in its policy of containment and the Soviet Union in its attempt at installing offensive missiles in Cuba have dealt with territory in a nuclear setting, but in pre-nuclear terms. In a conventional military setting, control over territory has retained its offensive and defensive functions; this has become obvious, for instance, in the relations between Israel and the Arab states. But a military conflict between the United States and the Soviet Union is bound to be, and one between the United States and China is likely to be, in the nature of an all-out nuclear conflagration. It is indeed the near-certainty of such a conflagration, if they should step beyond the lines of military demarcation of 1945 and 1949, respectively, which has contained the Soviet Union and China as well as the United States. The alliances we have concluded with nations at the periphery of the Soviet and Chinese empires, the military installations we have established in these countries, and the military operations we have performed there have fulfilled a political function by reassuring these nations of American protection, and they have performed a military function by presenting the Soviet Union and China with tokens of our military resolution. But they have no direct military relevance in a nuclear setting, save as additional targets for nuclear attack.

Thus by itself the policy of peripheral military containment, appropriate to a conventional setting, has really not contained the Soviet Union and China in being applied to a nuclear setting; it has only made the threat of nuclear retaliation against a conventional attack more credible. What has actually contained the Soviet Union and China has been the threat of all-out nuclear war. Thus the military policies we have been pursuing vis-à-vis the Soviet Union and China have confused the issues of conventional and nuclear containment. Instead of using conventional forces as means to the end of nuclear containment, we have tried to use them as ends in themselves. As such, the policy of peripheral military containment has performed a useful function only in so far as it has sought to discourage or counteract local expansionist policies, independent of those of the Soviet Union and China and hostile to the interests of the United States.

The paradox of the nuclear alliance reveals perhaps more clearly than the other paradoxes of nuclear strategy the nature of the dilemma and the fatal flaw in our modes of thought and action. Any attempt, however ingenious and forward-looking, at assimilating nuclear power to the purposes and instrumentalities of the nation-state is negated by the enormity of nuclear destructiveness. We have been trying to normalize, conventionalize, and "nationalize" nuclear power. By doing so, we have tackled the wrong horn of the nuclear dilemma. Instead of trying in vain to assimilate nuclear power to the purposes and the instrumentalities of the nation-state, we ought to have tried to adapt these purposes and instrumentalities to the potentialities of nuclear power. We have refrained from doing so in earnest because to do so successfully requires a radical transformation—psychologically painful and politically risky—of traditional moral values, modes of thought, and habits of action. But short of such a transformation, there will be no escape from the paradoxes of nuclear strategy and the dangers attending them.

9

The Seven Principles of American Foreign Policy

I F THERE IS merit in this analysis of the basic issues that confront the United States in its relations with other nations, then American foreign policy should be guided by certain general principles derived from this analysis:

1) The United States has one primary national interest in its relations with other nations: the security of its territory and institutions. The United States has a number of secondary interests in the world, such as peace and security everywhere, the protection and promotion of democratic governments, the containment of Communist governments and movements, the relief of poverty and disease. The pursuit of these secondary interests is subject to two limitations. They are not to be pursued at the expense of the primary interest of national security, and they can be pursued only within the rather narrow limits of available wisdom and power.

2) The security of the United States is today threatened not only in the traditional way by hegemonial powers in Europe and Asia—a threat to be countered by the traditional methods of the balance of power—but also by the exposure of the American territory to nuclear destruction, a threat to be countered by the novel methods of deterrence and arms control, and by the exposure of American institutions to ideological competition and subversion from abroad, a threat to be countered by the health and attractiveness of American society. American foreign policy must, then, move on three distinct and interconnected levels— the conventional, the nuclear, and the ideological. While these three different levels are interconnected, dynamically affecting each other, the principles guiding action on each are distinct. More particularly, the transference of conventional principles to the nuclear level is untenable on rational grounds and fraught with catastrophic risks, as is the infusion of traditional balance-of-power calculations with ideological considerations.

3) Nuclear weapons in the hands of both superpowers are not instruments of national policy; they only provide assurance that national interests can be supported with the conventional diplomatic and military methods. In the measure that the United States is unable to utilize these methods, it will be tempted to resort to nuclear weapons. Hence, effective diplomacy and strong conventional forces are an insurance against the suicidal absurdity of nuclear war.

4) The ideological decontamination of conventional foreign policy is a precondition of an American foreign policy that is both peaceful and successful. This has always been so; for accommodation and compromise, which are the aims of diplomacy, are incompatible with the contest of political ideologies, each claiming a monopoly of wisdom and virtue and trying to transform the world in its image. Foreign policies seeking the triumph of one political ideology at the expense of another have always issued in particularly fanatical and bloody wars, which have been inconclusive to boot unless they physically eliminated the supporters of one ideology altogether.

The irrationality of ideologically oriented foreign policies has been accentuated in our age by the polycentric character of Communism, the availability of nuclear weapons, and the great variety of techniques now at the disposal of governments for influencing foreign opinion, such as subversion and mass propaganda, foreign aid and trade. There is, then, much to be gained and nothing to be lost by a reorientation of American foreign policy on traditional nonideological lines. That is to say, the United States ought to subject its foreign policies toward all nations, regardless of their ideological coloration, to one ultimate test: Do they serve the security interests of the United States?

5) The ideological contest between hostile philosophies, social and political systems, and ways of life will ultimately not be decided by the political, military, propagandist, and economic interventions of the contestants in the affairs of other nations, but by the visible virtues and vices of their respective political, economic, and social systems. Throughout its history, this has been the source of America's ideological strength and attractiveness. It is at this point that foreign policy and domestic politics merge. Instead of embarking upon costly and futile interventions for the purpose of building nations and viable economies abroad, the United States ought to concentrate its efforts upon creating a society at home which can again serve as a model for other nations to emulate.

6) It is a novel aspect of the nuclear age that the United States not only has interests to defend and promote against other nations, but that it also has interests in common with other nations which can be satisfied without detriment to any nation. The avoidance of nuclear war is the principal case in point. Hence, the policies serving this aim, which the United States and the Soviet Union have pursued vis-à-vis each other—e.g., the avoidance of direct military confrontations, the nonproliferation treaty, nuclear arms control—stand apart from their traditional policies, which they pursue against each other or jointly against a third nation. The success of the former is a precondition for the very possibility of the latter. The ups and downs of tradi-

tional policies must therefore not be allowed to interfere with the consistent pursuit of the policies seeking to minimize the possibility of nuclear war.

7) The interests which the United States has in common with the Soviet Union and other nations have found expression in unilateral reciprocal actions, in bilateral and multilateral agreements, and in the United Nations and its specialized agencies. A new American foreign policy, intent upon broadening and strengthening the area of common interests and aware of the threat to world peace and order emanating from the balkanization of large sectors of the political world, must pay special attention to the unused potential of the United Nations.

The United Nations, created for the purpose of providing institutions and procedures through which the common interests of mankind could be realized, has been stifled by the immobilization of the Security Council that has resulted from the conflicts among the great powers, by the fragmentation of the General Assembly through voting procedures that give all member-states, superpowers and mini-states alike, the same numerical weight, and by the defense of national sovereignty against supranational tendencies in U.N. procedures, as exemplified by the refusal of financial support to some of its peace-making operations. The United States has an interest in resisting these crippling tendencies. It ought to make judicious use of the organization through its general policies, as well as support and promote specific moves seeking to reform the institutions and procedures of the organization.

No change in American foreign policy, however sound in itself, can guarantee success. For foreign policy is always at the mercy of accidents and, more particularly, of the foreign policies of other nations. However, America will discharge its responsibilities toward itself and mankind only if it maximizes the chances for success by putting into practice the principles on which a sound foreign policy must rest.

Index

COUNCIL ON FOREIGN RELATIONS

Publications

FOREIGN AFFAIRS (quarterly), edited by Hamilton Fish Armstrong.
THE UNITED STATES IN WORLD AFFAIRS (annual), by Richard P. Stebbins.
DOCUMENTS ON AMERICAN FOREIGN RELATIONS (annual), by Richard P. Stebbins with the assistance of Elaine P. Adam.

POLITICAL HANDBOOK AND ATLAS OF THE WORLD (annual), edited by Walter H. Mallory.

MIDDLE EAST POLITICS: The Military Dimension, by J. C. Hurewitz (1969).

THE ECONOMICS OF INTERDEPENDENCE: Economic Policy in the Atlantic Community, by Richard N. Cooper (1968).

HOW NATIONS BEHAVE: Law and Foreign Policy, by Louis Henkin (1968).

THE INSECURITY OF NATIONS, by Charles Yost (1968).

PROSPECTS FOR SOVIET SOCIETY, edited by Allen Kassof (1968).

THE AMERICAN APPROACH TO THE ARAB WORLD, by John S. Badeau (1968).

GULLIVER'S TROUBLES, OR THE SETTING OF AMERICAN FOREIGN POLICY, by Stanley Hoffmann (1968).

U.S. POLICY AND THE SECURITY OF ASIA, by Fred Greene (1968).

NEGOTIATING WITH THE CHINESE COMMUNISTS: The U.S. Experience, by Kenneth T. Young (1968).

FROM ATLANTIC TO PACIFIC: A New Interocean Canal, by Immanuel J. Klette (1967).

TITO'S SEPARATE ROAD: America and Yugoslavia in World-Politics, by John C. Campbell (1967).

U.S. TRADE POLICY: New Legislation for the Next Round, by John W. Evans (1967).

TRADE LIBERALIZATION AMONG INDUSTRIAL COUNTRIES: Objectives and Alternatives, by Bela Balassa (1967).

THE CHINESE PEOPLE'S LIBERATION ARMY, by Brig. General Samuel B. Griffith II U.S.M.C. (ret.) (1967).

THE ARTILLERY OF THE PRESS: Its Influence on American Foreign Policy, by James Reston (1967).

ATLANTIC ECONOMIC COOPERATION: The Case of the O.E.C.D., by Henry G. Aubrey (1967).

TRADE, AID AND DEVELOPMENT: The Rich and Poor Nations, by John Pincus (1967).

BETWEEN TWO WORLDS: Policy, Press and Public Opinion on Asian-American Relations, by John Hohenberg (1967).

THE CONFLICTED RELATIONSHIP: The West and the Transformation of Asia, Africa and Latin America, by Theodore Geiger (1966).

THE ATLANTIC IDEA AND ITS EUROPEAN RIVALS, by H. van B. Cleveland (1966).

EUROPEAN UNIFICATION IN THE SIXTIES: From the Veto to the Crisis, by Miriam Champs (1966).

THE UNITED STATES AND CHINA IN WORLD AFFAIRS, by Robert Blum, edited by A. Doak Barnett (1966).

THE FUTURE OF THE OVERSEAS CHINESE IN SOUTHEAST ASIA, by Lea A. Williams (1966).

THE CONSCIENCE OF THE RICH NATIONS: The Development Assistance Committee and the Common Aid Effort, by Seymour J. Rubin (1966).

ATLANTIC AGRICULTURAL UNITY: Is it Possible?, by John O. Coppock (1966).

TEST BAN AND DISARMAMENT: The Path of Negotiation, by Arthur H. Dean (1966).

COMMUNIST CHINA'S ECONOMIC GROWTH AND FOREIGN TRADE, by Alexander Eckstein (1966).

POLICIES TOWARD CHINA: Views from Six Continents, edited by A. M. Halpern (1966).

THE AMERICAN PEOPLE AND CHINA, by A. T. Steele (1966).